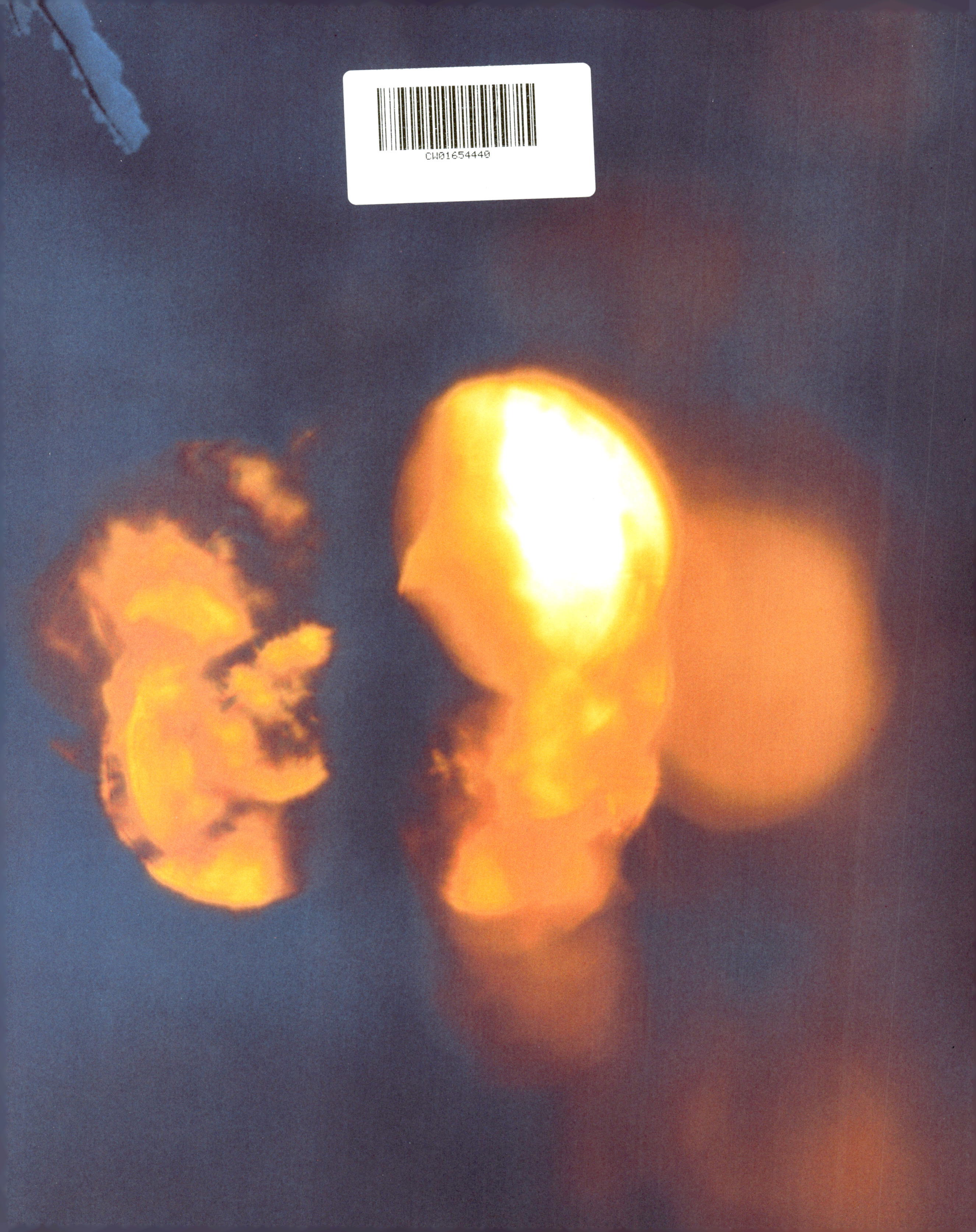

To Everything a Season

Hannu Hautala – Markku Lappalainen

OTAVA PUBLISHING COMPANY
LIMITED HELSINKI

To Everything a Season

A Year in the Finnish Wilds

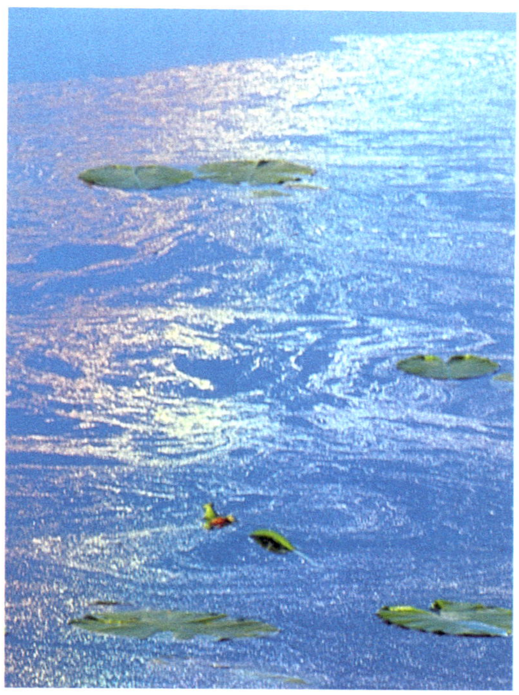

Photographs by Hannu Hautala
Written by Markku Lappalainen

Translated from the Finnish by Tim Steffa
with Riitta Kaatia

Design and layout Eija Hiltunen

Paper Galerie Art 150 g

Colour separation, typesetting, printing and
binding Otava Printing Works,
Keuruu 1997

ISBN 951-1-14888-5

Contents

THE SUN BEHIND IT ALL

The sun is coming up, the horizon glowing for a moment before blinding shafts of light pierce the landscape. The vast fiery orb rises into the morning sky, comes resolutely to the zenith of its daily course and inclines toward dusk. The sun sinks below the horizon, ushered out by a blazing sunset. It flattens and finally stretches into a fiery streak which is extinguished with a hiss by the deepening darkness. For a brief moment a few fleecy clouds glow, gilt-edged, until their brightness too fades.

As sure as day follows night and night day, so too do the seasons revolve, from winter through spring into summer and autumn, and again into winter. Gripped by snow and ice, winter goes surging into spring with might and main. Spring quickly matures into summer, which, marked by unchecked generation and growth, yields to the blazing hues of autumn. Inexorably, as life is reduced to another winter, nature falls silent.

Simple. Or is it?

In summer, Finland is bathed in light. In the south the sun disappears below the horizon for only a few hours. The farther north, the longer the summer day: in northernmost Finland it lasts somewhat three months.

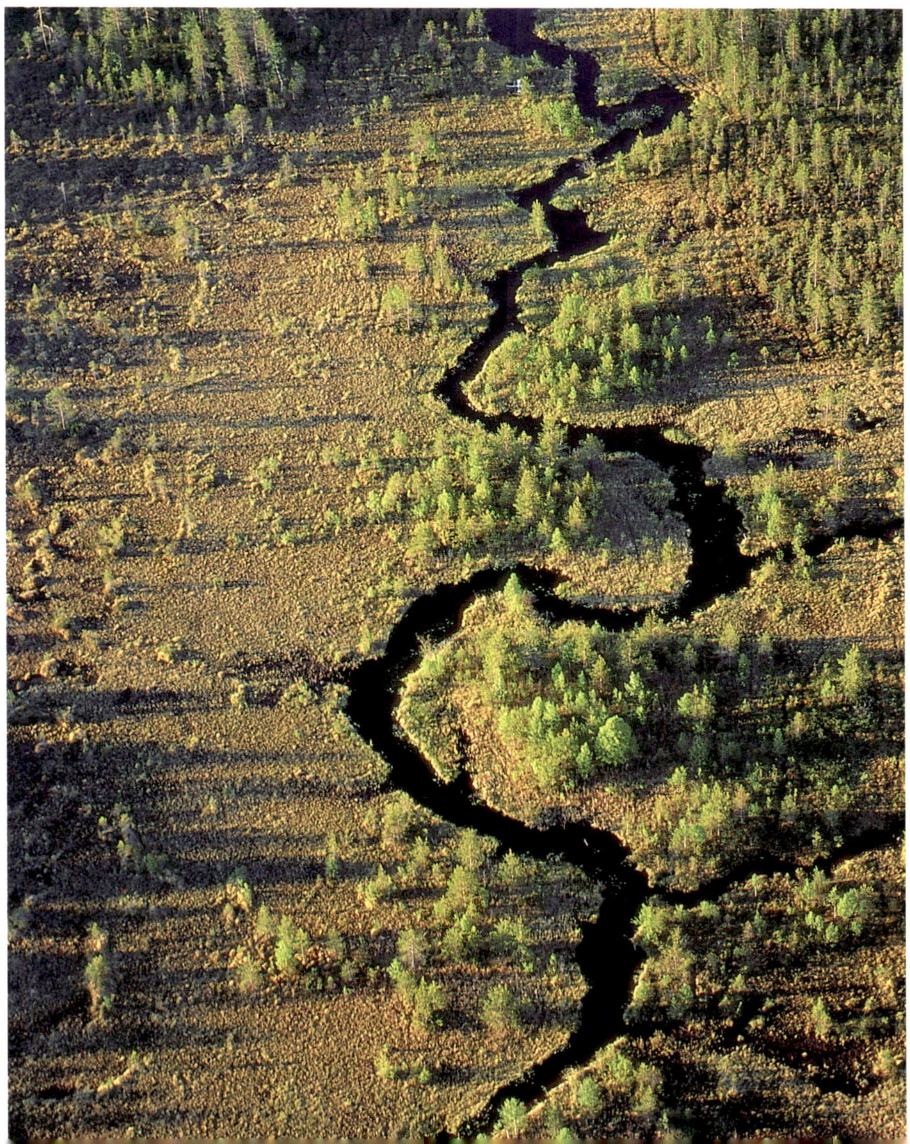

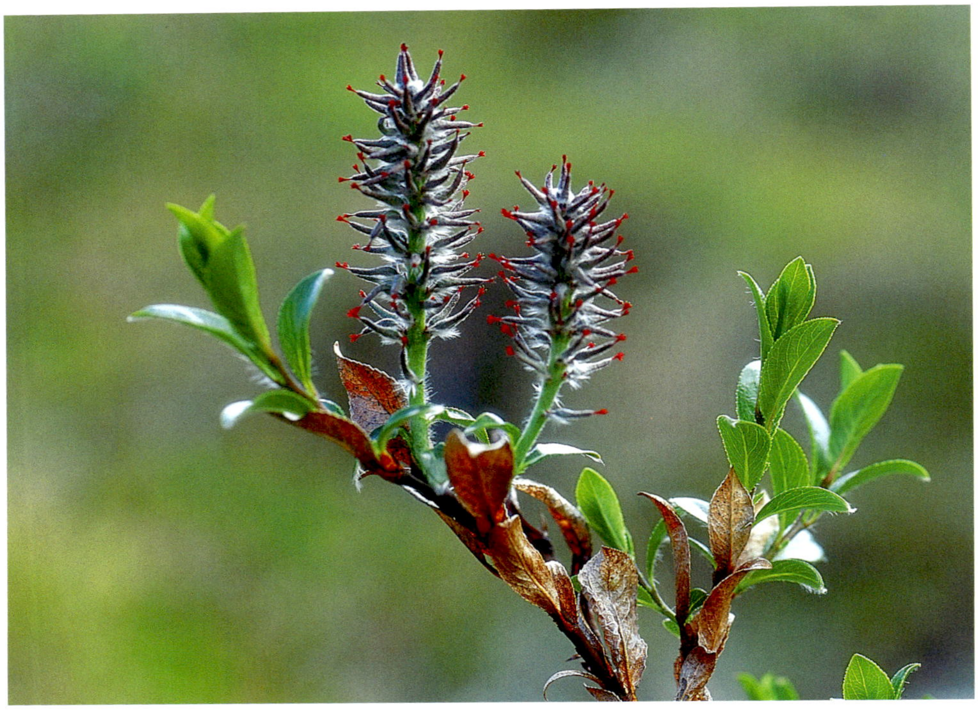

The small, low-growing wortle-leaved willow is a shrub of the rich marshes and fjeld slopes of the north. It is at its loveliest in June, when it comes into blossom and leaf at virtually the same time.

The cycle of the seasons is incomparable drama. Its script is in outline, providing a bearing. There is many an unexpected twist to the plot. Coincidences intertwine with seeming randomness but eventually form a cohesive entity. The pieces of the puzzle fit to make a vivid panorama. From year to year the theme is the same, but so extreme are the variations that the whole inevitably remains gripping.

Finland is located in a part of the world where seasonal change is unusually pronounced. Its northern situation guarantees that the extremes of nature's annual round may be experienced here. The period of winter darkness and the sunlit nights of summer mark the outside parameters of light. Temperature variations between the bitter subfreezing cold of winter and the most sweltering days of summer are greater in Finland than elsewhere at this latitude.

The weather plays the lead in the drama of the seasons. It determines how the inevitable course of events is depicted. Finland is not characterized by northernness alone; the country's location with respect to other crucial weather-making factors is also significant. There extend to Finland the influence of the Atlantic and the warm Gulf Stream flowing across it from south- to northwest and, by contrast, the continental climate of Siberia, rendering it a battlefield between two climatic zones.

Finland is located at the same latitude as permafrost-gripped Greenland, the tundra spanning Siberia, and arctic Canada, where climatic conditions are severe; the annual mean temperature is minus five degrees Celsius, whereas in Finland it is some one and a half degrees above zero. Here the average temperature of the warmest month of the year is over ten degrees, the threshold for the growth of forest and the ripening of grain. And Finnish winters bring snow, which protects life when the cold bottoms out.

The relative mildness of Finnish winters is a product of the Gulf Stream and the oceanic properties of its climate. The autumn storms and the low-pressure fronts that bring winter gales usually originate in the Atlantic. At times this oceanic climate type holds sway in summer, making it a common conversation piece. Winter's cold snaps, on the other hand, result from the continental climate insinuating its fringes over the Finnish peninsula. The hot spells of summer also emanate from the east.

The Baltic and Finland's nearly 200,000 lakes even out the climate. They retard cooling in the autumn and warming in the spring. Differences in the thermal economy of land and water systems also affect the way the seasons look: land warms and cools quickly, while changes are more deliberate in the water systems.

The intensifying greenhouse effect – the climatic changes wrought by the burning of coal and other fossil fuels, and the discharge of other pollutants into the atmosphere – also reaches Finland. The climate is warming. This inexorable development has already begun, and its repercussions remain virtually unknown. It is believed that extreme weather conditions – storms, torrential rainfall, drought – will become widespread. And all of it will occur at so rapid a pace, compared to the span of natural history, that it will be difficult for nature to adapt to the change.

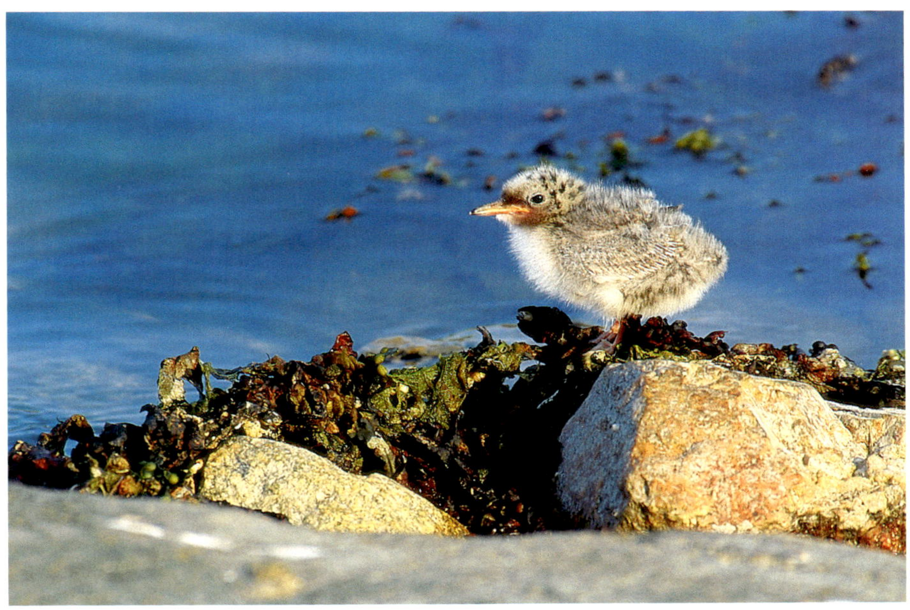

Ahead lies a global journey. Quickly learning to fly, a juvenile arctic tern sets out on a migratory trip that takes it to the region of the South Pole. It spends high summer and the dead of winter in landscapes where the days are long and the nights are bright.

But the warming of the climate does not alter the script of the grand drama. Without doubt climatic change forces nature to create new scenes for the stage, but the four acts of the play - winter, spring, summer and autumn - will yet long endure. Nature's year has no true beginning nor end. It will always remain a sequence of exquisitely linked events which may be joined at any point whatsoever. And, as always with a good play, it takes a while before the plot becomes clear.

Half of the winter's snow has fallen.

To be precise, it's the sun that's behind it all. It is the prime mover in the succession of the seasons: the true producer of the play, and in a way the writer and director as well. The conflagration one hundred and fifty million kilometers away sustains life on the small satellite circling it. It warms the land, water and air, generates the winds and the rains.

The never-ending fluctuation of sunrises and sunsets is in fact caused by the rotation of the earth. Flattened at its poles, the ball-shaped globe spins around its imaginary axis in twenty-four hours. Different parts of the world turn to hide from the sun at night and bask in its radiance during the day. As it spins about itself, the earth travels an elliptical orbit around the sun. It takes a year to make one circuit.

That the earth's axis is not vertical but inclined at a 23.5° angle is of significance where the drama of the changing seasons is concerned. This slight tilt has major consequences. Were the axis perpendicular, days would be of equal length everywhere on earth and there would be no difference in the relation of various parts of the globe to the sun: there would be no seasons.

Sea-blue and leaf-green, the burnished earth careens through space at a speed of thirty kilometers per second. Due to its list, its southern and northern hemispheres receive more sunlight by turns. In summer the northern hemisphere is inclined toward the sun. In winter the earth is closest to the sun, but the tilt is of no avail to the North: the warming beams are reflected past the regions in the grip of winter darkness.

JANUARY

A BEAR GIVES BIRTH IN ITS WINTER LAIR.

HARD TIMES FOR AN EAGLE.

THE SNOW HARBORS SMALL MAMMALS.

A DIPPER DIVES IN FLOWING WATER.

AN OTTER SUCCUMBS TO TEMPTATION.

WINTER DARKNESS ENDS ON A DAY OF LIGHT.

THE SEA AROUND THE OUTER ISLANDS FREEZES.

THE WIND SCULPTS SNOW-CLAD VISTAS.

LIFE AT A LOW BLUE FLAME

The sun traces its pitiful curve toward its winter's-day zenith. A long blue twilight precedes the golden glow of morning and the coppery glare of evening. Soft snow gently blankets a hushed landscape; white-glazed trees mope on a fjeld slope and even at midday cast lengthy shadows which, as the day advances, bend from west via the north to the east, steadily changing their character. So too, traced as silent mounds, do snow-mantled stones, anthills, the upturned roots of fallen trees, rotting trunks full length on the ground and all the minor features of the landscape which, when the earth is thawed, may be precisely named. Now they are but a single undulating expanse of snow.

The landscape is deserted. A solitary trail of fox tracks is sketched in the snow along the flank of a fjeld, a sensuously meandering chain. Nothing much of interest happened reynard's way as it roamed the twilight; no leaps break the winding line of prints to indicate pursuit. The silence is palpable. There is no wind, no raven croaks, not even a twittering flock of titmice chances by.

There is not a cloud in the sky, no trail of jet exhaust. Skis sink into the soft whiteness without a sound. Sojourners can feel their blood course, the pulse of the veins in their temples. One's muscles warm and sweat breaks to the surface of the skin, the breath freezes on one's whiskers and hair in a grey patina suggestive of ageing. On a break, a chill quickly spreads between one's skin and undergarments. So low is the sun that its warming rays are largely deflected into space. The great conflagration cannot yet provide the wanderer with warmth.

One mound among many, sheltered by the arching lower branches of a runt spruce on the north flank of a fjeld, a bear sleeps. Bruin's snoring is inaudible through the snow, there is no distinguishing between the mounds, but there it slumbers, just as it always has. People find this scree hard-going. The lair is out-of-the-way, on a suitably northward-facing slope which keeps the first vernal meltwater from running straight into the bear's lap. You won't find a better site.

The female bear, an experienced mother in good health, is giving birth to her young at about this time, to as many as three, all of them blind, helpless little tots a few hundred grams in weight. As soon as they're born, they seek out their mother's teat and begin to suckle on her rich milk, gradually growing into genuine bear cubs. In the spring, as the snows thaw, they exit, all three of them, given sufficient nourishment, big-headed cubs the size of Finnish spitzes.

The volume of crown snow on fljeld trees varies each year. It can be hard on them. Their crowns branches can't always bear the wintry burden.

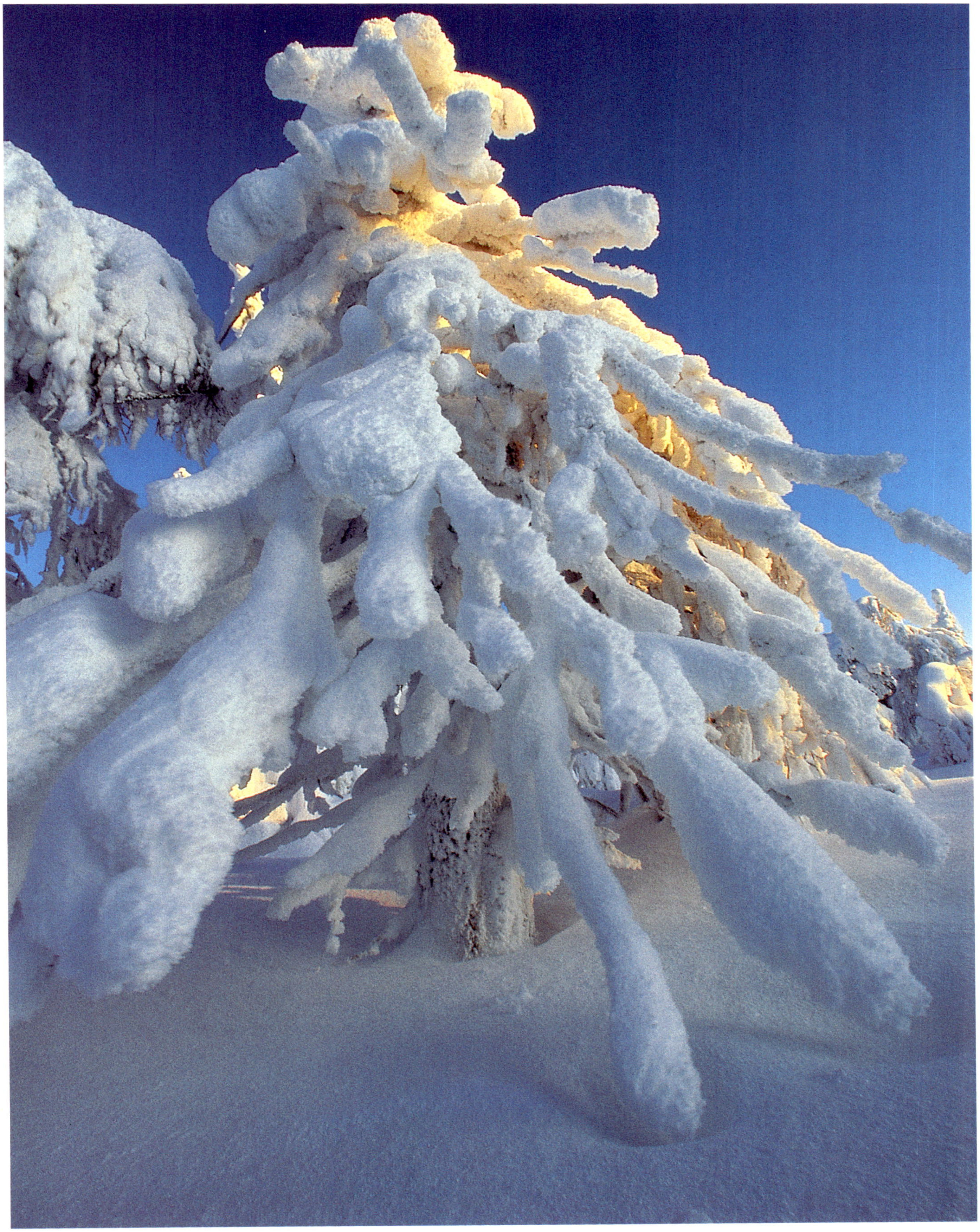

A bear huddled in its winter den sleeps almost normally. To offset the periods of deep sleep, it also spends long stretches awake, monitoring the sounds in its surroundings and raising its huge head. If need be, it is prepared to react almost instantly, if somewhat listlessly and groggy with sleep, when disturbed. It undoubtedly dreams as well, when it isn't sound asleep, or awake and wondering at the human skiing by.

The body temperature of a bear in winter sleep does not approach zero, as does that of bats and hedgehogs in a dormant state. It does drop by as much as five degrees from the normal 37, and its heartbeat slows from the usual fifty beats per minute to a rate of ten or fifteen. This conserves the energy stored beneath its skin as a thick layer of fat.

Let it snow; this eagle's craw is full.

Nonetheless, consumption is intense: even at complete rest, in a sheltered cubbyhole, blanketed by thoroughly insulating snow, it burns up the equivalent of a packet of butter, a quarter of a kilogram, each day. It's no wonder that when the once corpulent bear comes crawling out in the spring it is visibly leaner. Even ample reserves dwindle to a minimum over the six-month rest. But sleep is a better option than wallowing about desperately in deep snow in pursuit of nimbly fleeing prey. The fact is that a bear has no alternative.

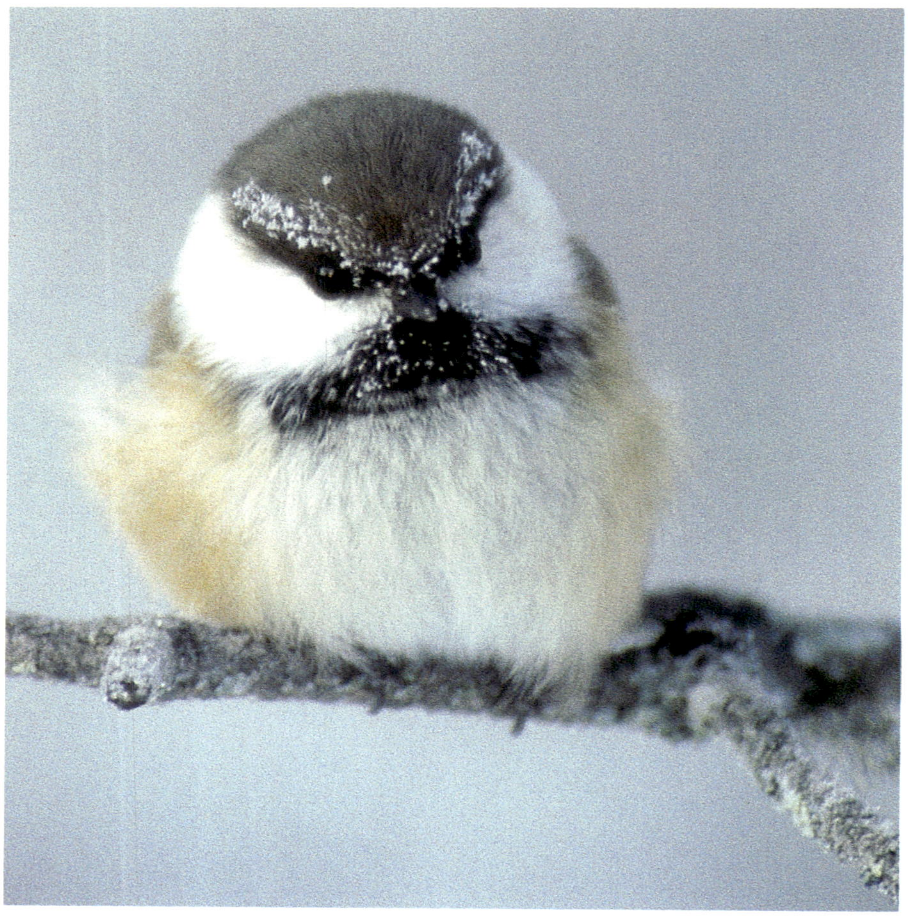

It's nearly minus forty degrees Celsius, and this Siberian tit's expression shows it.

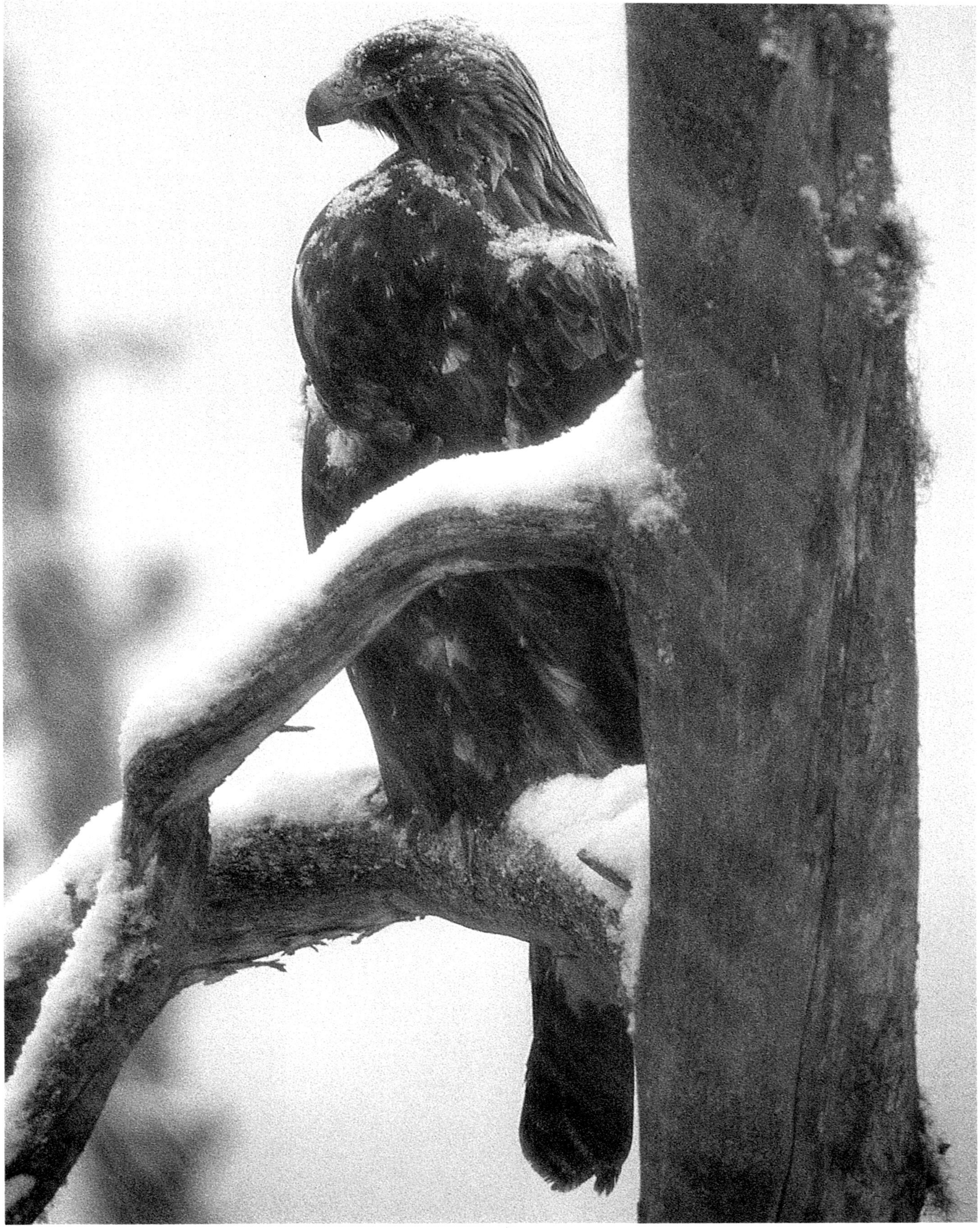

Midday at the Arctic Circle
in the dead of winter.

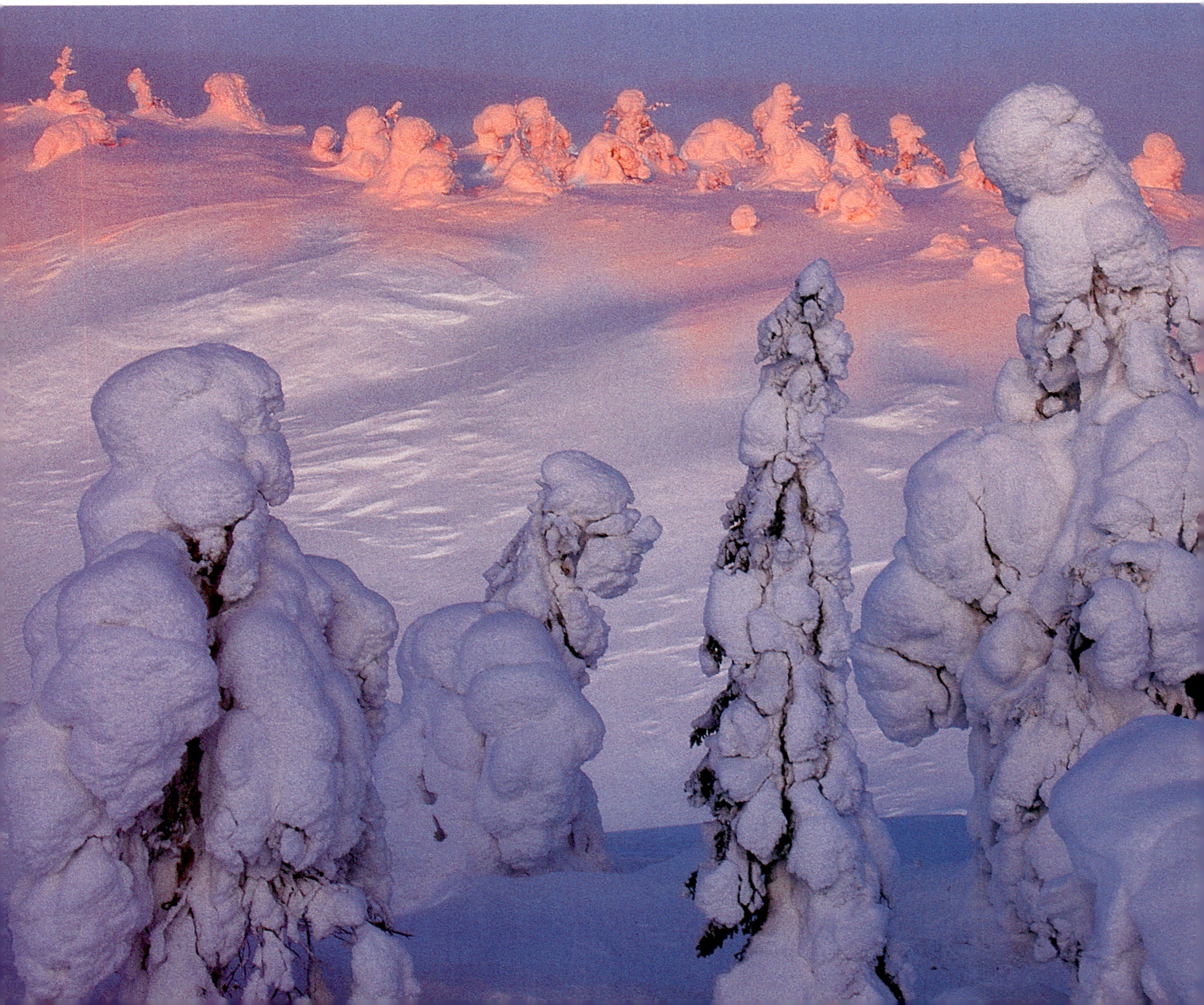

A vole's death certificate, signed by a great grey owl.

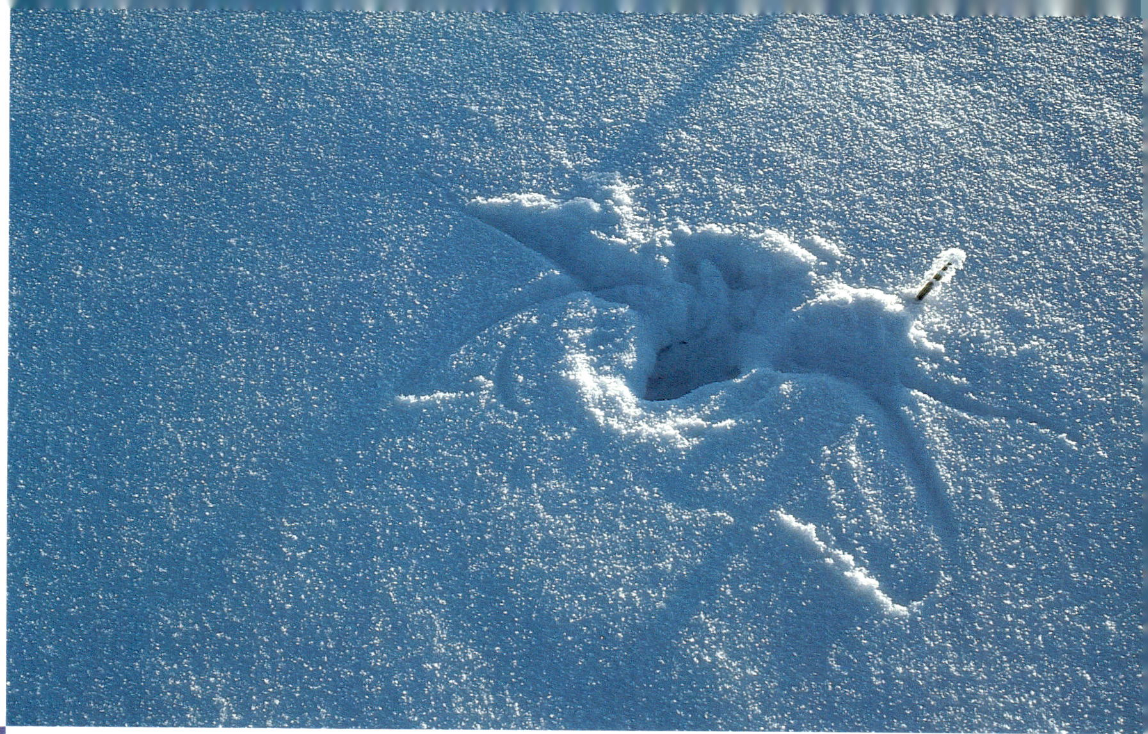

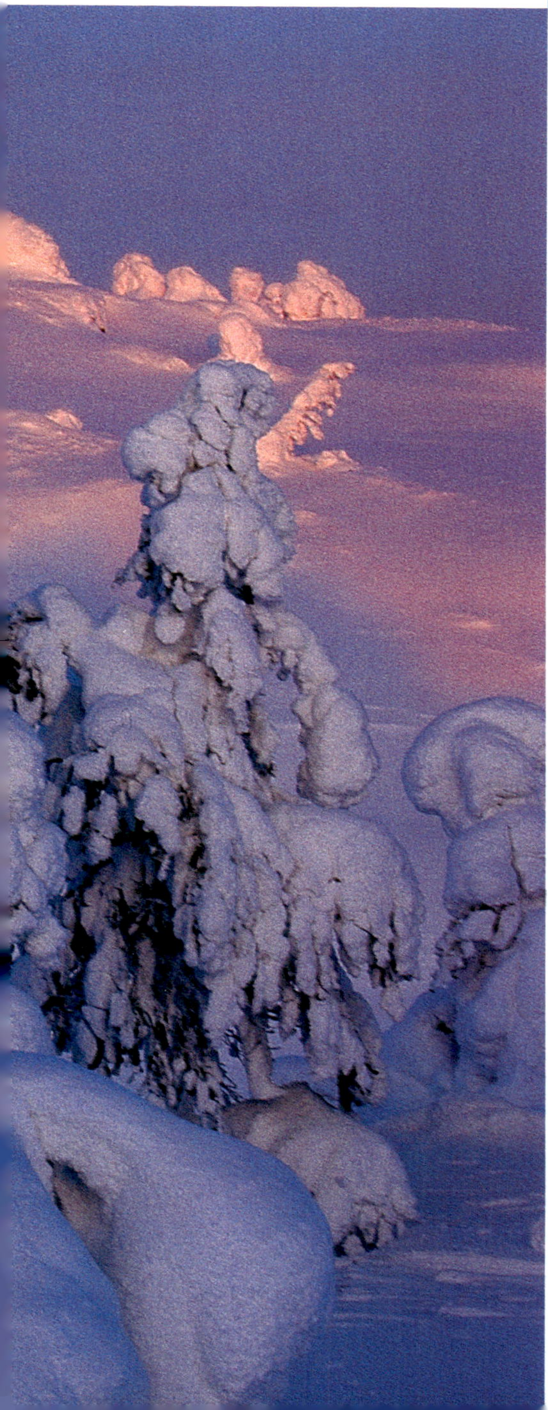

What is perhaps most remarkable, though, is that the bear gets through its winter sleep without excreting. It empties its bowels during a brief fast prior to going to sleep. But urine may not be disposed of like this, in advance. A few days of urine retention can be fatal to a human. The bear's system breaks up the urine and recycles its essential components.

A moist blast pushes in from the sea. Recoiling from the grip of subzero cold, the watershed is draped in dense fog. Greyness in all its shades dominates the scene. Sky and snow-clad earth are one and the same continuum; the horizon vanishes somewhere on a great reach of marshland. Distant stands of trees float like clouds in the greyness; the periphery of the marsh emerges from the mist like a darkening wedge. The green of the spruce trunks, the rusty color of the pine crowns and gnarled limbs, and the mustard hue of the beard moss draping snowy branches are visible only from a few paces away.

Willow grouse tracks criss-cross a birch thicket bordering the marsh. Clad in a white snow suit, the bird leaves a caterpillar-tread pattern in its wake. The movements of an entire covey create a modern painting in the snow, the compact tramping of the little feet tracing an endless crosshatching. For all its haphazardness, the work of art by the grouse does indicate deliberate movement: the birds have shifted from one feeding place to another, plucking buds from boughs bent to the snow and climbing aloft, as indicated by broken upper branches and snow knocked to the ground.

The white mantle on the chill earth is, in fact, water. Snow is formed when moisture in the air is condensed by cold into a solid form. The resulting ice crystals combine and form light, airy flakes which, as they accumulate on the ground, act as insulation, like down. Continued below-freezing temperatures ensure that the snow stays fluffy.

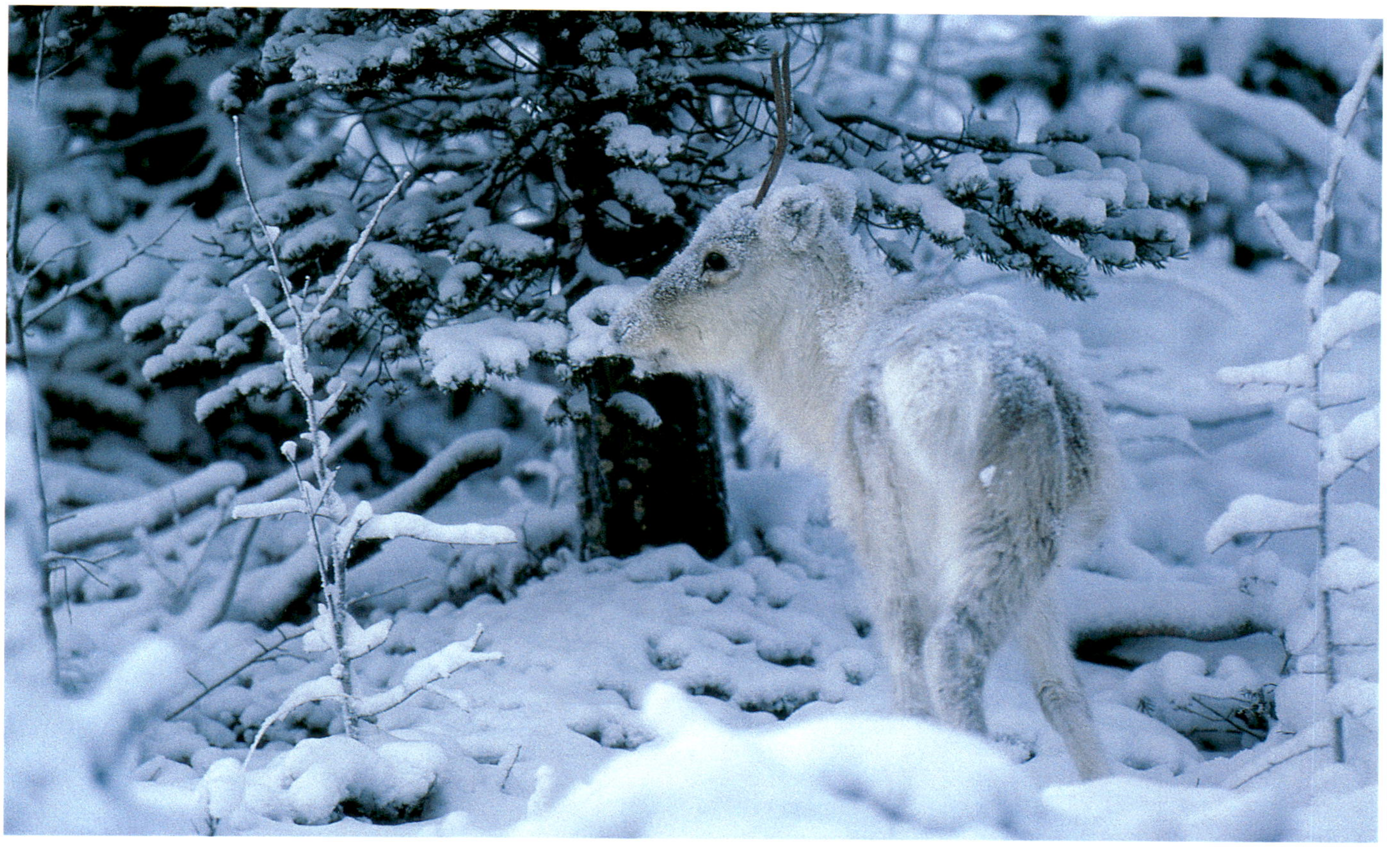

Their first winter taxes young reindeer.

Suddenly the snow trail of the grouse ends, for no apparent reason. Their tracks stop where the wings of birds launching into flight scooped at random into the snow. The crust does not reveal what frightened the wildfowl. Judging by the tracks, each of the dozen or so grouse went barrelling off on its own – in all likelihood to congregate again somewhere nearby. There are no signs of a predator in the snow, no traces of either a duel or a beast on the prowl.

From a misty stand of woods a great, dark shape takes wing. With a few sinewy stokes, it gains speed and lifts into flight, borne along by a breeze within the fog. The golden eagle seems incredibly huge and pitch black in the slushy greyness of the short winter day. The broad wings seem to envelop the sky, the wing-tip feathers spread like fingers. After wheeling widely, the monarch of the skies swings into a shallow descending glide which ends in a felled area on a slope rising from the margin of the marsh.

In late autumn the carcass of a dead moose still provides food, though the ravens are always at ready should the eagle look away. And the eagle is not alone. Its lifelong companion also spends the winters in its native haunts; only the young and the hungry move away for the winter. Breeding-age golden eagles are rare visitors to the carcasses put out in the south specifically for them. Adult pairs maintain their territory all year around.

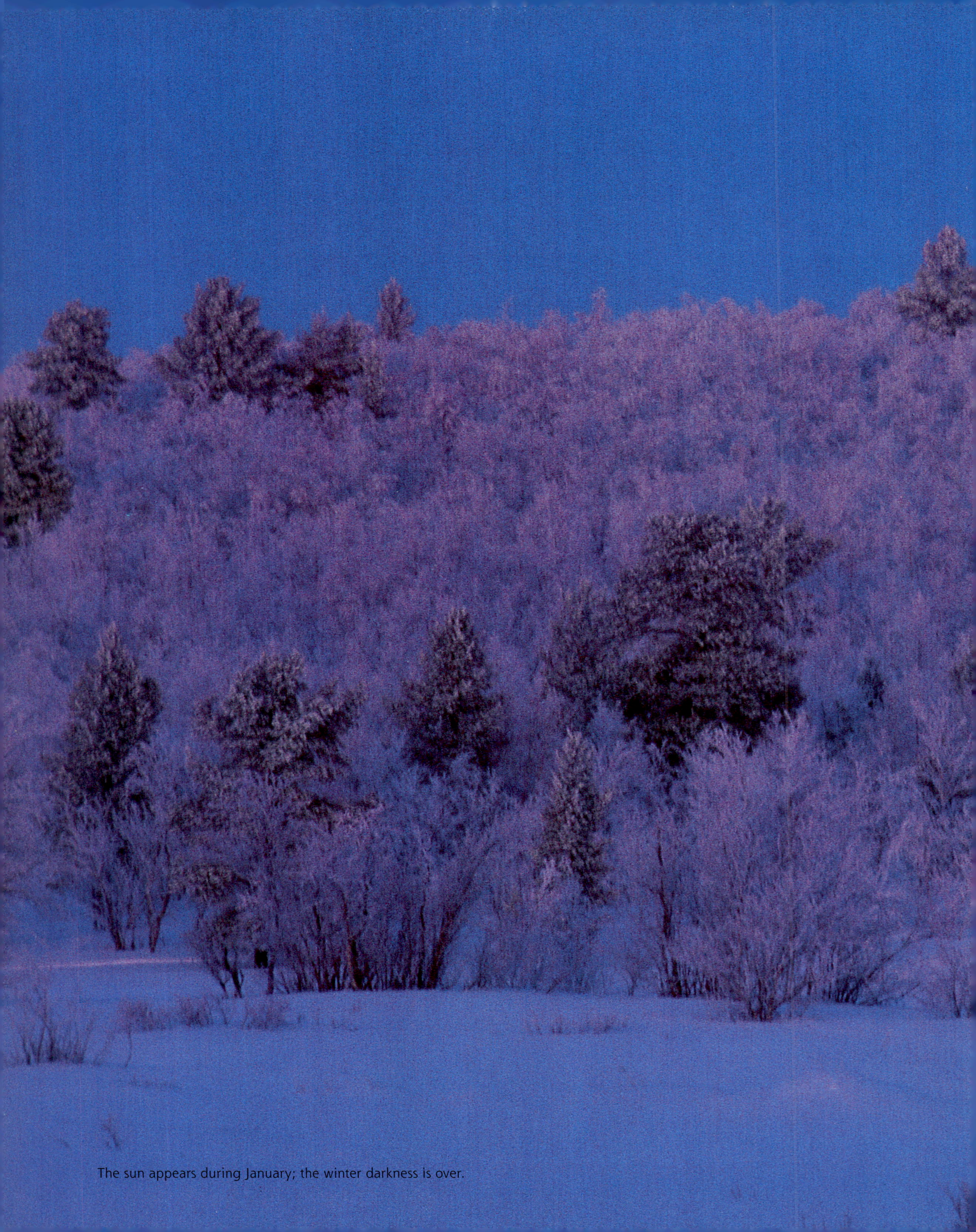

The sun appears during January; the winter darkness is over.

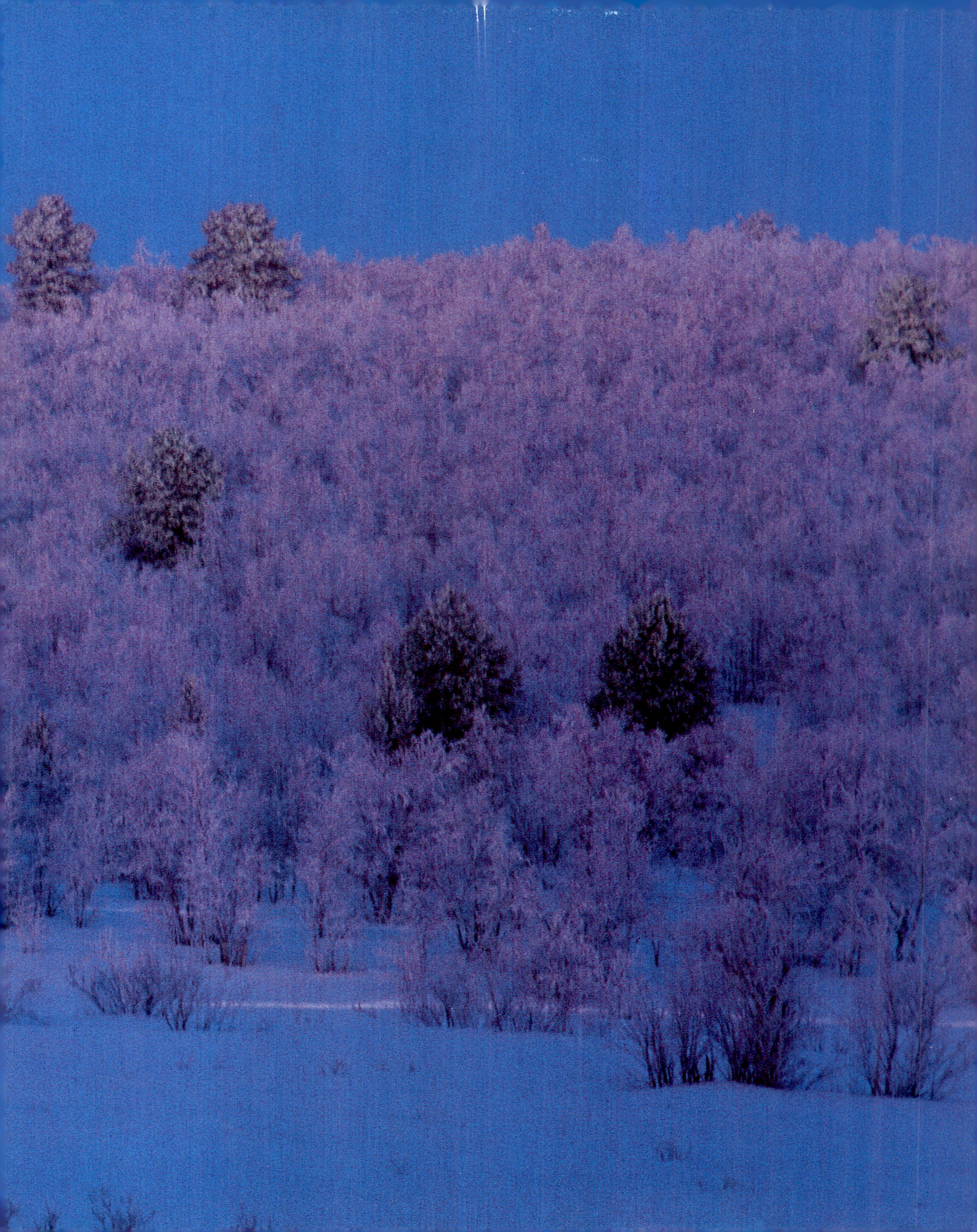

Larger than its mate, the female shows determination at the carcass. The ravens willingly keep their distance, especially as the handsome male eagle, its senses honed, is on sentry duty in the crown of a nearby dead pine. A careless raven may end up in the poised talons, though this is extremely uncommon as ravens can avoid surprise attack. Sometimes in the early hours or at dusk a raven blind with hunger or exhausted from overeating may drop its guard for a moment; and this the eagle ruthlessly exploits.

The gun-blue twilit day looms up out of the darkness of the night as though in stealth. A cloudy sky sees to it that not even the faintest glimmer shows on the horizon. A pallid light glows from a farmhouse window, and within its compass birds flit about, snatching crumbs to augment their winter fare. A great spotted woodpecker and a great tit quarry some hard-frozen tallow; a bullfinch and a yellow-breasted bunting enjoy a sheaf of grain.

The birds take flight when the door opens, but soon return to continue their activities, only to be flushed again promptly. A few vehement whistles, a sharp rustling of wings, and, as if exploding, the fugitives scatter in all directions.

Something grey darts by on the ground, which is strewn with droppings from the avian restaurant. The birds' warning calls also send the small gate-crasher on its way. Vying with the birds, the ball of fuzz bolts for its nook beneath the snow, its sweetly snuffling snout protruding as the first of the birds return to their repast. Cramming its cheeks with seeds and bread crumbs, the creature humps it to its hiding place, where it stores the provisions for its future needs.

The yellow-necked field mouse has found choice pickings. Via a burrow beneath the snow, it reaches the wall of the house, slips between the foundation and logs into the cellar, whence it scurries on into the floor structures. Its nest is near the bake oven, in the warmest corner of the house, where the big-eared little rodent is laying in supplies for a rainy day.

Long-tailed, glossy-coated, well muscled and in fine fettle in every respect, the mouse nibbles the sunflower seeds, nuts and barley grains it pilfered from the bird feeder as a squirrel would. Once its belly is full, it continues its stockpiling. That moderation exists and that the offerings on the feeder will last until spring are beyond its ken. Occasionally is snoozes for a few hours, but then it's off again to gather grub. A short sortie beneath the open sky entails risks.

A pigmy owl is a keen observer as the birds feed, for any moment might offer a careless bird or a plump mouse or else a vole, it too drawn to the birds' feeding site as an uninvited guest. The household environs are also patrolled by a domestic cat.

But in the tranquil stillness beneath the snow there squeaks a creature which has not the slightest interest in seeds or bread crumbs. Almost tirelessly, the shrew stalks all manner of small terrestrial creatures. The common shrew weighs but a grams and its nutritional requirements equal three quarters of its own weight daily. Because it feeds on small insects and spiders, winter means round-the-clock diligence.

The shrew has an unusual way of greeting winter. In the autumn it shrinks, its system breaks down the cartilage between its vertebrae, and even its skull collapses slightly. This little beast is unable to store up in advance the required amount of nutrition. It's a mode of living that is extremely taxing; the price is pays for its efforts is a short life: this cone-nosed insectivore never sees two winters.

As sheltered as life is beneath the snow, mice, voles and shrews sometimes fall prey to beasts that dwell on its surface. Carbon dioxide produced by respiration accumulates in subsurface passages, and the animals drill holes in the snow to vent it. They also visit the surface for fresh air and to excrete waste. That's when owls strike. Or stoats. The smallest of the mustelids family, the least weasel, may even force its way into a burrow and drive its inhabitants out into the open for slaughter.

Flume water is not readily curbed. Free water is a rare natural resource in winter.

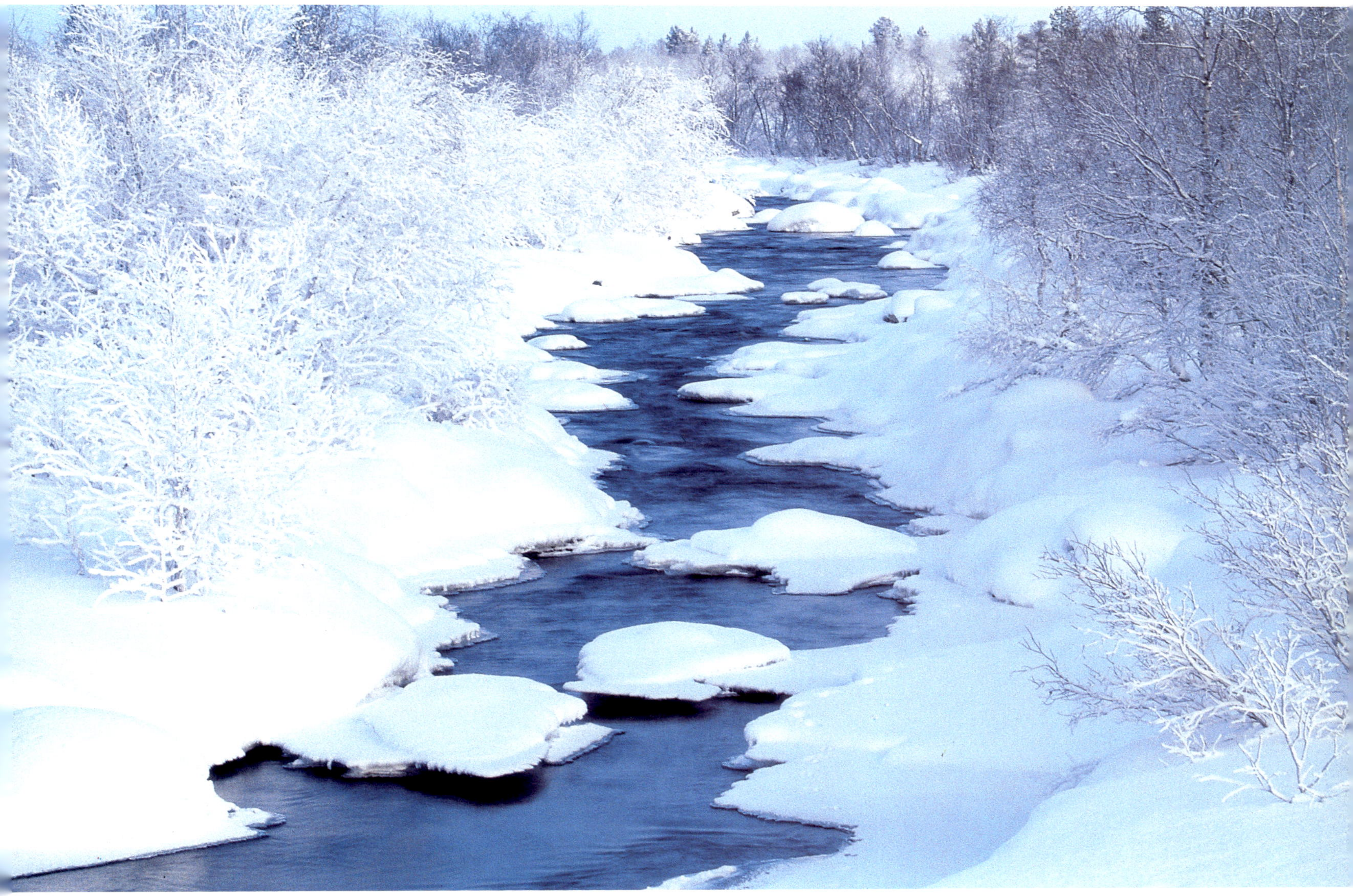

The rush of flowing water is heard through ice. Now and then the current flings a wave into an air pocket beneath it, and a hollow thud resounds. The stream dives into view over the rim of a waterfall, the black mouth of the landscape, steaming in the cold. A dipper curtsies beside the open stretch, pipes gently in a cracked voice, and goes flitting back downstream. It maintains its winter territory with incessant vocalizing and patrolling, unless it happens to be diving to the riverbed for its sustenance.

A diving dipper swims to the bottom by scooping at the water with its wings and thrusting its beak obliquely into the oncoming current, the flowing water thrusting it toward the river bottom. From the sand, rocky crannies, and vegetation the dipper extracts the larvae and pupae of aquatic insects. It even catches fingerling fish. Cute, the size of a starling, and also known as the water ouzel, it sports a white bib as it devours its prey on the edge of the ice. It beats the grubs to death and hastily bolts them. And dives again into the dark maw of the stream.

Tracks meandering along the bank lead straight to an opening in the ice. Another of nature's intrepid winter divers, an otter, wanders the river without leaving a single opening uninspected. This handsome member of the weasel family is after fish numbed with cold and frogs hibernating in the riverbed. It is endowed with a diving suit of a dense underfur impervious to water. As absurd as this may seem, the colder the temperature, the warmer the water feels.

The otter is a denizen of pure and unspoiled water systems. Pollution hampers hunting and toxins reduce vitality and fertility. Dams and dredging render currents so artificial that otters' hunting prospects are reduced. It's no wonder that younger individuals in particular find the allure of fish farms irresistible, as adults already have the best aquatic environments staked out. And for their visits to the farms the poor otters must often pay with their lives.

Bitter cold and dazzling radiance are typical of February.

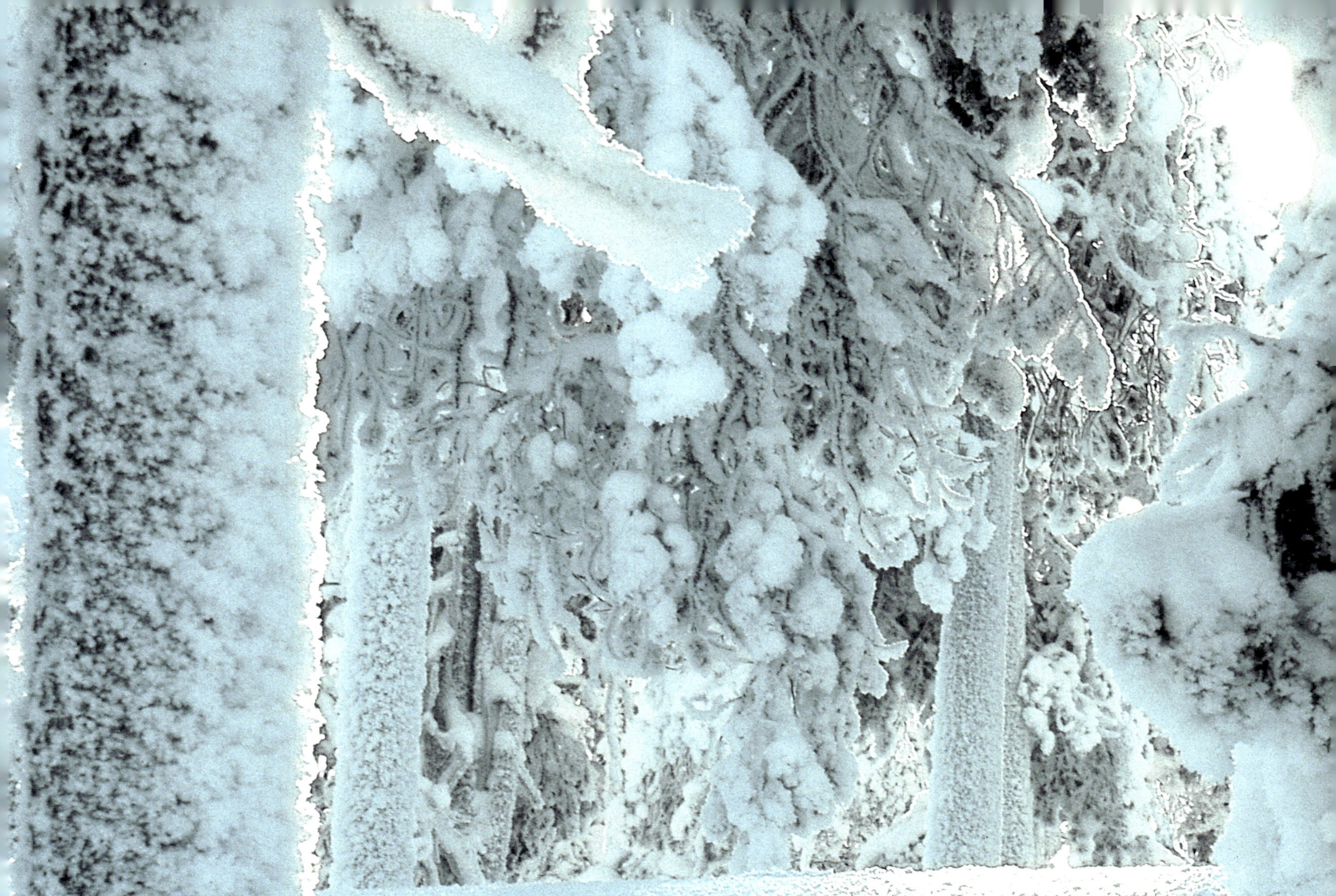

February

Tracks in the snow reveal secrets.

Burbot spawn beneath the ice.

Crossbills find bliss among spruces.

Trees are crushed by their burden of snow.

The year at its coldest.

Trees pop in the bitter cold.

A beaver, hare, fox and wolf in heat.

The vernal restlessness of the crow family.

The first icicles suggest spring.

Freezing Cold and Snow Flurries

A small grey-brown bundle of fluff scampers over the sunlit snow. The creature peers from of a clump of grass and springs off at a brisk pace, dives beneath a spruce sapling, and vanishes. The beast comes into view for a second or so. The keen observer identifies it as a vole: a ball of fur with virtually no tail or neck. On snow softened by daylight, lasting documentation remains: something has signed the snow with its tracks.

The pattern indicates it was a vole, but more precise classification calls for conjecture and in the end is often based on guesswork. One must content oneself with the fact that those who inscribe these hieroglyphics on the crust cannot always be identified by species. And what difference does it make anyway? Tracks aren't merely an autograph; they too have tales to tell.

A hare in dark-season forest cannot vanish without a trace.

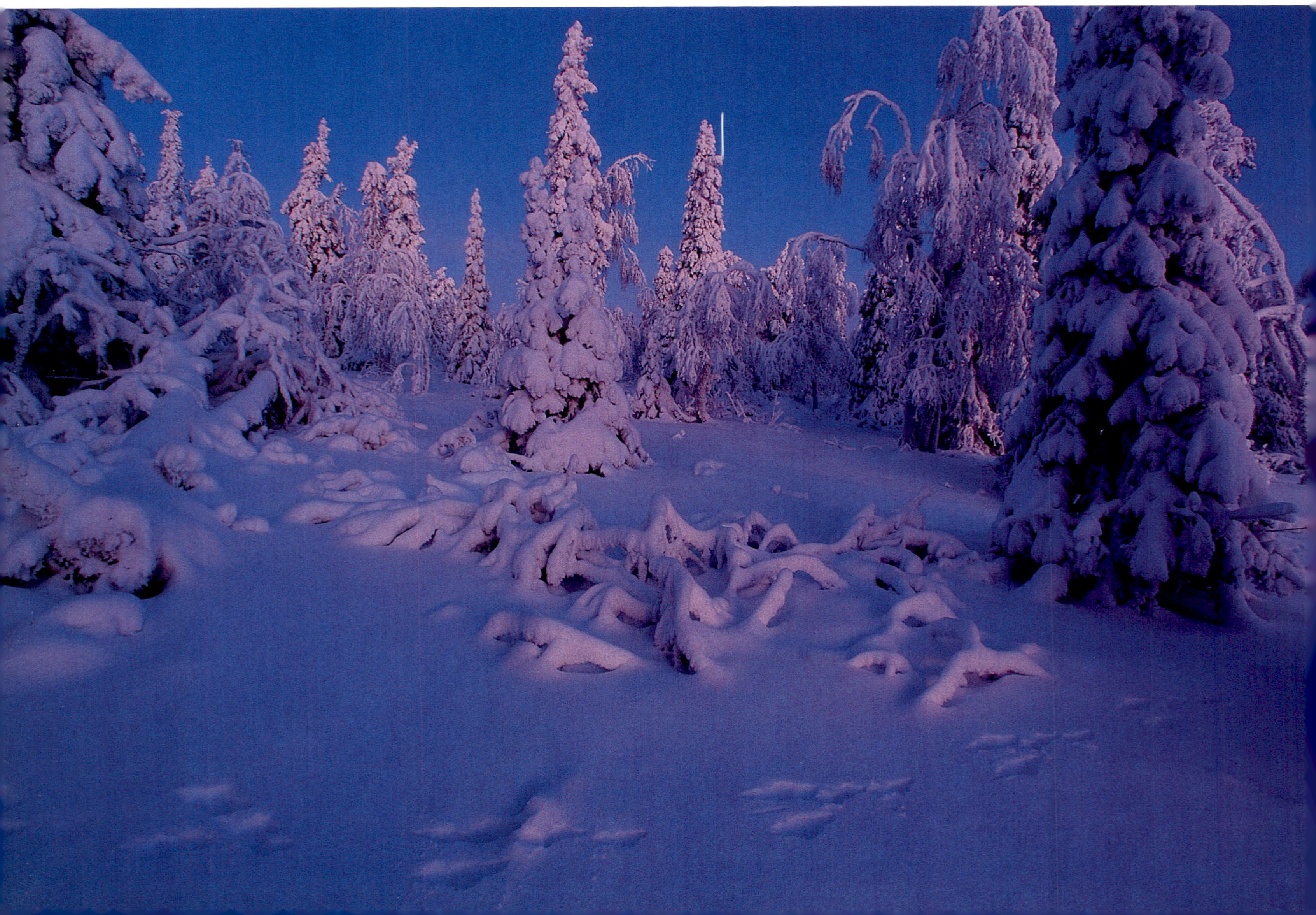

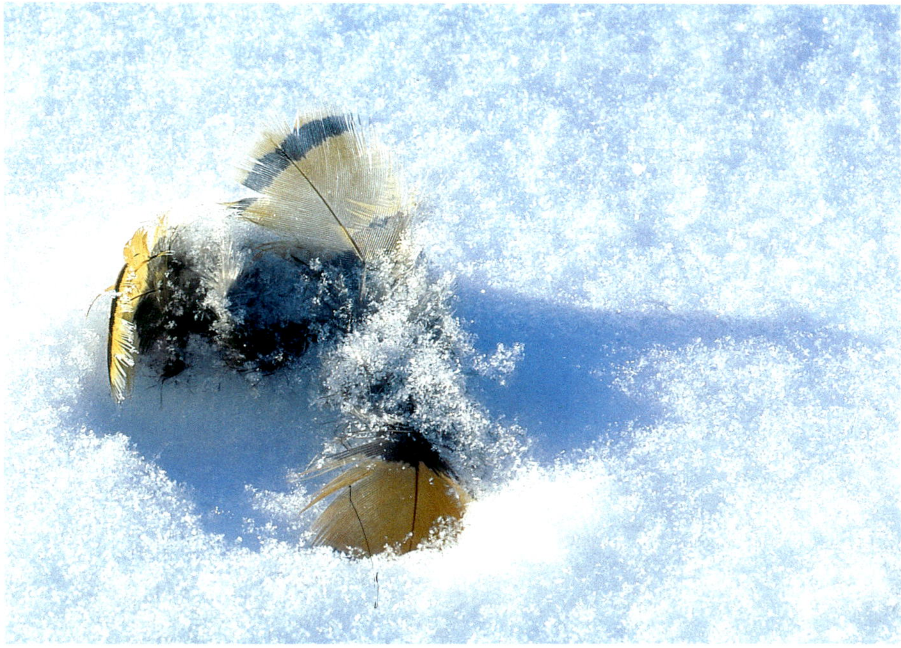

A goshawk's calling card. The feathers remaining from its prey, a capercaillie hen, will end up warming birds' nests.

Snow tracks reveal the secret life of their creators, be they the sunken footprints of a large beast, the tank-track patterns of small mammals, or the imprints of birds' wings. Trails display droppings, scraps of food, signs of struggle, tufts of fur snagged on barbed wire or the tips of twigs. Following these clues throws light on the activities of these prowlers of the twilight and darkness.

The lengthening day melts the crust, the snow living out its life. The trail traced by the vole widens slightly as the day progresses. The dry, light snow, turning wet during the day, freezes again at night; and tomorrow, if the sky provides a full measure of sunlight, the vole's tracks will dilate even further. Thawing temperatures and the wind also alter the tracks. In the end fresh snow wipes the slate clean for the next instalment.

There is a distinct imprint of cleaves in the bottoms of the tracks left by a moose wandering a stand of saplings. Piles of faeces, pellets the size of a grown man's thumb-tip, appear at a glance to contain pine needles the beast has nibbled as it went along. Broken pine crowns indicate the feeding habits of the large animal. Its hooves slash the deep snow from print to print. On broken twigs and in resting places there are hairs in shades of black and grey, the hollow fibers typical of the moose.

A fox has sketched a necklace of tracks across the moose's trail. It gently veers to the margin of the copse, where reynard leapt over a forest ditch toward a field opening out nearby. Lunges indicating a vole hunt interrupt the evenly winding curve of tracks. From a corner of a manor house the light gait proceeds to a lake and, there, from one ice-fishing hole to the next.

On the edge of habitation the features of the fox's handwriting are highlighted as the cavorting of a dog appears beside it. The fox is sparing of movement, while the dog clearly squanders its energy. A raccoon dog also meanders constantly to and fro, every so often changing direction; this is not in keeping with the purposeful progress of a fox. In fact, a raccoon dog avoids being out on snow, sleeping through the harshest period of winter and occasionally emerging but briefly to stretch its legs before its den.

The familiar paw prints of a hare adorn a willow-clad shorescape. Just to make sure, the broad-pawed mountain hare, arrayed in snowshoes and a white camouflage suit, gnawed at some willows and, somewhat farther up the bank, a clump of young aspen shoots. The wealth of droppings strewn along the trail betrays a whole community resident in the area. Long bounds and signs of gambolling show that the hares are already feeling the effects of spring. At night they thrash about in the throes of heat.

The paired tracks of a mustelid, advancing in hops, ends at the open field. The creature thrust itself into a vole's vent hole and came up under the open sky again a good ten meters on. A drop of blood on the snow and drag marks leading to a cluster of junipers affirm the least weasel's success at the hunt.

A strong glow flushes the landscape. A lake cove resembles Swiss cheese; dozens of holes have been drilled a few meters apart in the ice. Ice fishermen chat is hushed voices and smoke – one a pipe, another hand-rolled cigarettes, a third blows rings of his own breath into the calm, chill sky. A beautiful spring-like day draws to a close, and in celebration an eagle owl launches the year's first hollow call into the air. A long subzero night studded with stars lies ahead. The goal is a hefty catch of burbot.

Beneath the ice there reigns an eerie silence and darkness. The boom of an ice rift expanding out on the lake is like a reply to the hoot of the owl a while before. The ice will strengthen still, though the clock has advanced many paces toward spring, and people's minds, even further. Ashore the pistol of frost goes off in the bole of a tree, the wood freeze-dried until its cells finally yield.

The rising sun tinges the landscape while the moon lingers on in the sky.

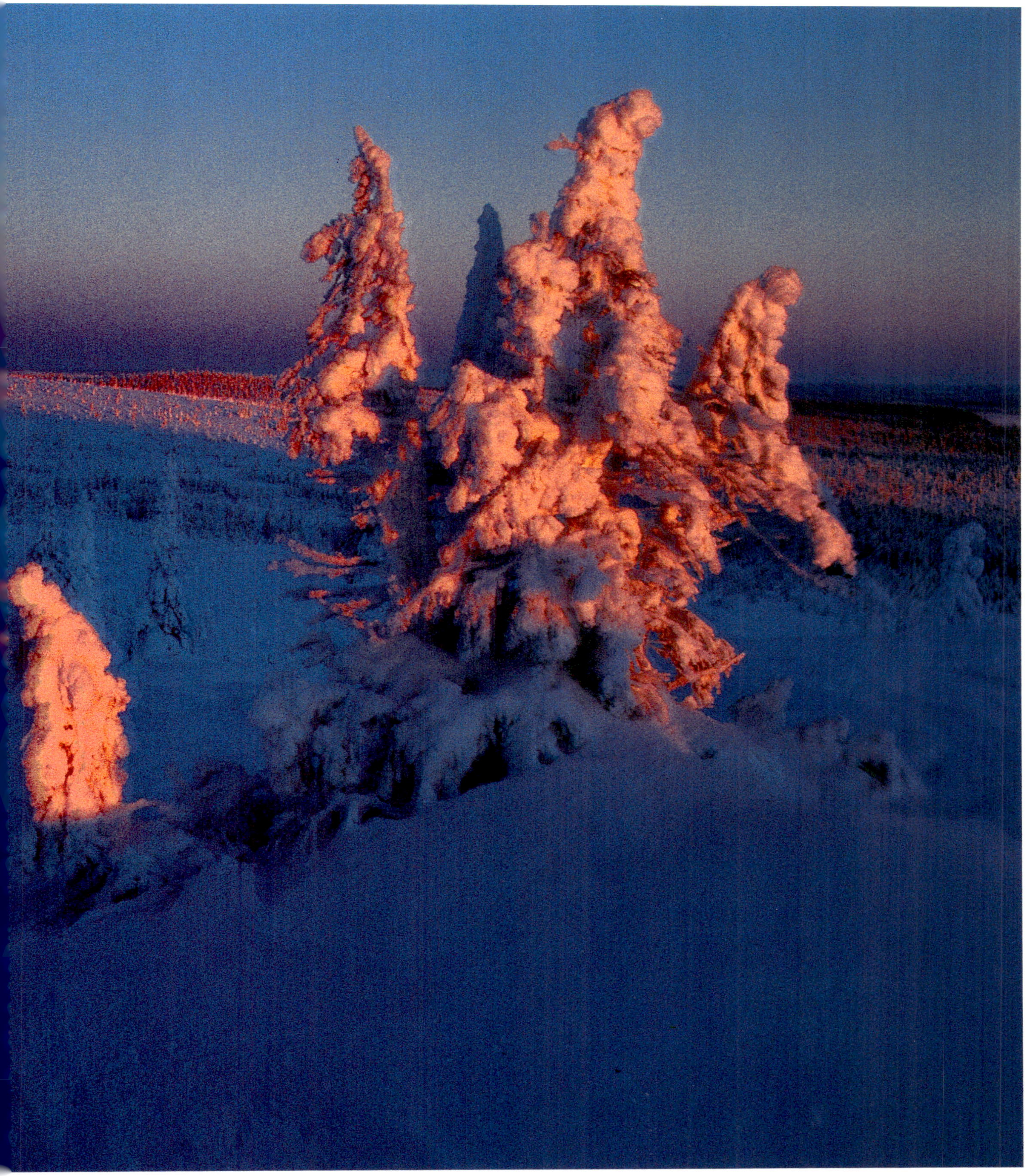

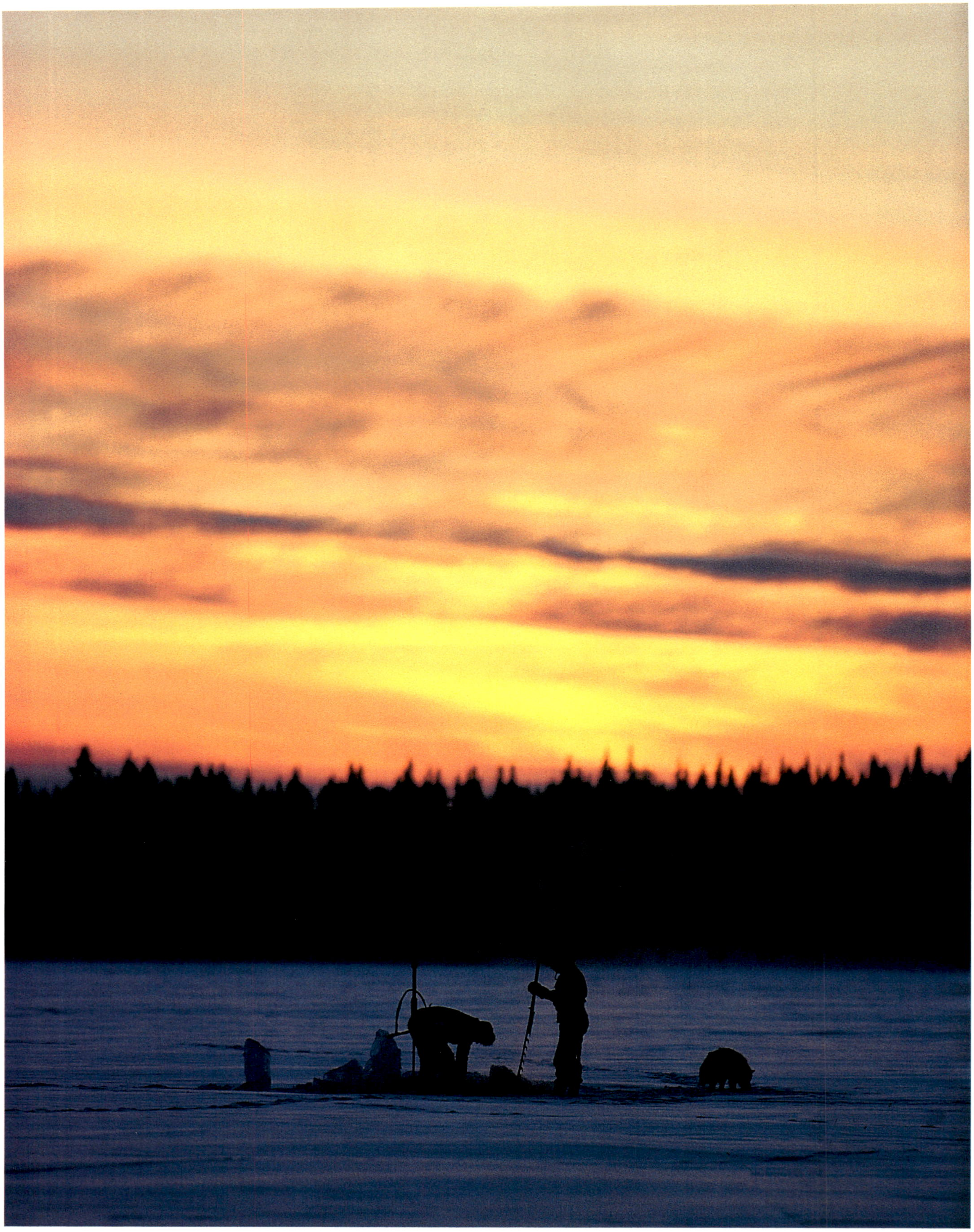

The dark eye of an opening in the ice appears lifeless. Somewhere in the depths lurks a pike. This ruthless predator goes on lengthy fasts, seldom eating in winter and hardly so much as moving. It may sometimes lash out indolently in event of unusual provocation. The perch is somewhat more active, though in plucking larvae and plankton from the lake bed it doesn't exert itself all that much. Inactive bream occupy the depths at the mouth of a bay.

But the lake bed is not as quiet as it appears on the surface. The area teems with burbot: pot-bellied matrons and old codgers somewhat less rotund. The female wriggles in its courtship dance, flashing its pale belly and thus enticing the male into becoming its mate. A fitting companion having been found, the couple hunkers side by side on the lake bed.

As they dance, the fish whisk the bed of the lake with their tails and fins, creating a sort of spawning pit. There the pair casts their reproductive cells, which the female scatters by flicking its tail. This also spreads a little protective sediment over them. Each fertilized egg contains a drop of oil which keeps it afloat enough to prevent it sinking to the bottom.

The dance of the burbot lasts hours and is repeated over and over until the female has laid its eggs. A four-kilo burbot can hold as many as five million of them, all perfectly safe in mid-winter. In the chill darkness, roe predators are scarce. As it favors oxygen-rich waters, the burbot and more particularly its roe may suffer from that scourge of shallow, eutrophic lakes over long drawn-out winters, oxygen depletion. Acid masses of water flushed into waterways via melting snow can also trouble burbot and their roe; the hardest hit are the fish in waters sterile by nature.

Boring holes in the ice, the fisherman are callous gatecrashers at the burbot nuptials. Through the openings, they lower to the lakebed lures furnished with hooks. Engaged as they are in spawning, the fish are not much interested in lures, as they do not feed during their wedding celebration. So fishermen attempt to insinuate their hooks into a fish's path; and when the line registers movement produced by a passing whopper, it's given a yank. The fish is gigged in its side or tail, not necessarily in its mouth.

The fisherman pull in not only females bearing the coveted, delectable roe, but also many male and undersized burbot, some of which are left on the ice. None are returned to the water. The burbot is considered a disreputable devourer of valuable varieties and its elimination en masse, maintenance of the water system. The discarded fish wind up fare for foxes and ravens in reduced circumstances.

Subaqueous produce from beneath the ice.

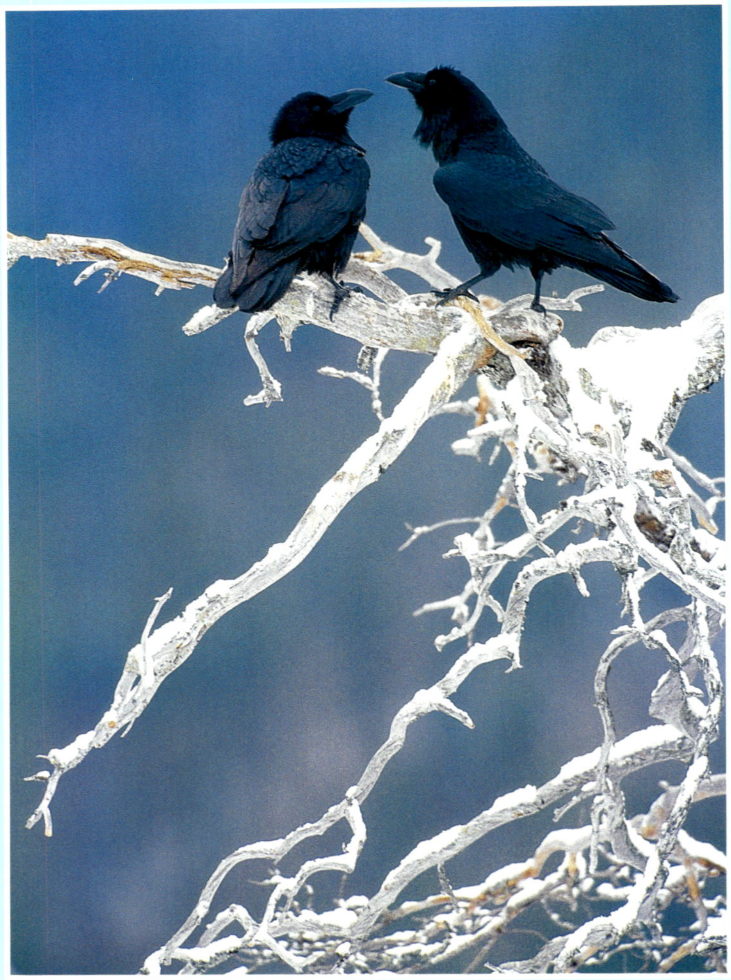

The effect of early spring. The scuffle for the best sites begins as soon as the sun's rays warm the ravens' meeting place. Their black plumage absorbs the sunlight reflected off the snow. Soon the birds will launch into displays seasoned with special sounds and choice aerobatics. Ravens nest early. The carrion exposed by melting snow provides fine fare for these scavengers as they hatch their eggs.

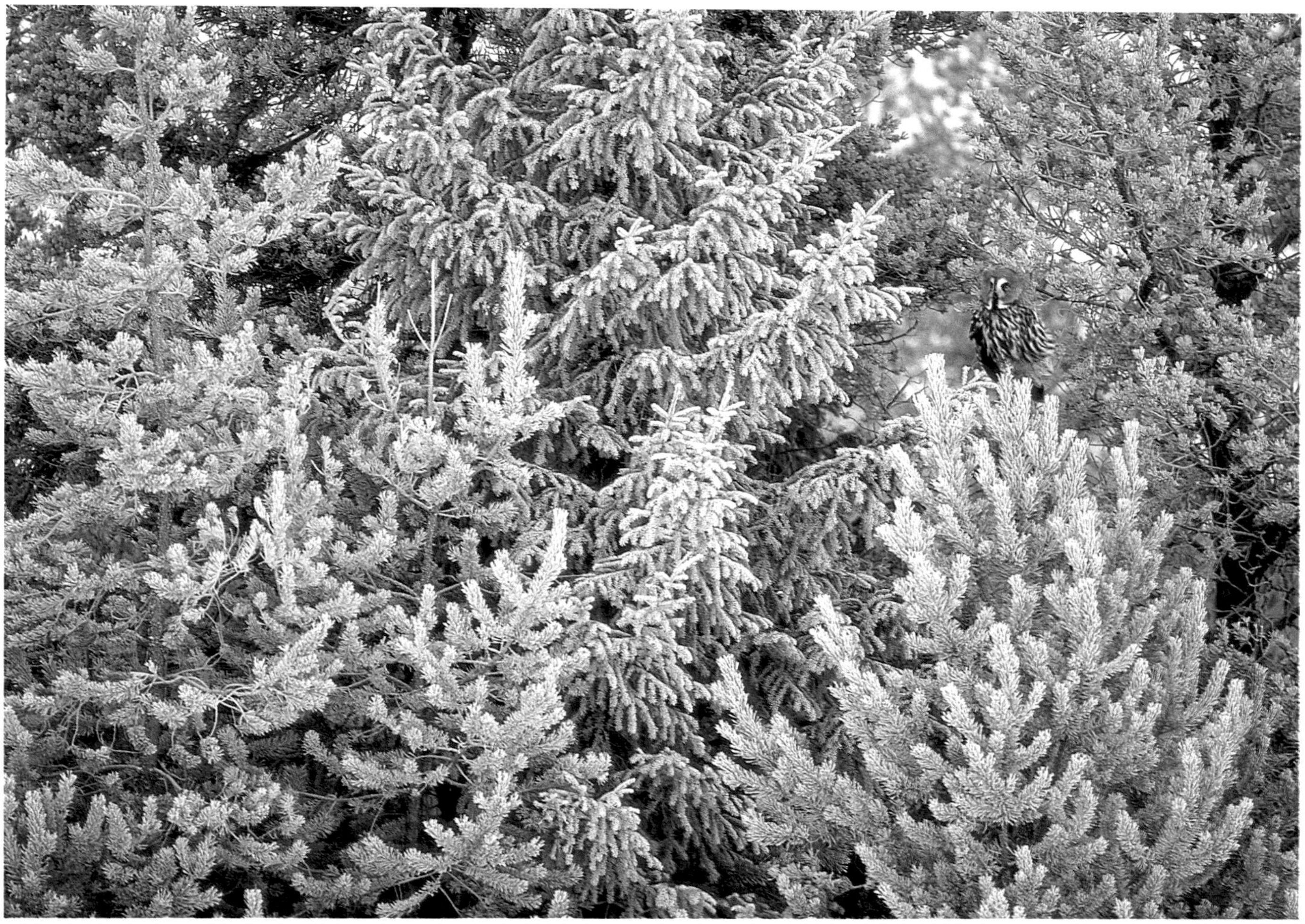

A vole-killer knows how to hide; a great grey owl's vigil is rewarded with a careless vole.

From a spruce grove at the base of a cliff a bright trilling and sharp ringing accompanied by metallic clinks strike the ear. The snow-clad spruces bear a heavy burden: their canopies are literally laden with cones, the branches bowed beneath their weight. Hoarfrosted moisture and the glistening white snow increase the trees' load. After a moment's silence the birdsong commences anew in moist noodlings immediately followed by an animated reiteration of the idiosyncratic themes.

On the top branch sits a vivid red bird whose parrot-like beak crosses at the tip. The male common crossbill firmly grips the bough, looks up toward the blue sky and wafts its song out over the landscape. The spruce has yielded a bumper seed crop and, under its inspiration, the crossbill sends forth its best tunes. More modest in its coloration, the green female broods on a nest fashioned in the canopy.

This comely denizen of the air specializes in consuming spruce seeds, and nests where the best nourishment is on offer. A wanderer, it seeks out areas in which the spruces are fruitful. It ranges unimpeded from country to country, even deep into the Orient when necessary, if its favorite food is unavailable nearer by. It's of no concern to the crossbill that the fare is best when winter is at its coldest.

Having quietly endured the darkest phase of winter, the crossbills begin to warble their mating songs and fashion their nests as soon as the darkness shows signs of easing its grip. The nest, constructed of twigs, is lined with a thick layer of beard moss and lichen. From snowless patches and exposed bases of long-boughed spruces they gather moss and grass as insulation.

The young, hatching in subzero temperatures, survive without the brooding mother's protection even when quite small due to the thick down covering on their backs. The mother birds extract spruce seeds from cones for its offspring. The helpings are large and served up at an unhurried pace. The female pre-digests the seeds in its crop and regurgitates the gruel thus created into the nestlings' craws. Unlike other passerines, crossbills do not remove the faeces of their young; once frozen, it serves as camouflage. The nest resembles the lichens and rime on the tree.

After their winter nesting season, the crossbills set out to range with their young, eventually coming to a halt in an area which offers good provisions for the next nesting season.

A blizzard strikes, the air is thick with wet, sticky rags which the wind jerks carelessly about. The landscape is grey throughout. The snow adheres to windward surfaces and, aided by eddies, even reaches into sheltered areas. It piles up, getting deeper before one's eyes. Ever higher drifts form at the bases of trees and glacial erratics. Snow, snow, snow without end, after days of nothing but blizzard.

Slender birches bow beneath their burden, electric lines sag under the weight of the snow, but the spruces stand in place like sugar loaves. The crown snow amassed in early winter swells apace. The gaunt, narrow-shouldered taper-like spruces put on snowy muscle, conjuring up creatures to inspire the imagination. The spruce wood is like a band of pensive figures, slightly stooped but dignified looking in their white robes.

The crown loads formed of frost and snow are a commonplace of winter in the northern forests; in the south, thaws and the wind lighten the trees' load. But on the forested fells and the flanks of fjelds the snow-laden trees are at their most splendid. In the cold, the moisture in the air crystallizes as rime on the tree trunks and branches. Wet thaw snow adheres very firmly to frozen surfaces, and eventually dry, cold-weather snow also stays on the rough surface thus formed.

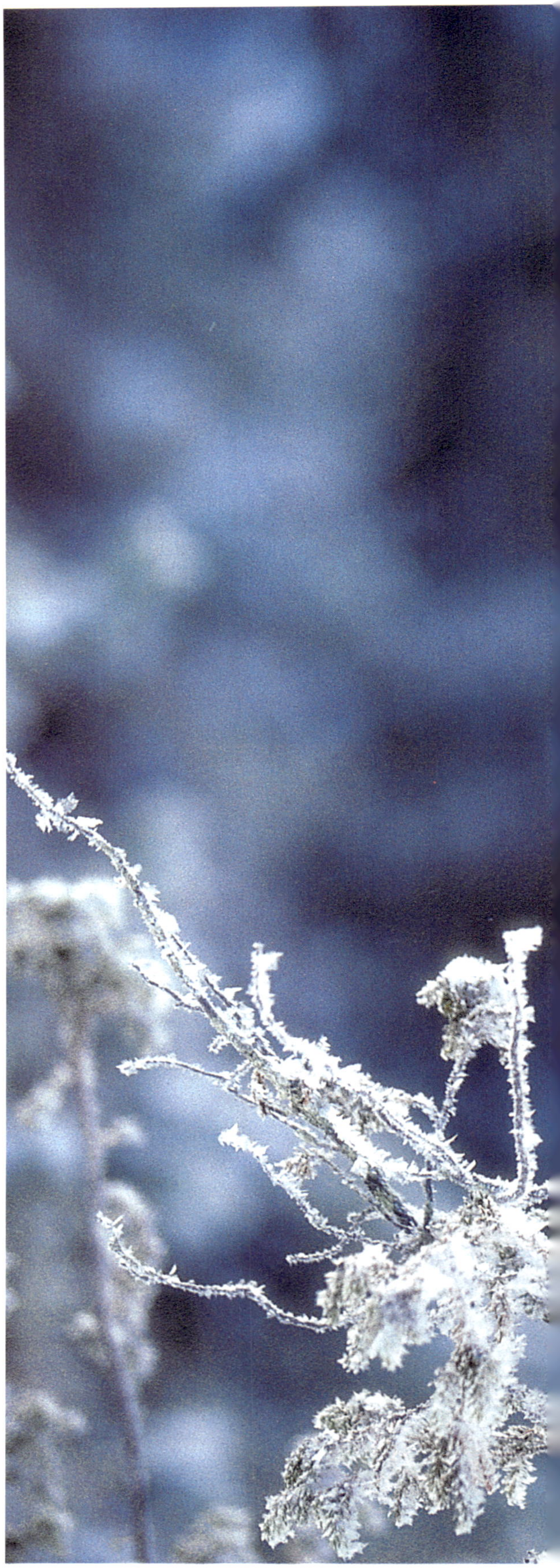

There is no giving in;
willow tits squabble.

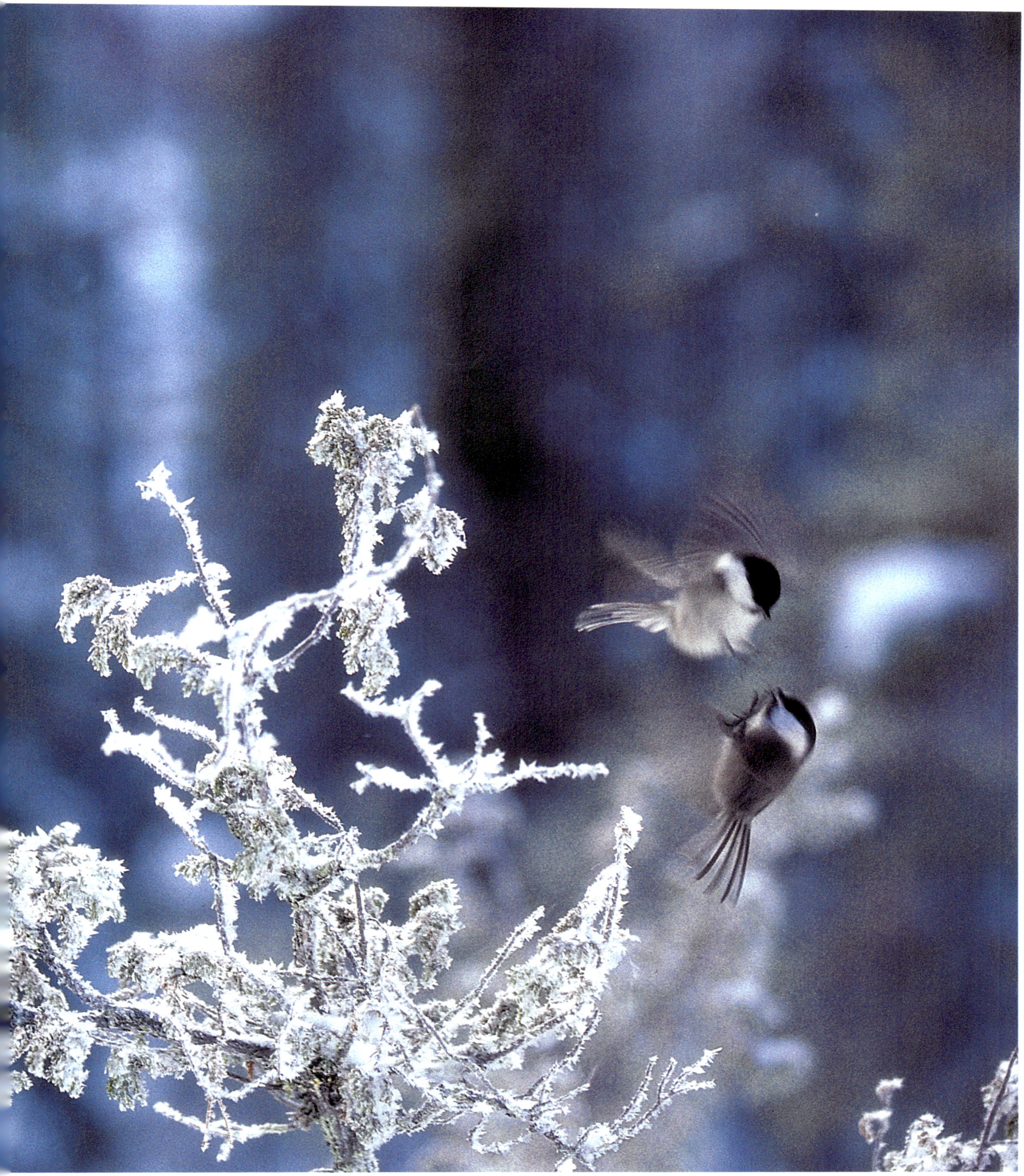

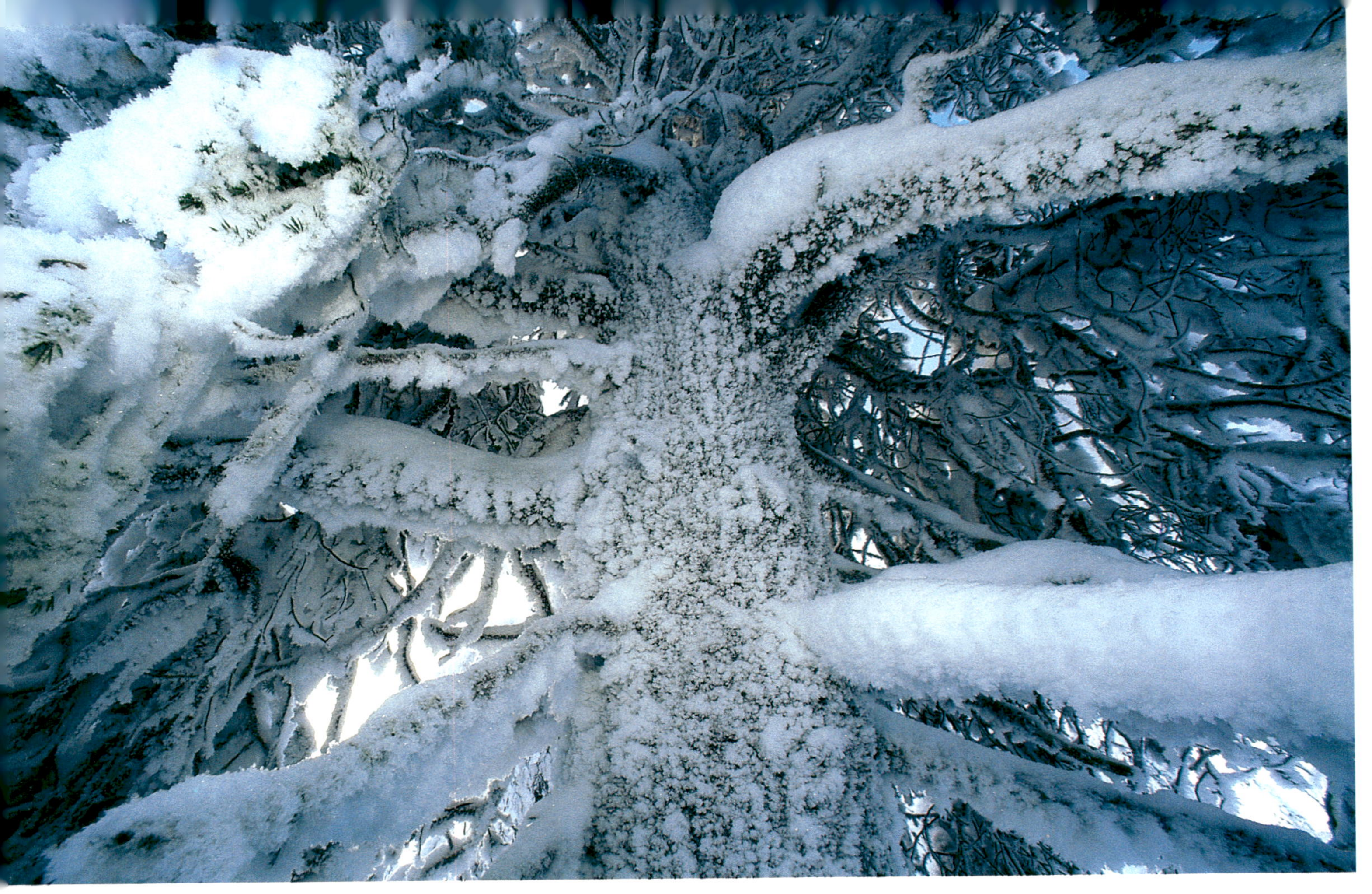

Now and then supercooled rain freezes as a tree's snowy livery, the weight over the winter reaching as much as four thousand kilograms. It's little wonder that the spruce, which in the south grows long, broadly reaching branches, has adapted to crown snow in Lapland by becoming narrow. Despite the differences in appearance, they are the same species.

The narrow taper-shaped spruce does not come through the hazards of winter unscathed. The higher the elevation at which a tree grows, the more deformed it is by crown snow. On many an arctic fell, more than half of the trees have lost their tops and a conspicuous number of limbs display stress injuries induced by burden snow. Only the most stately of trees may survive virtually undamaged. If a tree's top bends under the weight of snow, breakage is almost inevitable. The resulting wounds pave the way to the tree's interior for rot fungi.

The thick mantle of snow also acts as protection against the harsh winter, inhibiting the effects of the freezing cold and bitter winds. On the other hand, crown snow may exacerbate stress produced by air pollution. As the snow begins to melt in early spring, the acid compounds it contains damage the needles.

Crown snow protects insects and spiders overwintering in the bark, in fissures and the crotches of branches, which also means that the tits hunting them for winter food have problems during the period of thick crown snow. They must toil more than usual to satisfy their daily energy requirements. If necessary, they may leave the area of crown snow. For a titmouse fleeing a bird of prey, the recesses in a load of crown snow offer excellent cover.

Crown snow swathes the trees to the core.

The lengthening day occasions the first icicles.

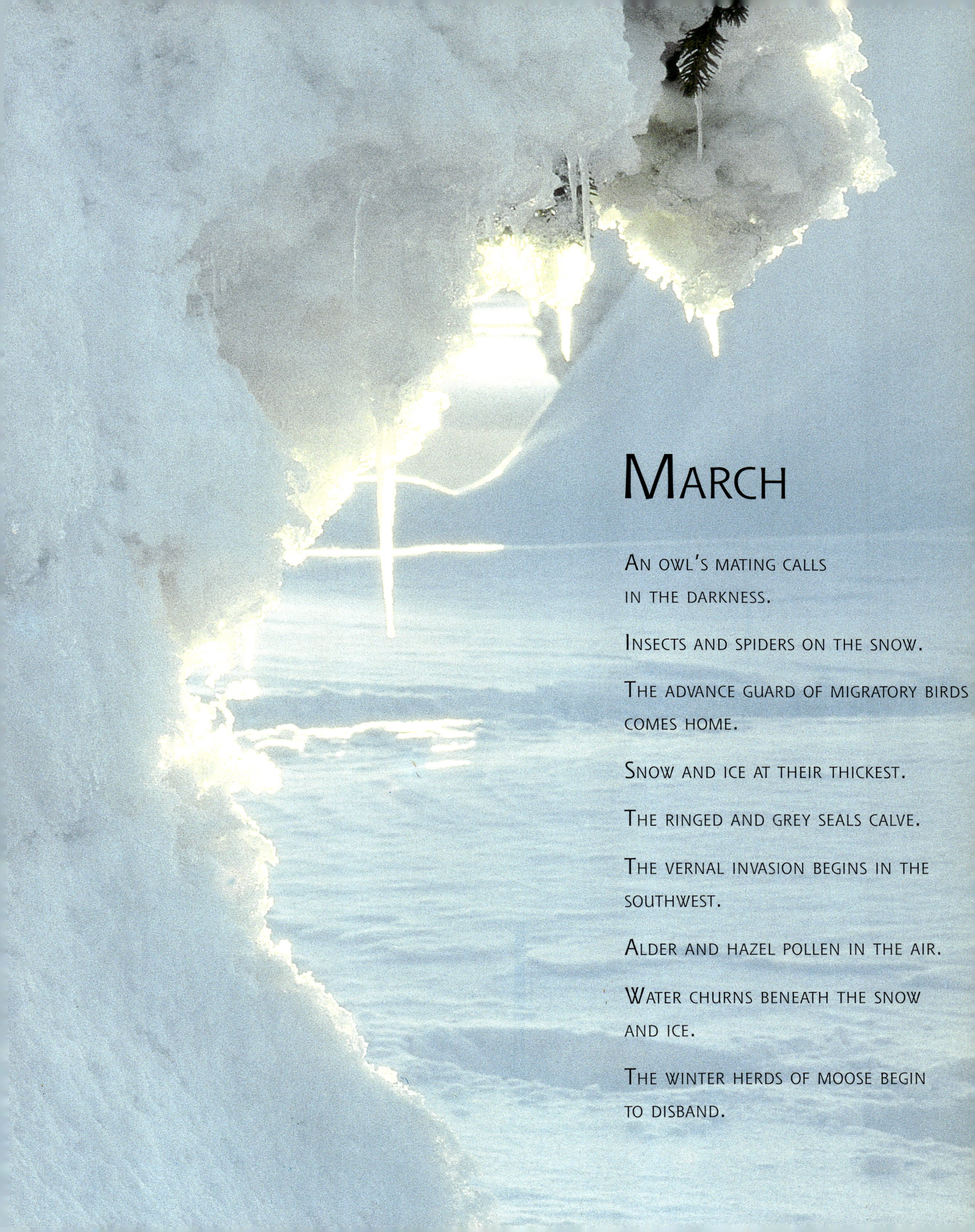

March

An owl's mating calls
in the darkness.

Insects and spiders on the snow.

The advance guard of migratory birds
comes home.

Snow and ice at their thickest.

The ringed and grey seals calve.

The vernal invasion begins in the
southwest.

Alder and hazel pollen in the air.

Water churns beneath the snow
and ice.

The winter herds of moose begin
to disband.

PRELUDE TO SPRING

Day gives way to evening, wet snow encumbers spruce branches, the timorous light of the moon glimmers among thick clouds. The lungs of a city ready for bed sigh with a grating wheeze. In a grove the first moments of night echo with the sounds of spring. The wet weather yields to a light frost, invigorating the wanderer as well. The gnarled limbs of trees trace forms against the star-spangled sky, firing the imagination.

A hooting like the miaowing of a cat sounds from among the vaulted trees. The tremulous lovesong of a tawny owl is interrupted by a shrill clangor that reflects the fervor of the owl's courtship. This night there will be no battling over food - that is, squealing voles; this night is consecrated to life and its perpetuation.

In the depths of the grove, in a hollow hewn by a black woodpecker, any night now a mother owl will lay a few pale eggs which

Day thaws, night freezes. The dark boughs of a fjeld birch are bathed in blazing sunlight by day. Its roots remain frozen until the threshold of summer.

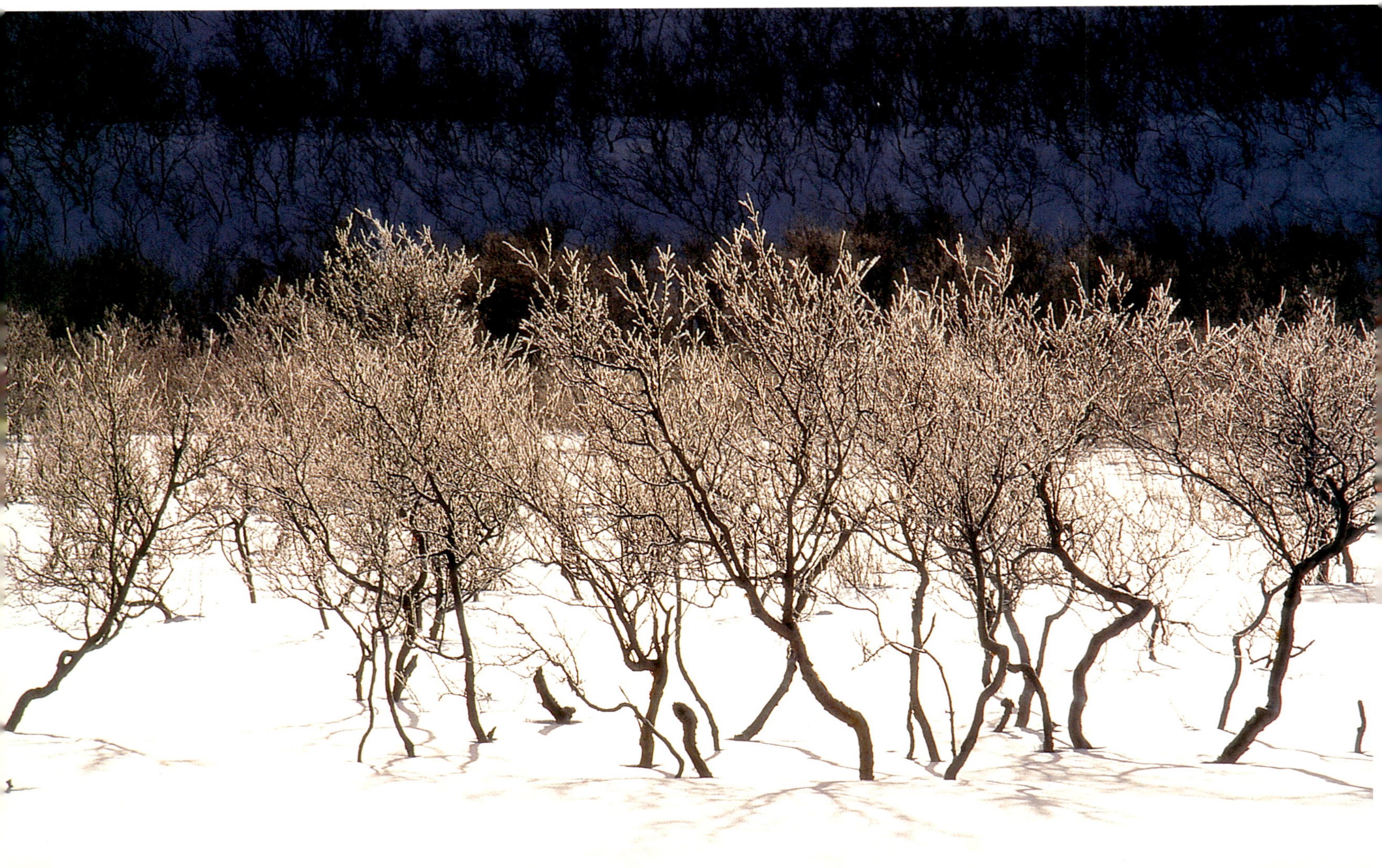

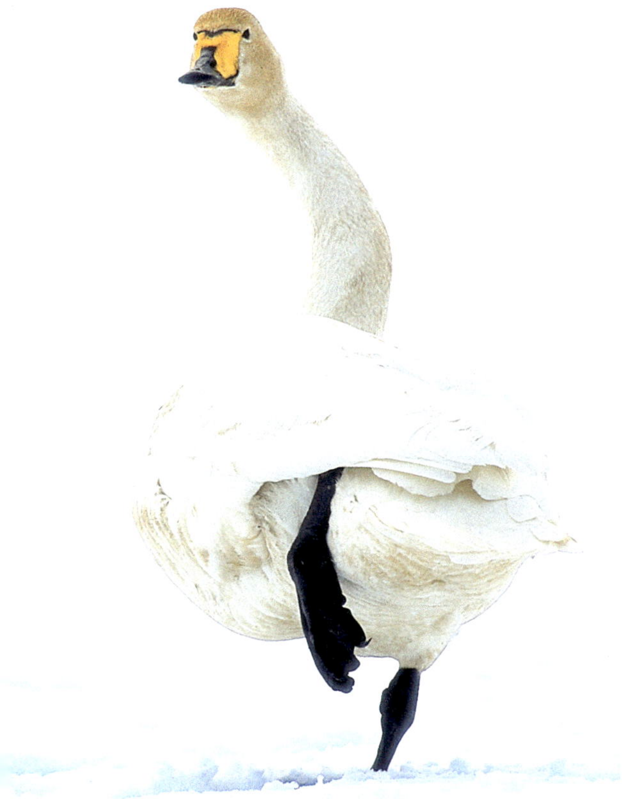

The first swan of spring in the hinterlands: white on white.

will hatch into young that will test their wings in early summer. By then the terrain will be teeming – if not with the owl's favorite food, voles, then with fledgling thrushes and other young birds. They make prime practice quarry for owlets in the toughest phase of learning by doing.

As evening draws on, any wisps of cloud drifting in the sky flee. The warmth generated by the spring day escapes into space. Ice crusts a pool of meltwater. The steam from exhaled breath freezes. The cold pops in a roadside signpost.

And just then a hollow "oo-woo! oo-woo!" rebounds from the sky. The colossus of the night, an eagle owl, speaks. In the heart of the forest towers a rocky crag, an ancient stronghold in which this horned sovereign has dwelt since time out of mind. In the stillness of the night this booming avowal of love carries for kilometers. The eagle owl lays its eggs in a hollow scratched into the south face of a steep bluff. During this time this monarch of the night is at its most vulnerable; those inspired to roam by the resplendent weather at the onset of spring can, if they happen on the nest, cause untold damage.

Deep in the forest a ridge dominated by old pines descends into marshy wilds. As moonlight cannot penetrate the dense network of spruce boughs, a soft darkness prevails in these parts. Among the trees Europe's smallest bird of prey, a pigmy owl, busies itself. The soft sequence of whistles made by this miniature owl is barely audible at two hundred meters: "Yi-ou, yi-ou, yi-ou-yi-ou...." In summer an owl pair may be found in the spruce grove, zealously defending their privacy. Along, of course, with a troupe of beady-eyed little gnomes who were given their start in the glory of early spring.

The snow crust bears a human's weight in the pygmy owl mating territory, where the distant calling of an eagle owl also lends its own enchantment. A fox unexpectedly lets out a howl of desolation. Its true mating urge is now on the wane, but Sir Reynard is still up to expressing his feelings.

Its screeches are interrupted by a message from an Ural owl: "Hoo-woo, woof woof...." On the margin of a fallow field the large owl bays gutturally like a distant dog. An intriguingly soft hooting. The Ural owl, a consumer of small rodents that will also hunt more substantial quarry when hungry, is renowned for its willingness to attack when its progeny are threatened by humans. This laid-back courtship barking does not give a true picture of this hot-headed owl.

Soon, almost furtively, the ear detects a familiar, somewhat wistful pooting. The best-known soloist of the vernal night, a Tengmalm's owl, is at last expressing itself. Specialized in rodents, the little owl is often the most common sound of March nights, but it falls silent if beset by a dearth of provender.

To culminate the trip, there sounds from the sky a series of sharp cries, familiar from very different surroundings: a dipper. Having wintered beside flowing water, dippers travel to their native habitat with the starry sky as their map, their destination perhaps a brook in Norway.

The rapids thrust a dark cone into the open lake and this grows in length and breadth even as one watches. The strong current consumes the ice from beneath, and the warmth of the lengthening days enlarges soggy patches, some of which burst free as rippling pools, despite the wintry surroundings. The gradual shading of the forest suggests that spring is gaining a firmer hold. The trees shed snow which the sun causes to evaporate, but night freezes glaze these parts white, with the pools too given a sheath of ice. Snowfall, even a full-fledged blizzard, is still possible at any time.

The dipper chimes brightly on the edge of the ice. A blue tit, feeling the effects of spring, does acrobatics on birch boughs dangling over the water. The snow along the shore is dappled with shreds of birchbark, twigs and crumbs of lichen. Strewn over the snow by the wind are spruce seeds, needles and entire twig tips from which a squirrel has nibbled buds to supplement its late winter diet. The melting snow looks cluttered.

There is power in the take-off of a white-tailed eagle.

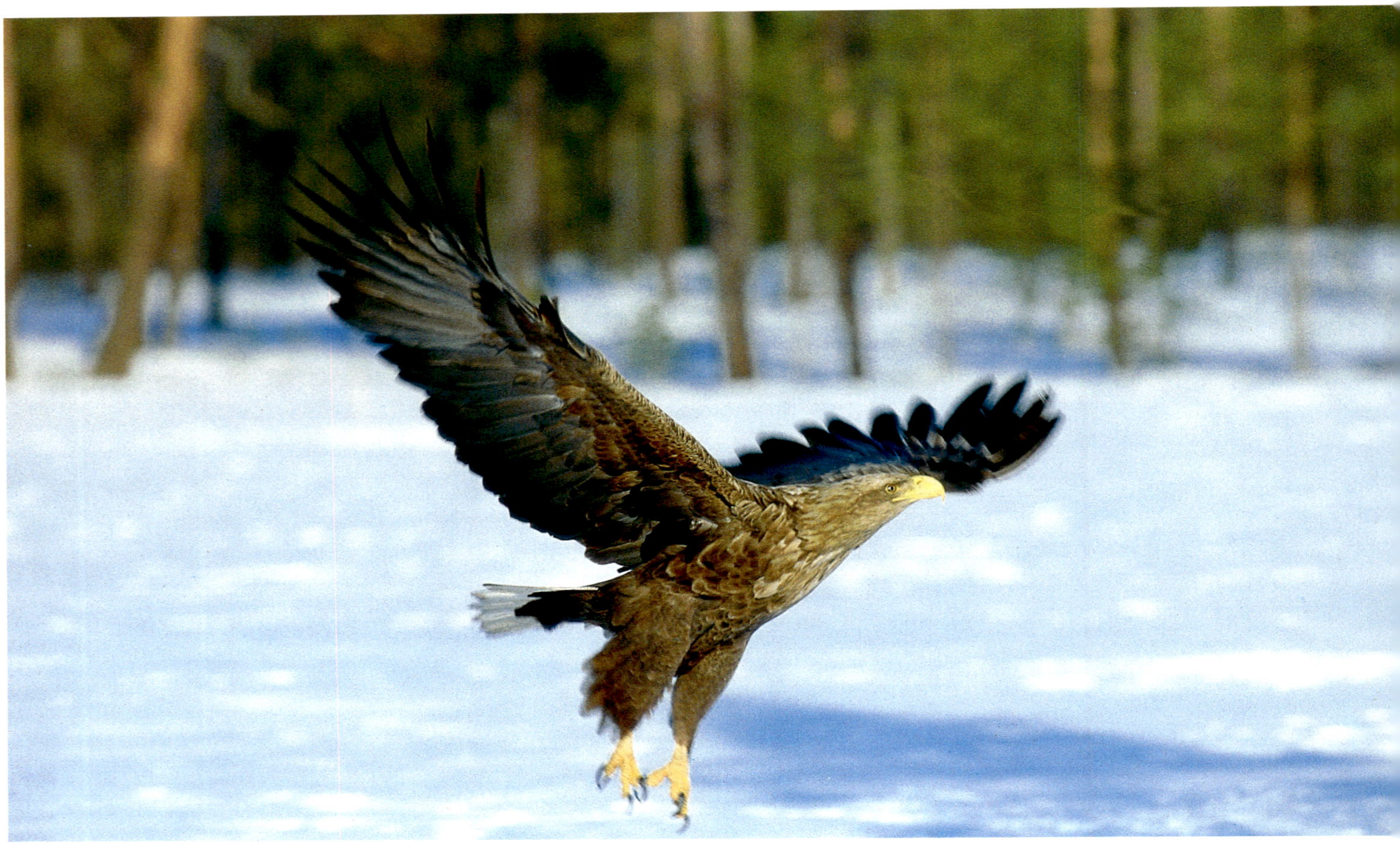

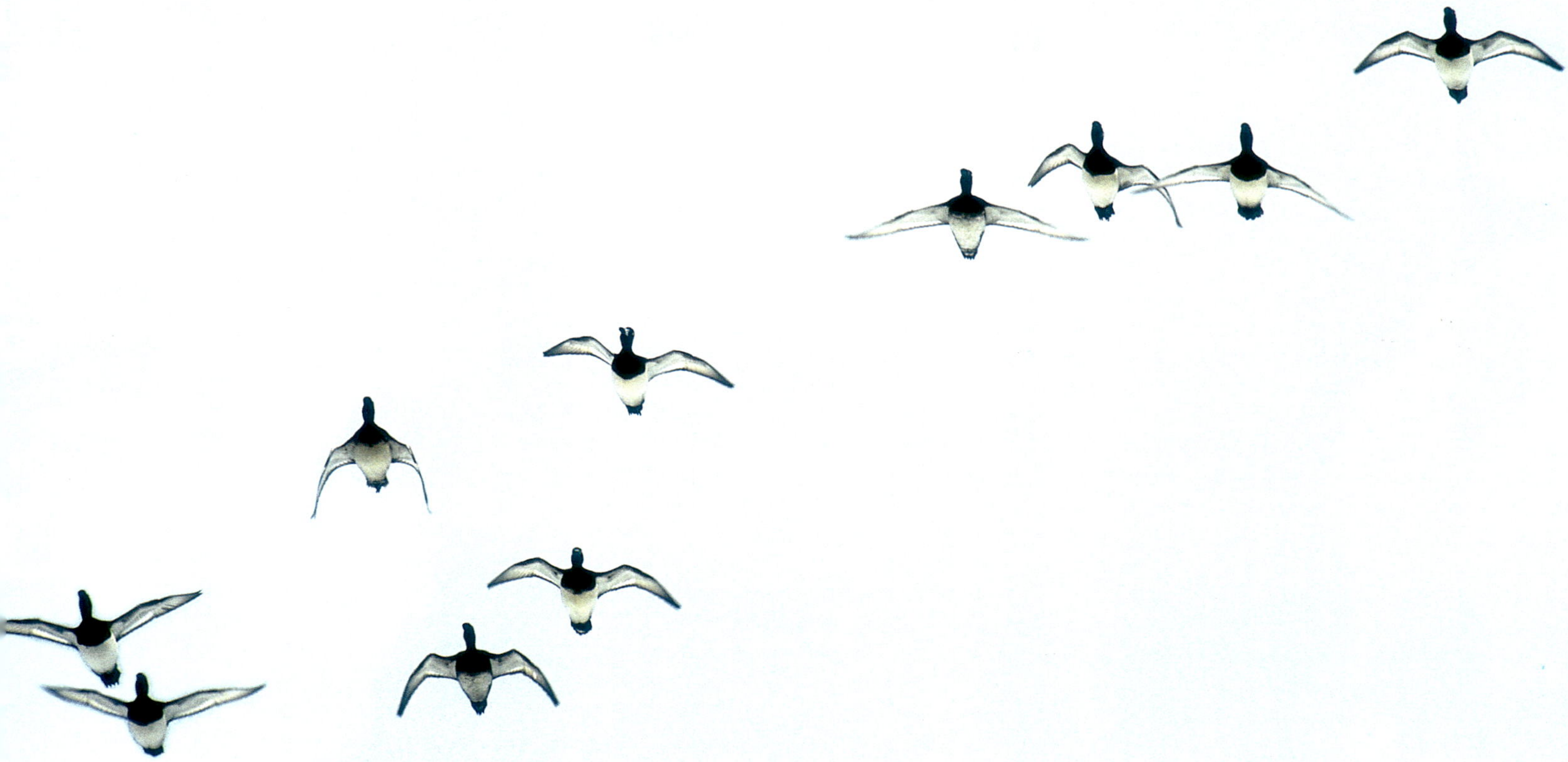

The sun reflects a flock of migrating tufted ducks on the crust.

There is movement among the fragments on the snow, a community of grey-brown insects is on the march. Small nymphs emerge from the water, throw off their mantles and molt to become insects; the spring festival of the storeflies is taking place unobserved on the snow. When the invasion is at its height, these wingless nymphs even pour out onto the ice through the holes made by ice fishermen. They make fine bait, as many a winter angler knows.

A trek of a few meters suffices for these nymphs, which settle into a recess in the snow and molt. The larval appearance as well as the long antennae, narrow forewings and broad hind wings distinguish the creature. The storefly isn't much of a flier. As a rule it flees on foot, and speed is of the essence when a bevy of blue tits happens by and spots the mass of delectable bugs.

The adult phase of the storefly lasts but a few weeks in late winter. Having mated on the snow, the ground or in the cover of shoreline brush, the female hovers above the water, dropping its fertilized eggs into the current. Sometimes it even takes a dip as it lays its eggs. The larva which hatch from the eggs eat the moss, grasses and grubs of other insects on the bottom. Storefly larvae are an important component of the dipper's winter diet.

The nymphs are by no means the only bugs active when snow holds sway. Things are all abustle beneath the snow; and as the surface melts, more and more insects and spiders make their way out under the open sky. In mild weather it may be several degrees above freezing on the surface, and even the snow can be around zero. At subzero temperatures the surface of the snow is coldest, and then only the most inured of insects and spiders are encountered.

Moving about on the snow are the insects known as snow fleas, wingless crane flies, true bugs, certain flies, small butterflies and winter gnats. The best known of the creatures that creep about on the snow are probably the lovely, hairy larvae of the ruby tiger moth, which anyone skiing the spring snows has doubtlessly seen. Having spent the winter as a larva, the furry "grub" seeks out a place to pupate at the first sign of spring.

And where there is prey, there are also predators. Snow insects and the spiders pursuing one another are found moving about even in a slight frost. There is a dark spider which, warmed by daylight while out on the brilliant crust, manages to kill a meal. Another species even lays its snares in such snowy surroundings. In the cold, a spider's energy consumption is minimal; prey its own size provides fuel for many weeks.

A blue tit sings its fervid song, and a greenfinch frantically slurps. To top these off, a yellowhammer trills and a bullfinch whistles. A hooded crow alights atop a spruce and belts out its rasping squawk. Spring achieves miracles. The lengthening day makes the creatures of the air slightly daffy. Feeling its oats, the blue tit ruffles itself, flies through the yard on stiff wings, as if in slow motion, and examines the birdhouses with a proprietary air.

The crow studies a stick with an eye to taking it to its new home, which is evolving in the depths of the forest. Soon, twig in beak, it flaps off into the trees. A flock of the birds that wintered across the Baltic heads north. This nest-builder spent the winter on the southern coast of Finland and, rising in its reserved seat, it croaks harshly: taken.

As the morning frost eases, more singers join the choir. A great tit titters cheerfully, a coal tit ardently recites its stanza over and over in the treetops. The vibrato of a crested tit sounds, as does the plaintive melody of a willow tit. A treecreeper's melancholic song, resembling that of the yellow warbler, also reaches the ear. Magpies squabble among willows on the edge of a village. Flocks of jackdaws sweep by, cheerfully babbling on their passage inland. Croaking and bonking, a raven airs its expressive vernal calls; as its numbers increase over recent years, this black bird settles ever closer to human habitation.

Near meltwaters the noble cackling of a herring gull is heard. A whole choir of large gulls hollers out loud, the shores amplifying the echoes. The hoarse cries of a great black-backed gull sound the most dreadful, but the day, exuding a vernal sweetness, mellows the air of ferocity.

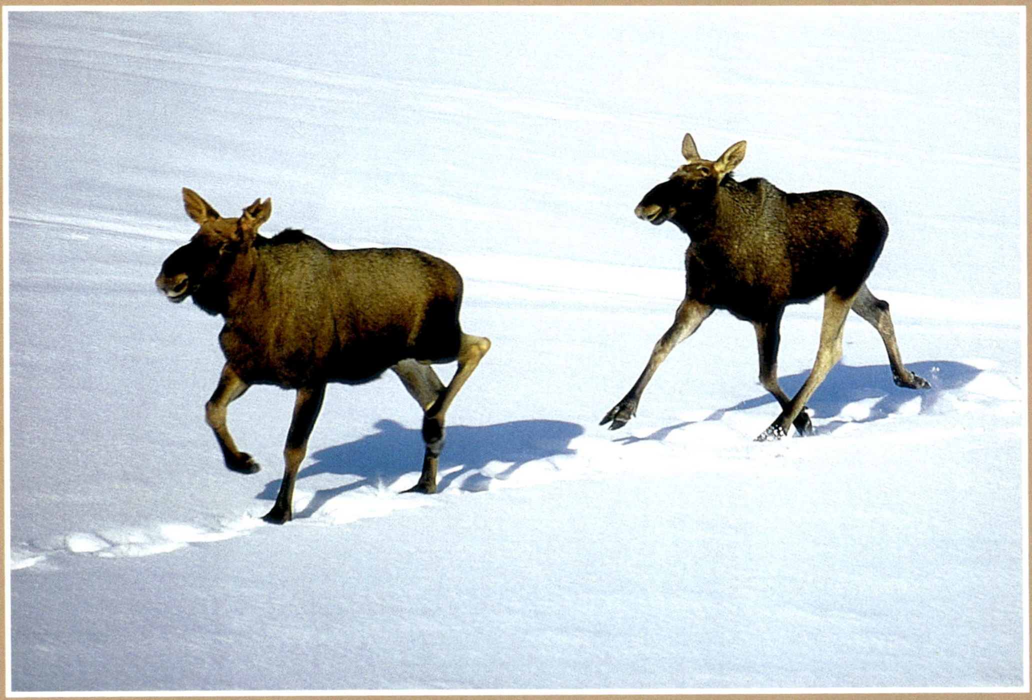

The availability of food and the amount of snow govern the life of the moose as well. They live the winters in loose herds in copses and marshes with little snow, and at the onset of spring seek out their summer pastures. Their migration may measure tens of kilometers and they travel accustomed routes. In the south the move begins in March and continues in the north well into May.

The creamy plumage of a male goosander glints like enamel on the waves. The drake burbles nasally at a comely red-headed female and rivals. The wings of a goldeneye male whistle melodiously; the individuals in the water eagerly engage in brawls and perform special aquatic dances, wriggle their necks and hold swim meets.

Arriving earliest, the gulls and ducks congregate in huge masses in the first open patches, on ferry quays and in current-swept narrows. Eiders and long-tailed ducks also appear where the ice is out. Few stray to the coast or inland, but the archipelago channels actually teem with these handsome swimmers. The raucous squabbling of these attractive birds imparts intense atmosphere to the change of seasons.

Puffing themselves up, mute swans also chase each other about; air currents howl in their wings, the slap of huge webbed feet accompanying the white birds' movements. Whooper swans on their way inland remain aloof from the fights of their half-tame cousins. They have their own matches in their home territories, where they head forthwith, vying with the snow buntings and crows as the first birds of passage.

Spring has come to the hinterlands. Crows are its advance guard.

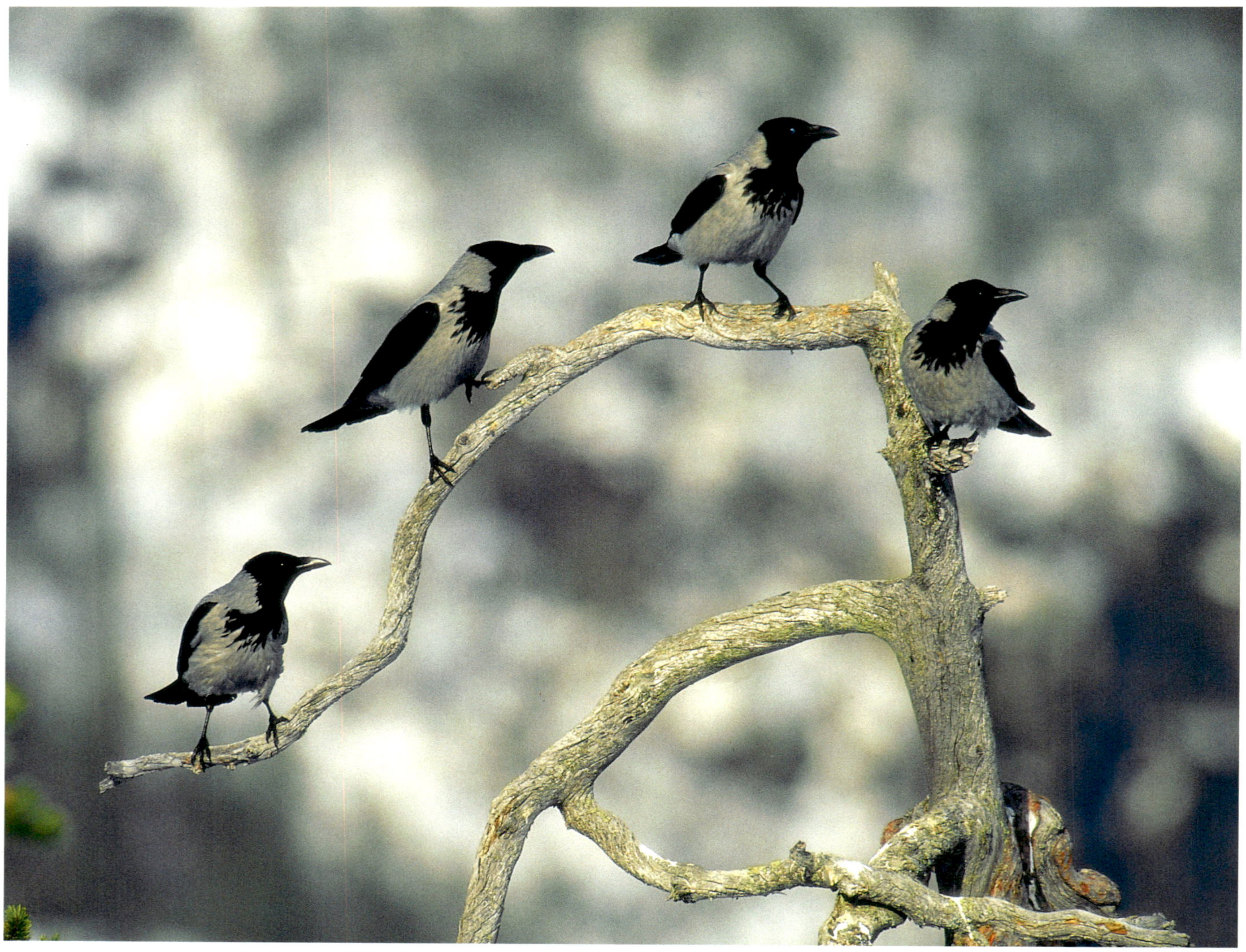

MARCH

Tonight an eagle owl
proclaims spring.

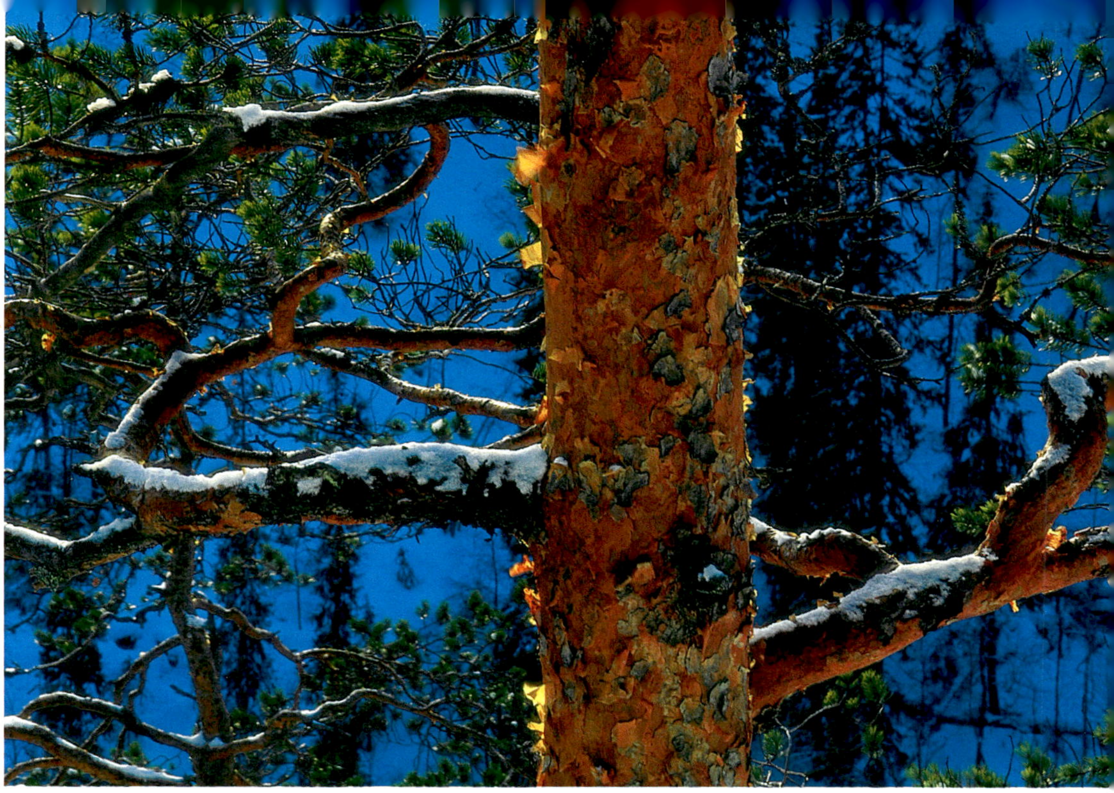

Winter shows its might.
Birches bend but do not yield.

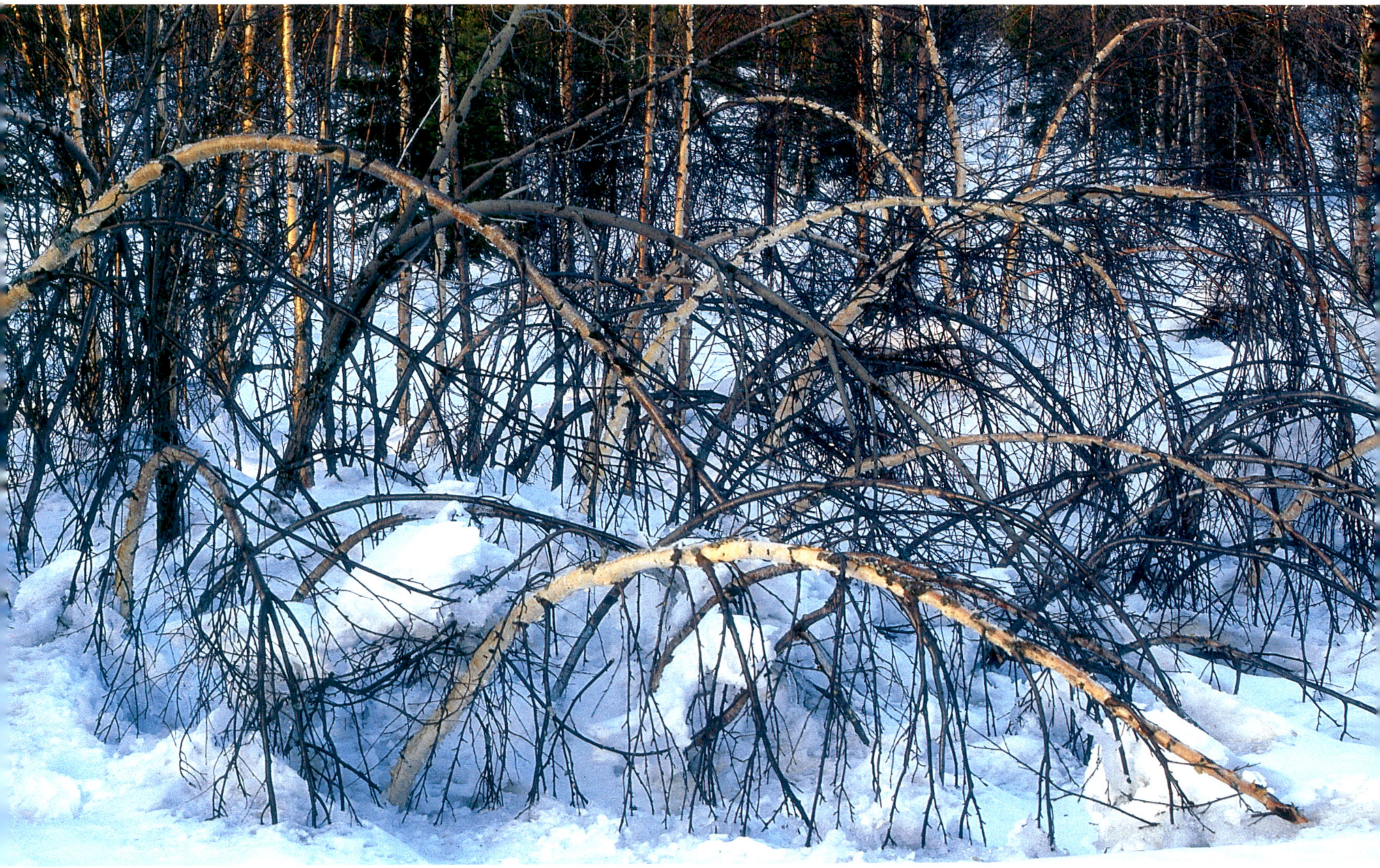

Hooded crows and jackdaws pour northward in droves, by the hundreds and, on the best days of migration in early spring, by the thousands. Rooks also tack the same winds, on their way to gladden summer in the coastal towns on the Gulf of Bothnia.

Among the first arrivals are skylarks burbling softly to themselves and snow buntings flitting across the view like white snow flurries. Both species appear along roadsides in open country. The skylarks settle on dark exposed ground or, lacking this, darkening roadbanks to await the thawing of the fields. The dulcet-toned snow buntings, for their part, make swiftly for Lapland, as if competing for the title of first harbinger of spring. While awaiting its eventual onset, they sustain themselves by gobbling springtails and other sun-roused insects with which the dazzling surface of the snow literally teems.

Crane tracks have appeared on marsh habitat still under snow.

In the afternoon hours, water flows in a trickle from the icicles on tips of branches. The snow has compacted, its surface a watery porridge of coarse granules which freezes hard during the subzero periods that come largely at night, but which the drizzle of milder nights continues to melt as if of its own accord. Subsurface meltwater seeks low ground. This gradually spills over, the water breaking out as brooks that join to culminate in streams and, beyond them, in lakes.

The rush of runoff sounds through the snow, and it will be some time before the ultimate onset of spring banishes the whiteness entirely. The snow yielding to spring is grubby. In addition to the twigs, needles and scraps of bark from trees, algae grow in the snow, giving the whiteness a dark and grey cast.

But the snow also holds impurities originating in human activity, and in spring they produce harmful effects when runoff conveys them to these wild water systems. Over the winter long-distance air-borne acid compounds accumulate as pollutants in the snow. When spring transforms the snow into fluid form, the pollutants layered in it are also set in motion.

The acid meltwaters are particularly problematic in the small lakes, streams and brooks of wild environments. There are many such water systems, unable by nature to tolerate acidity, in Finland. Even a temporary cresting of acidity can prove fatal to some fish species, lampreys, crayfish and molluscs. Fish roe and hatchlings are at special risk; adults may survive an acid attack with nothing more than stress.

Perch, pike and river trout are fairly resilient to temporary periods of acidity. Fishermen have cause for concern if the size of fish caught increases but no small fish are caught at all. By then the worst has already happened. Even as adults, salmon and roach are singularly susceptible to acidity. It is also worth noting that acid waters look deceptively pure, actually as clear as spring water.

Acidification affects plankton. At worst, the entire ecosystem breaks down, and nature is slow to recover from damage caused thus. Once the threshold has been crossed, the rehabilitation of an ailing environment is slow, wearisome and costly.

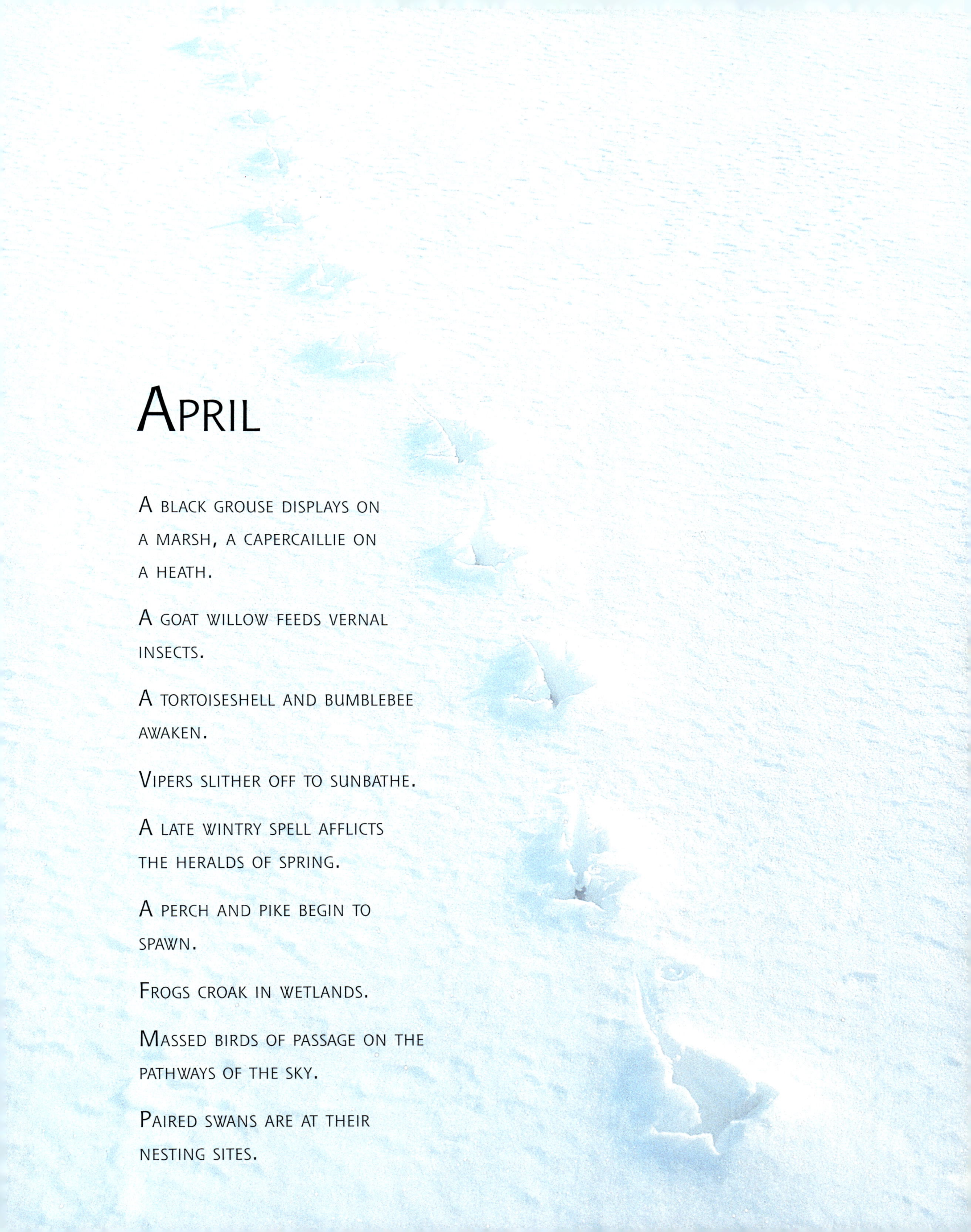

April

A black grouse displays on a marsh, a capercaillie on a heath.

A goat willow feeds vernal insects.

A tortoiseshell and bumblebee awaken.

Vipers slither off to sunbathe.

A late wintry spell afflicts the heralds of spring.

A perch and pike begin to spawn.

Frogs croak in wetlands.

Massed birds of passage on the pathways of the sky.

Paired swans are at their nesting sites.

The Feverish Days of Spring

A full moon looms above a treeless marsh. The features of the blue-tinged landscape are clearly distinguishable, although the night is still dark. Stunted pines form park-like compositions on the dark hummock ridges of peat moss, the pools between them gleaming in the pale moonlight. Nocturnal cold has rimed the open margins of the pools, their centers are sheathed in splintered white ice. It would scarcely support a human, but it does serve as the battleground of black grouse.

The twittering of migrating redwings sounds from on high. Orienting themselves with celestial navigation, the birds return rather inconspicuously from their wintering grounds. One morning a familiar shape flits by, and by evening its melancholic song carries from nearby woods.

The wintry aspect of a marsh quickly changes when a heatwave collapses the crust.

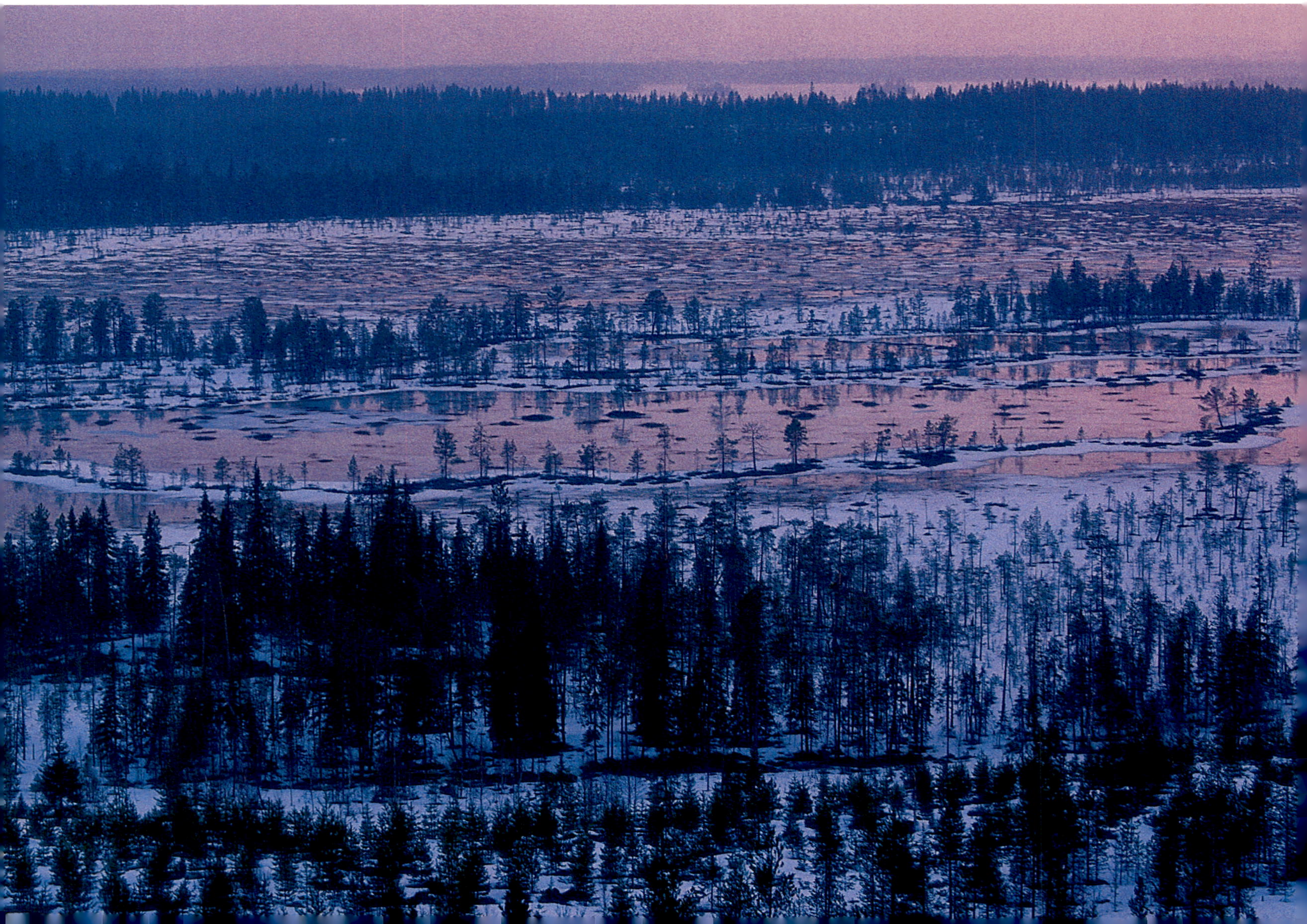

While the social calls of the thrushes still fill the air, the rustle of wings can also be heard. A large bird appears in the top of a pine, finding its balance on a slender bough and then tensing to listen to the nighttime sounds. The song thrush makes sharp cheeping sounds. And then another large pair of wings beat the air, a third, fourth, fifth.... The area seems to fill with black grouse.

The first cock begins in total darkness. It gabbles, throat ruffled and lyre-shaped tail fanned. It is silhouetted against the moon and the star-studded sky. Amid the gabbling, a sharp noise sounds like the lashing of a whip. A second grouse replies from an adjacent tree. Soon the whole troop descends, continues cackling on the ice and the carpet of sphagnum moss. The more ecstatic blackcocks pull out all the stops before the sun flushes the eastern sky.

The day dawns. Beyond the saw-toothed horizon the great pyre blazes, the brightening sky extinguishes the twinkle of stars, and finally the molten copper of the sun pours over the landscape. The plumage of the black-clad grouse cock glows with a metallic sheen, the coiled tail feathers flap like coattails, and its under-tail coverts gleam like a white shirt in the rising sun, which weirdly accentuates the blood-red wattles above its eyes.

Reindeer ascend the fjelds with the first bare patches.

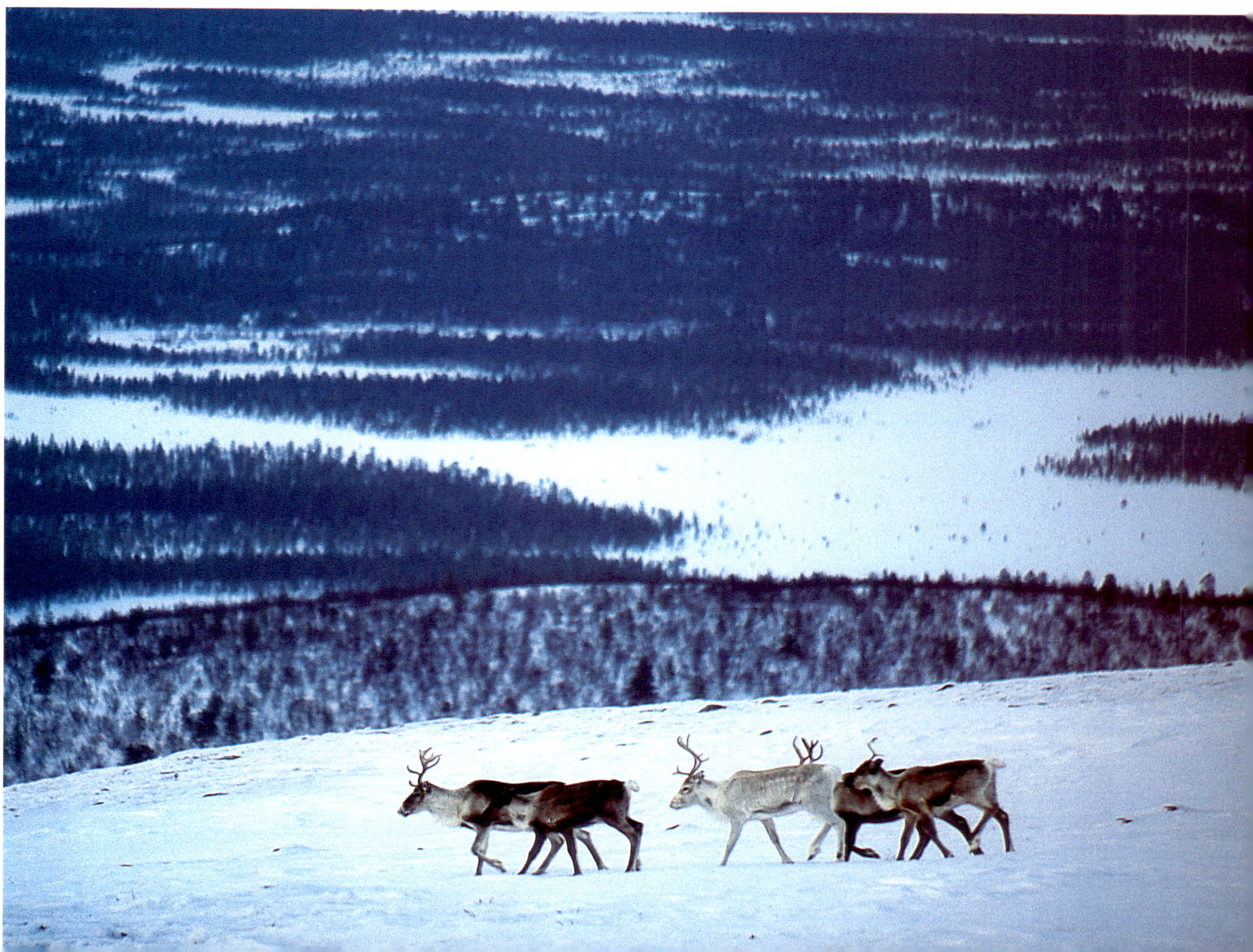

Throat inflated, the black grouse babbles and strolls its lek like a gladiator. The bird halts and lashes the air with its whipping sound, springs into the air and flaps its wings, and then goes on pottering about. When it crosses paths with a neighboring male, the beaus take each others measure with threats. If required, the adversaries attack one another, striking out with their wings and clawing. Feathers flutter to the wrestling mat.

A dozen or so cocks tussle during the courtship display, the strongest, most self-assured adults in the middle. The youngsters, who have no business with the best positions yet, loiter on the fringes of the lek. They burble listlessly, hiss softly, and hop about. The youths may forget themselves, and pluck at twigs and scratch at the moss in frustration.

When a loose flock of hens arrives at ringside, the fervent display builds to a free-for-all. It's time for the cocks to strut their stuff. At first the greyhens observe events from the trees, but then descend and select their mates. More often than not, it is the strongest of the males who is permitted to continue the line, but the fracas also provides other blackcock beaus with opportunities.

The worst is past. Expanding exposed areas offer fresh fare to ptarmigan preparing to nest.

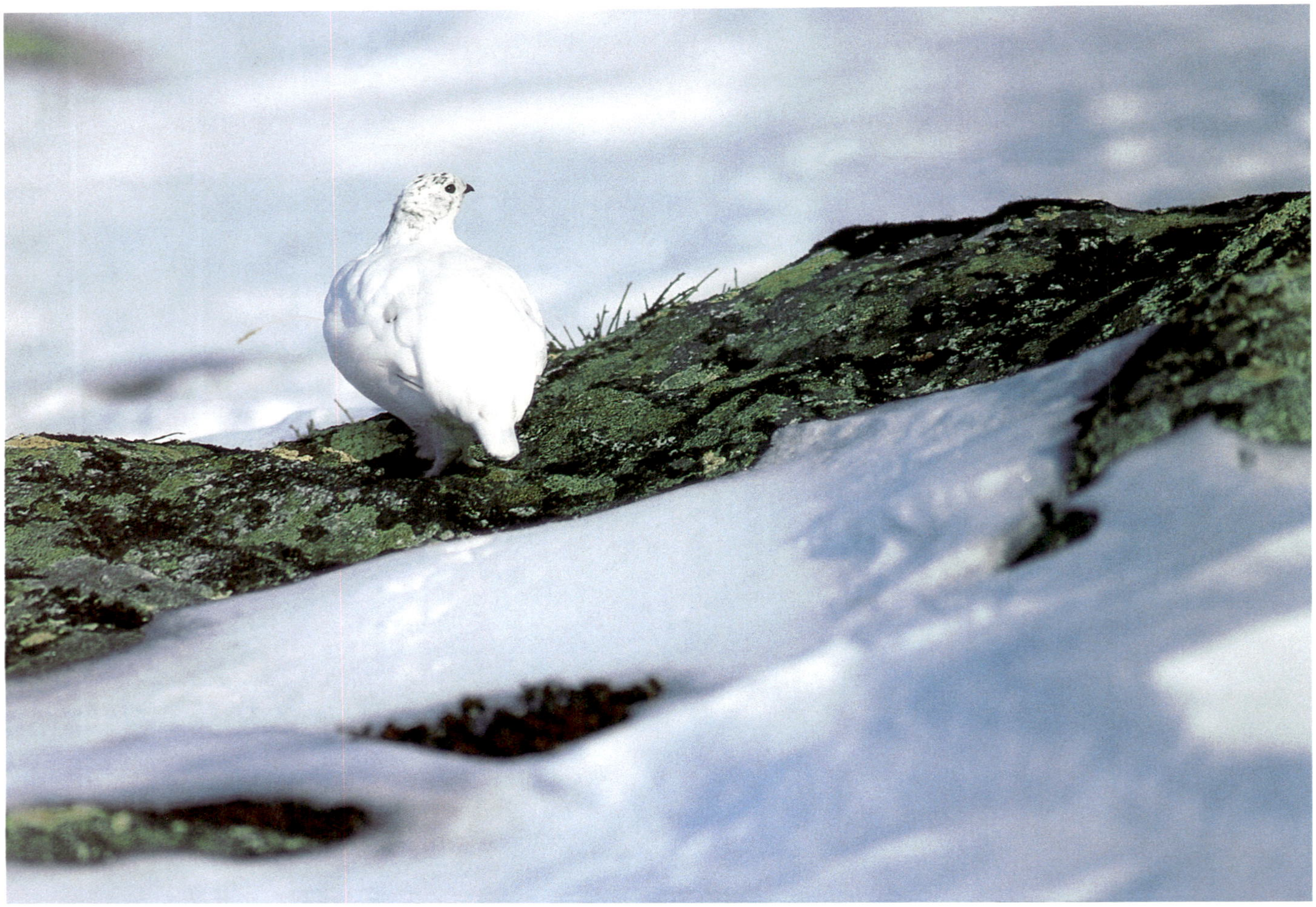

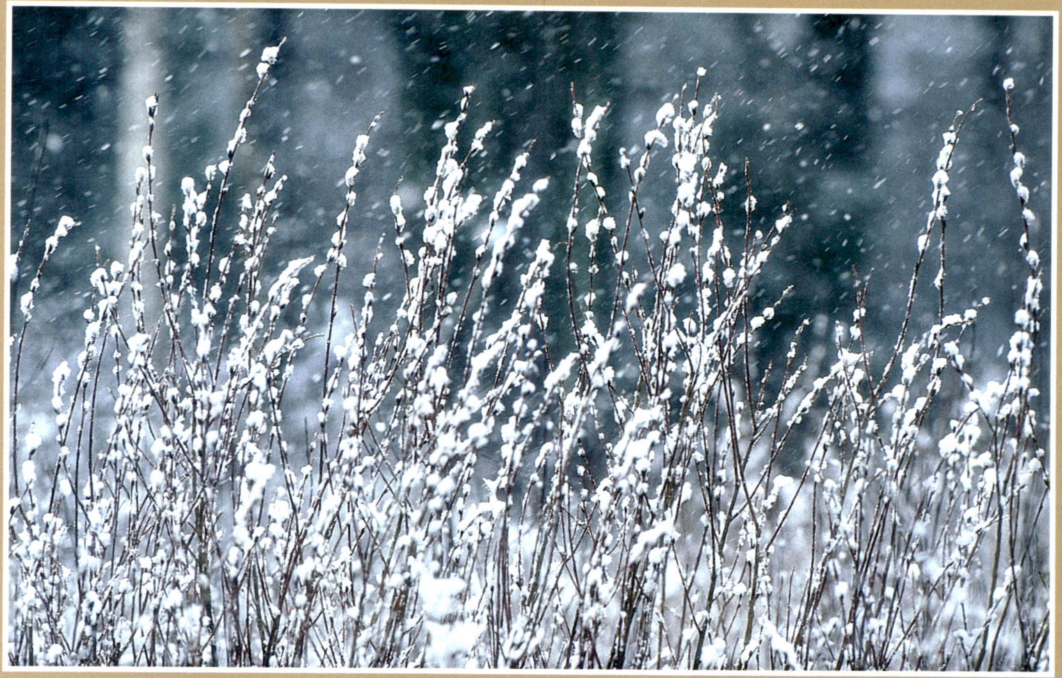

As the willows blossom, winter and spring clash.
The cap-like scales covering the downy buds known as catkins
are borne away by the wind early on. The yellow blossoms do not open
until the sun has also awakened pollinators. Wetland willows are largely
bushy shrubs which generally bloom before coming into leaf.
There are of course exceptions to this rule among Finland's
two dozen willow species.

The hens attend the display for only a few mornings, lay their eggs in nest depressions excavated in the woods, and eventually stay on to incubate the eggs and tend their offspring. For black grouse cocks, life centers around the peat bog for somewhat longer, for a few more weeks of spring. They begin to rehearse their mating songs and dances as winter shows the first signs of breaking, long before the females are attuned to procreation. The cocks also continue their gradually abating display until the onset of summer.

Flood waters bathe a field ploughed in autumn, its surface, now free of snow, glinting brown in the springtime brightness. The branches of white-boled birches show dark red; silver-sheened aspens stand expressionless in woods along a field. The even green of the conifers seems somewhat lifeless after winter. A black woodpecker wails forlornly and raps in short sequences, the hollow limb of dead-standing pine providing an excellent resonator for the black bird's amorous declarations.

But at the forest margin the gaze is drawn to a goat willow which glows as a eye-catching splash of color in the greyness. Having grown large in this rich soil, it is a tree whose presence also makes itself heard, for the wealth of nectar in its yellow blossoms has drawn swarms of insects to the place. The drone of tiny wings is like soft music in this cheerless landscape, its sound enhanced by the babble of a brook flowing not far away.

The first deciduous trees to blossom sow their pollen on the wind; alders, hazels and birches hold no particular pleasure for the human eye, nor nectar for winter-ravaged insects. The goat willow and others of the Salix family rely more for pollination on insects attracted by their gaudy yellow flowers. The buds on the naked branches open early into white catkins. These offer copious nectar and bounteous pollen. Early flowering assures popularity among insects.

The yellow blossoms buzz with bumble bees and other wild apian varieties which fly, legs dangling, from flower to flower until entirely coated in pollen. The blossoms are also visited by a whole throng of flies and small, steady-paced beetles. In addition, they provide desperately needed fuel for tortoiseshell, Camberwell beauty and brimstone butterflies after their overwintering as adults. As evening arrives, moths also steal up to replenish energy supplies depleted by winter.

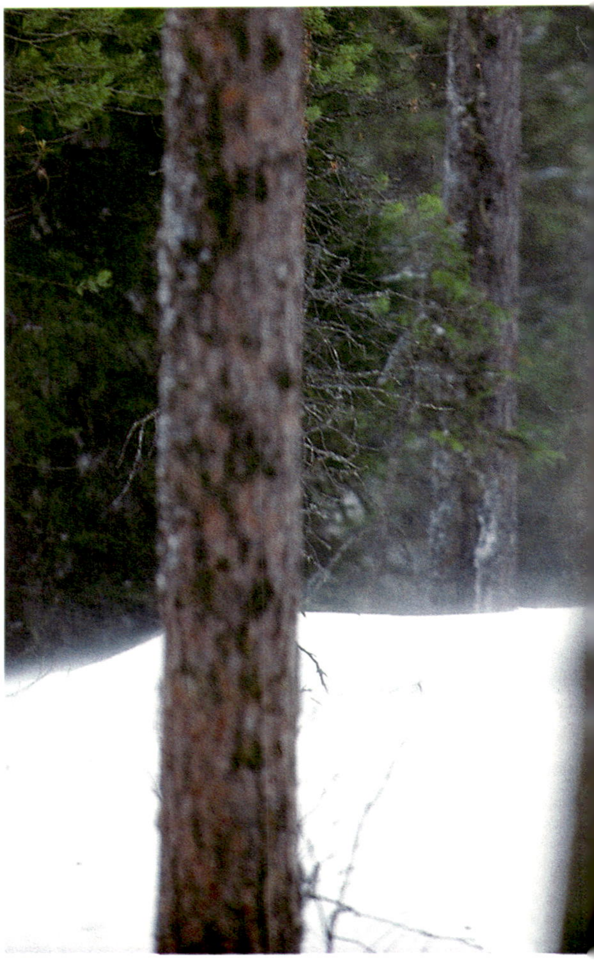

These winged visitors are a crucial element of plant reproduction. The yellow sea of invitingly scented flowers is of vital importance to the insects. The goat willow provides one of the few sources of early springtime sustenance.

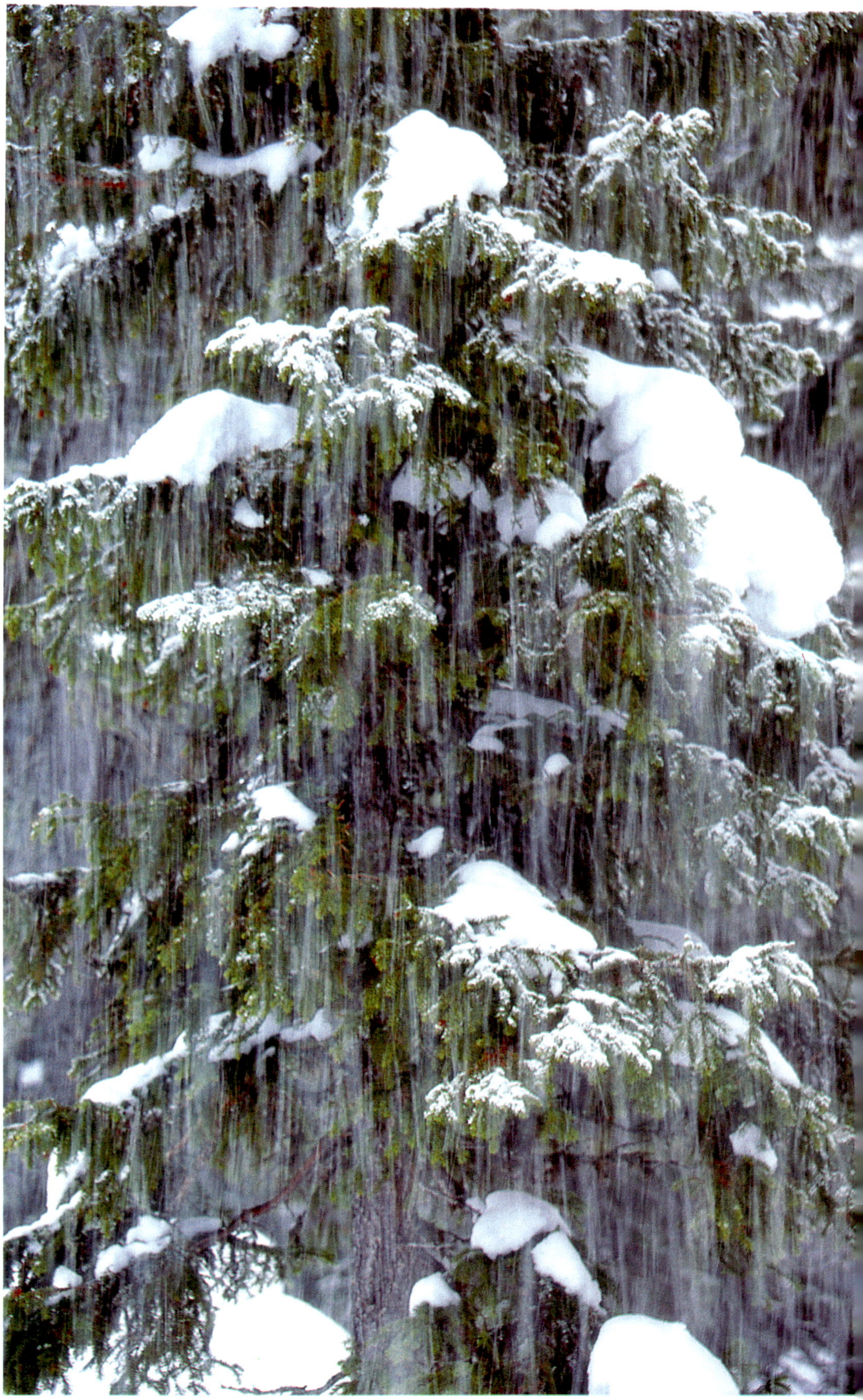

New snow does the old snow in.
Even a wet flurry advances spring.

A final spring flurry lashes a bear
waking from its winter sleep.

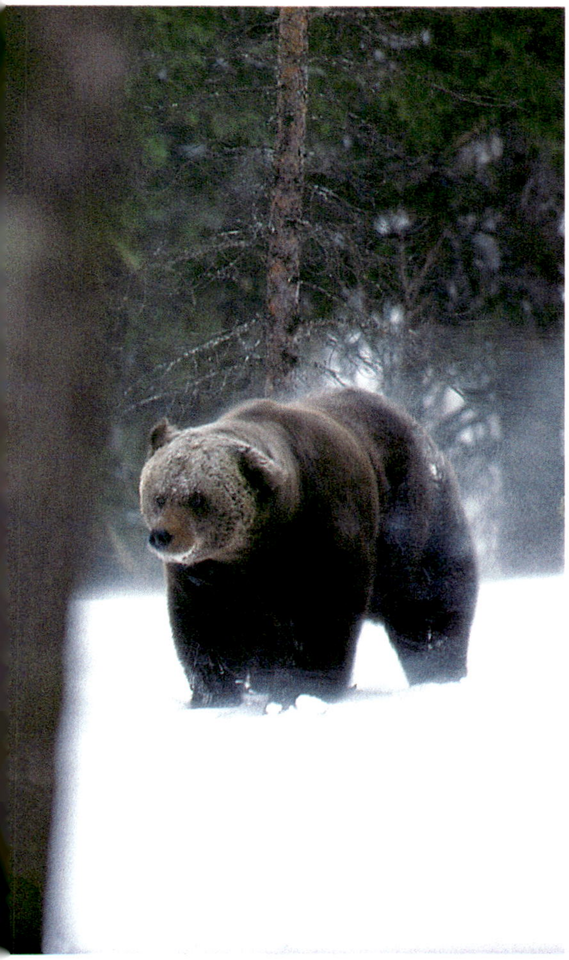

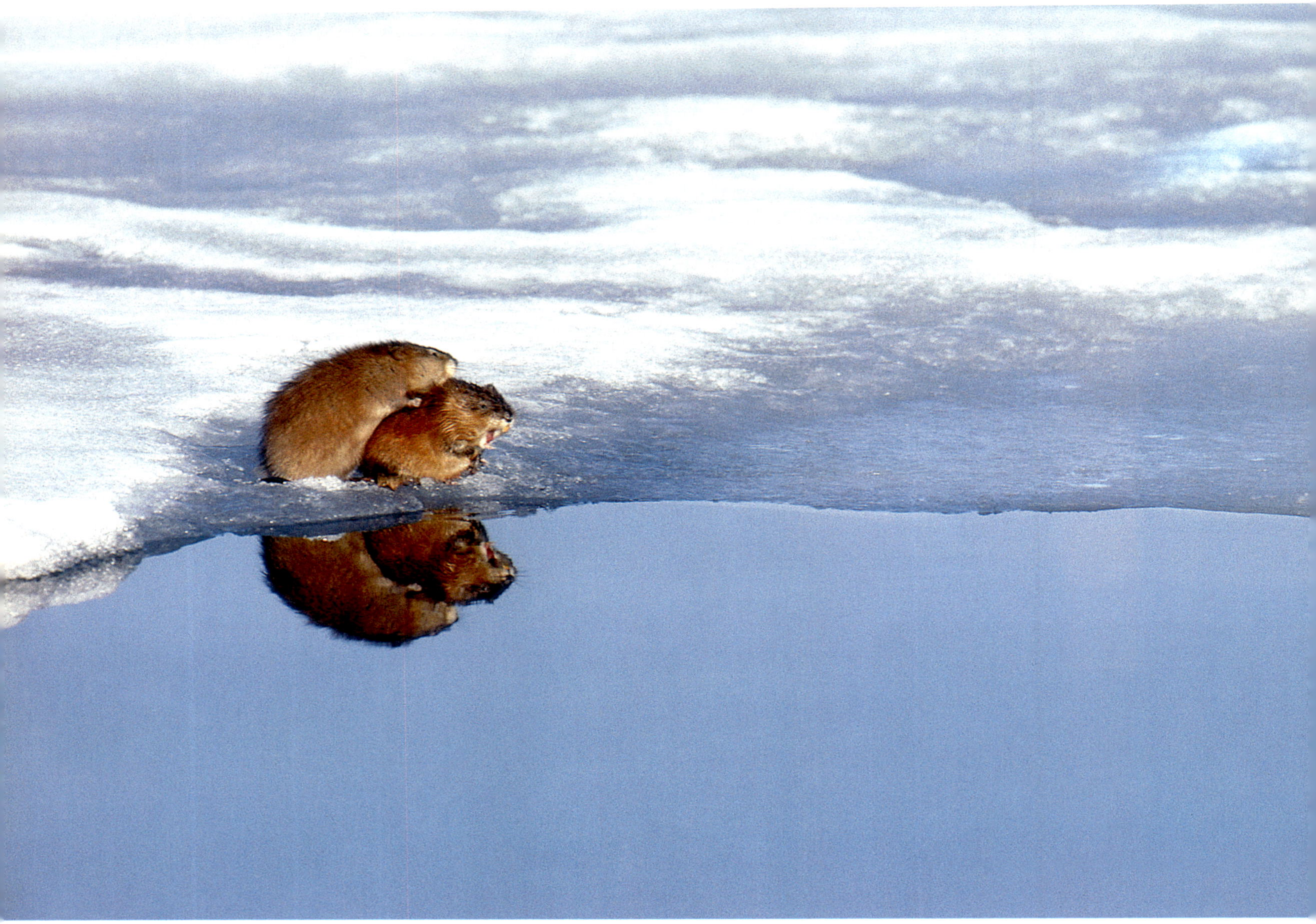

"May I?" whisper muskrats in the vernal warmth.

The sun, parching the bedrock, brings on a sweat. The ice on a pond peeping through the trees darkens in the heat. Glinting in the sun along its north shore is an open stretch where a black and white goldeneye contorts its neck for its unassumingly mouse-colored mate. Along the tree-shaded south shore there is open water only in name. The sheet of ice floats on the pond like a raft. In the woods the coarse granular snow whispers as it melts. A brimming ditch thrusts water into the pond.

An outcrop, long free of snow and basking in the sun, literally radiates the warmth of spring. On a ledge of its south flank rests a becomingly coiled viper that has spent the winter in outcrop scree. A prehistoric beach, this bed of stones is a traditional hibernation site for vipers. The stones form bunkers that provide perfect winter cover.

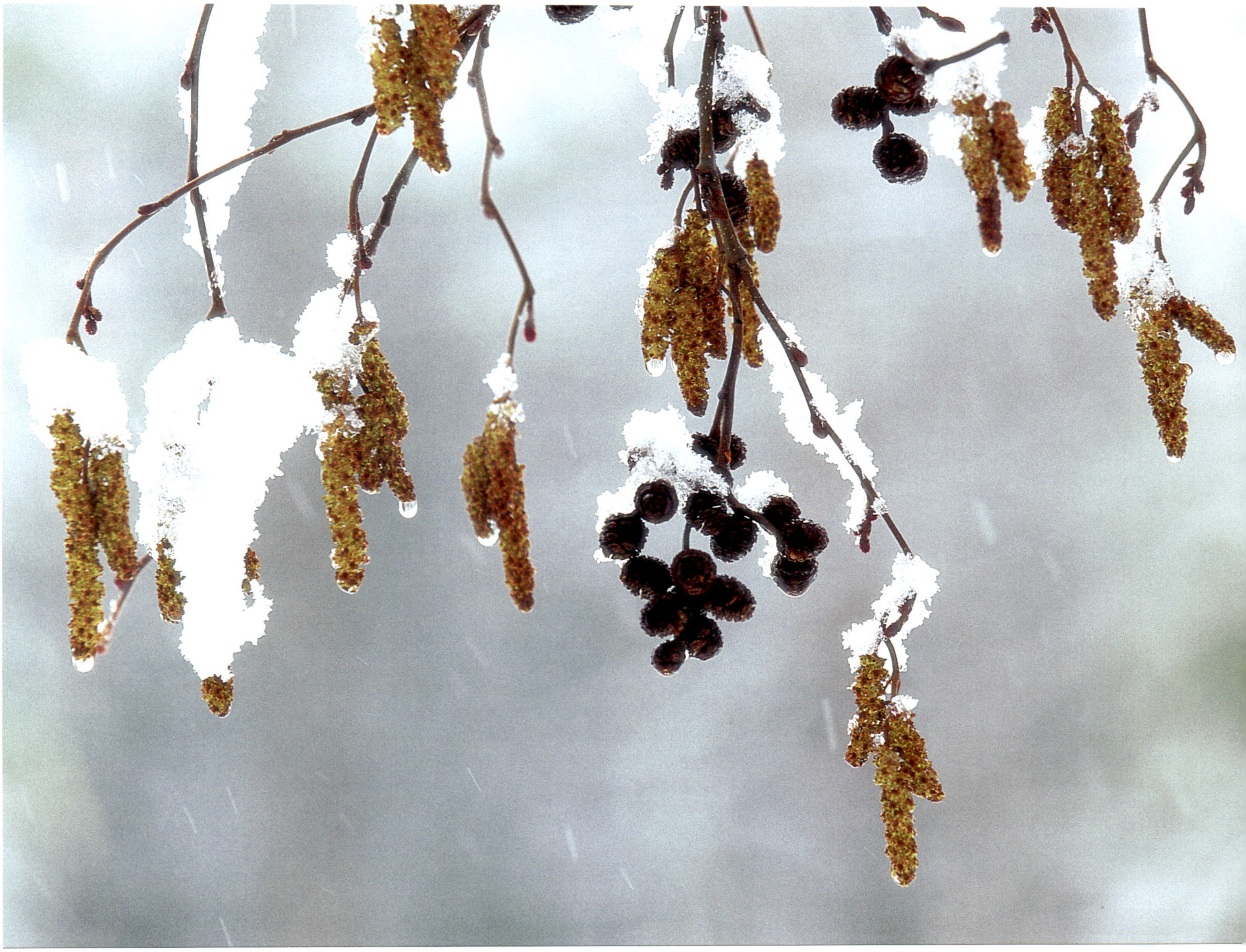

Alder catkins broadcast pollen the instant winter slackens its hold.

A bundle of dozens of snakes rouses in late winter as the springtime warmth and the moisture indicative of thawing snow also reach into their crannies. The males are the first of these reptiles, which have been close to the freezing point, to revive; and they slither off to sunbathe and ripen their sperm in the vernal warmth. Winter is extremely taxing to vipers; individuals weakened by bacterial infections and viral diseases do not wake up at all.

Male vipers prepare for their wedding by basking in the sun. They slough their skin and go off as if in their Sunday best to seek a mate; the females do not revive until a couple of weeks after the males. Wandering hundreds of meters, the male constantly flicks out its forked tongue, groping for an impression of the odors in its surroundings. Eventually the tip of its tongue encounters scent molecules denoting the presence of the opposite sex.

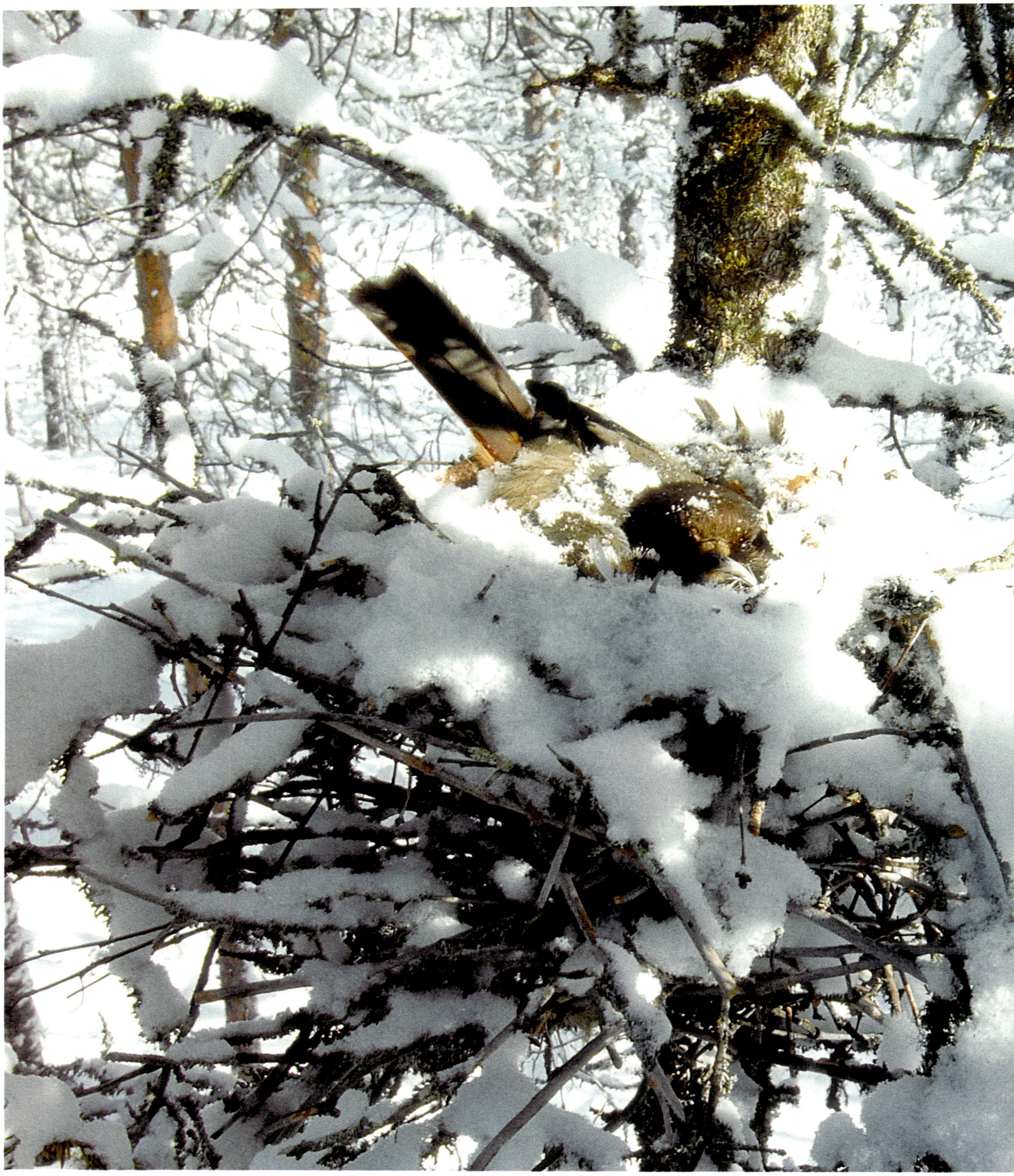

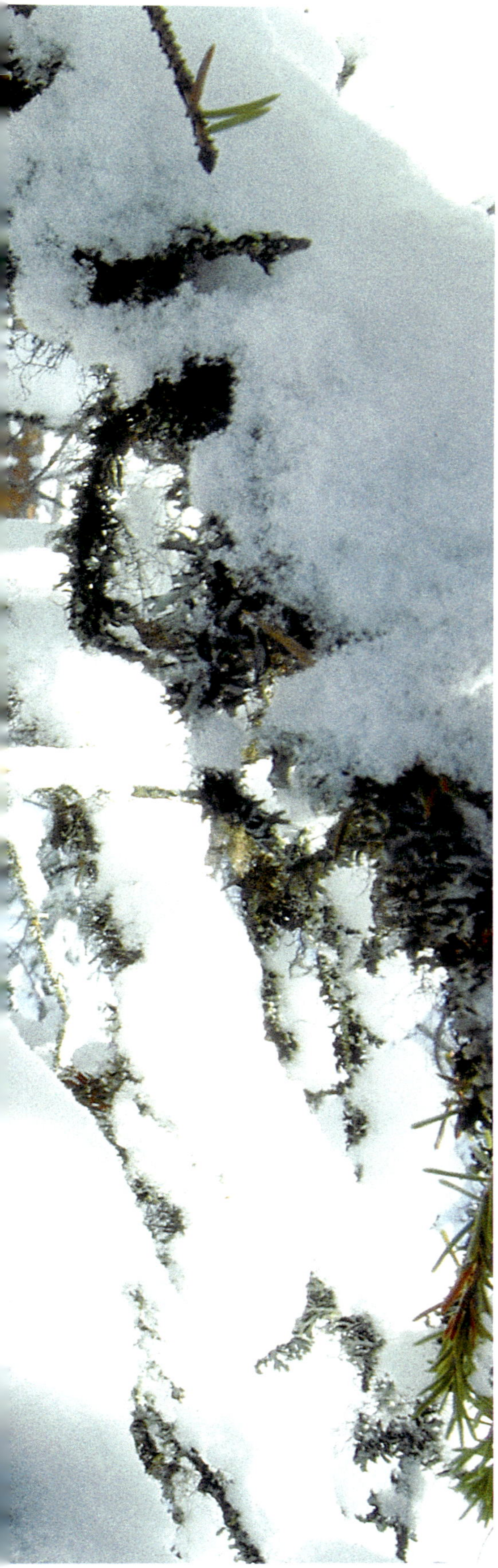

However, the noble prince is by no means the only serpent attracted by the arousing fragrance. Any rival must be fought. In competition for the same female, the animals butt and battle on the moss, throttling and flailing each other with their tails, puffing and rearing up. The stronger lifts its head higher than its opponent, which backs down, defeated.

The winner of the duel proceeds to mate with the female. The couple rub their flanks together for a moment, the male nibbles its companion with its fangs, they entwine, and the male inserts its forked penis into the female. Following hours of copulation, the male ejects a frothy plug into the female's oviducts, thus foiling any attempts by other males at subsequent mating with her.

The mated female seeks out sunlight, where it fasts and incubates the eggs developing within. These also hatch inside the female. The viper gives birth to its young live at the height of summer. A female viper bears young only every other year. During alternate years it eats and gains weight to stay in good condition for the next reproductive period. The male, on the other hand, vanishes after mating to hunt and lay down fat so as to be in good shape for hibernation and in fine springtime fettle once again.

A long spell of warm spring weather has filled the coast with birds. The snow-free mainland blossoms with coltsfoot and, on warm southerly slopes, anemones peep forth. Looking industrious, ants trudge off to drink birch sap and gather nesting materials to refurbish their snow-ravaged hill. Butterflies flutter and gnats soar in the sunlight. Lizards bask on stony ground. The first litters of voles squeal in the grass.

And suddenly everything changes: a chill blast surges down from the north and over the entire country. The weather turns cold just like that, a chill wind howling around corners and blustering among tree branches. Spring, advancing in backward steps, now actually leaps in the wrong direction. Soon the sky is flinging cold rags of snow in one's face; the ground, green with burgeoning shoots, is covered with slush; the prospect is enveloped in grey. Harsh winter returns to conquer the land.

The return of the migratory birds comes to a complete halt. Waterfowl and gulls stop off at wetlands and open stretches of water; for large birds able to find food in such places, winter's return poses no great problem. But small passerines and waders glean their living from the ground. They are hard hit: skylarks, thrushes, chaffinches, wagtails, lapwings, curlews and many others. The singing goes silent, the courtship revelries go cold, the birds fall into a funk.

When a Siberian jay broods, it's often in genuine need of nesting insulation.

But those most stunned don't go on watching the flurries for long. Even the birds that have found their native haunts are set in motion again by the return of winter, seeking cover, sustenance. Large concentrations throng dumps and permanently thawed roadsides. Thrushes and chaffinches panic, fleeing into retreat migration. Huge rafts of thousands upon thousands of birds drift southward to escape the vicious gales. Mournfully gurgling skylarks and lapwings in droning flight also beat a retreat as winter again tightens its grip.

The birds do not survive winter's return without losses. The weak are the first to succumb, but those that do survive are among the first to occupy the best territories when the cold eases, as it inevitably must before long. Wintry spells in early spring are less an exception than the rule, but the risk of a relapse declines with the approach of summer. In Lapland snow in June is not an impossibility, though usually of short duration.

Spring continues its triumphant progress as winter's grip slackens. The birds turn their beaks northward once again. The bird gatherings on snowless patches disband and song rings out as joyously as if nothing at all had happened. The poikilothermic reptiles, insects and spiders that yielded to torpor during the cold spell swing into action again. Even the flowers, humbly at rest in their buds beneath the snow, straighten and reach, petals wide, for the sun.

Long-legged cranes navigate a landing.

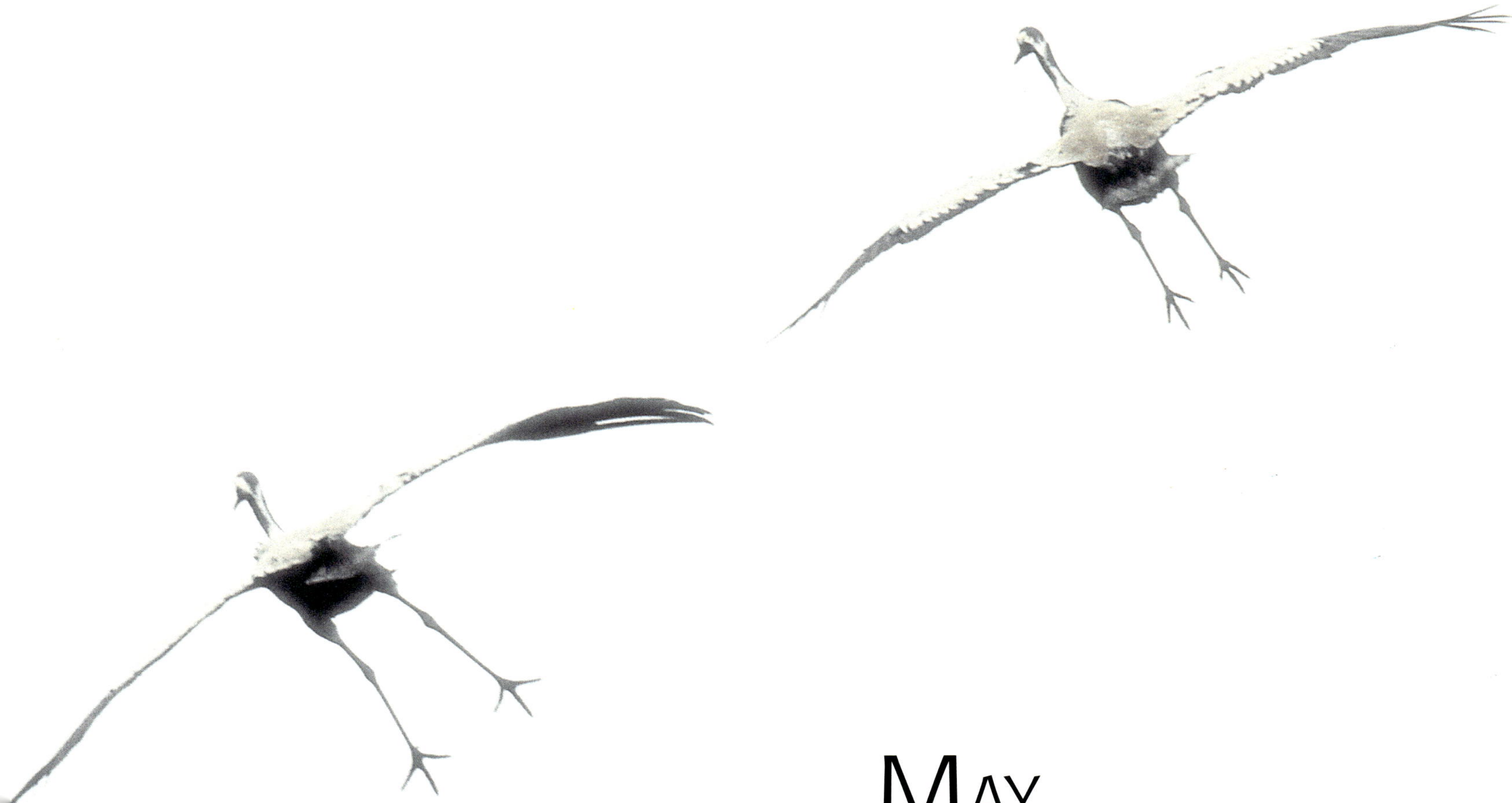

May

Southwestern groves in full blossom.

Arctic birdlife on review.

A moose cow defends its calves.

The thaw in southern lakes.

A birch blossoms and bursts into leaf.

Roach and bream spawn in bays.

A hedgehog and bats awaken from hibernation.

Lapland's sunlit summer night begins.

The majority of birds busy with nesting.

On the Verge of Summer

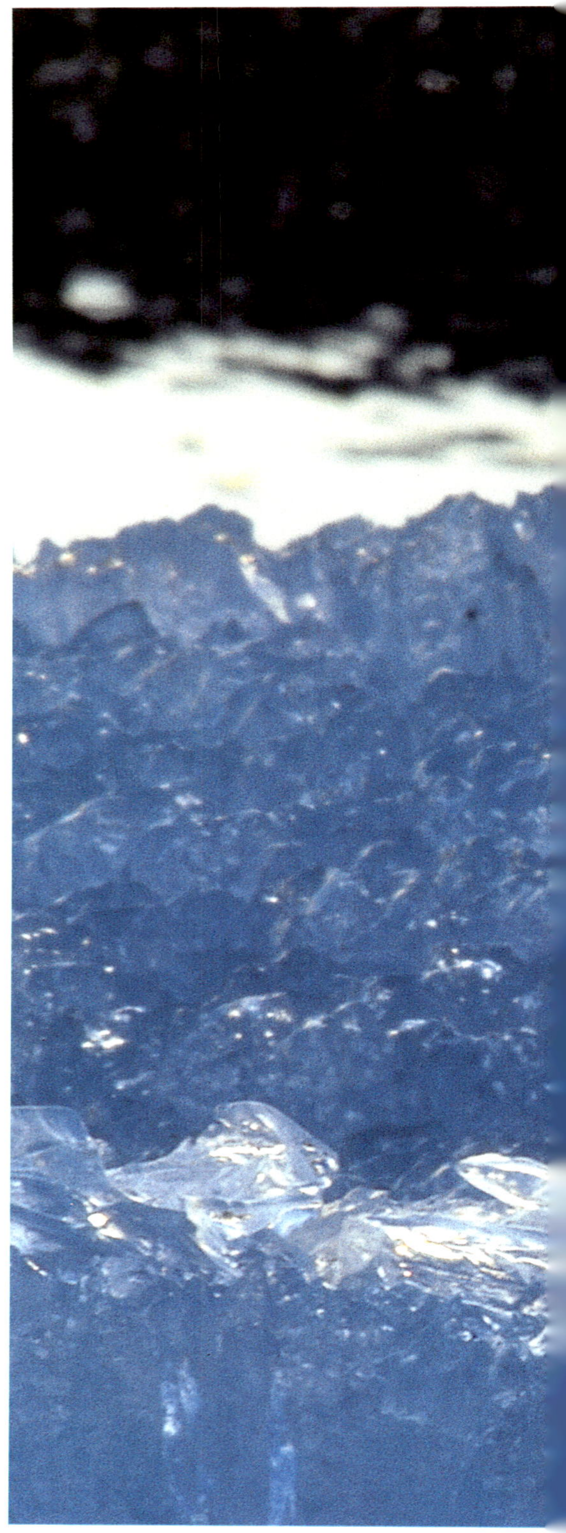

The tremulous hooting of a tawny owl rents the morning twilight in an oak wood. The grey assassin of voles glides in ghostly silence to its nesting hollow, its daily tasks as hunter completed. Its young whine for a moment as they attack the morning's final catch, a bank vole that disappears down the greediest gullet. The owl nest opening gapes like the lifeless eye of a Cyclops in the dawning day. The knothole in a mammoth rotten oak was previously in use by a stock dove and a goldeneye; the initial work was carried out by a black woodpecker.

A blackbird flutes mellifluously; the jet-black, yellow-beaked bird tours its territory proclaiming its proprietary rights in song. Its spouse huddles on the nest incubating five blue-grey eggs. A chiffchaff scatters is rhythmic stanzas on the air. The avian choir crescendos as day breaks. Chaffinches and willow warblers join the singing meet; a woodpigeon coos fervently and the pumping, furtive burble of a stock dove also reaches the ear.

Proud hardwoods lift their boughs to the sky. Their swollen buds have not yet burst into the first small leaf. The leaves of the previous year rustle on the ground, something a warm brown skittering among them. Dark eyes alertly scrutinize the landscape, small ears are pricked, and a snout framed by thin whiskers voraciously devours scents. Leaping a few times, the least weasel sits up on its haunches and scans its surroundings. It inspects the hollows under roots and mounts stumps. The creature pays a standing human no notice; it seems to have tuned its instincts to the hunt: voles and shrews, beware!

On the edge of the grove is a summer sheep pasture, its turf glossy as a purple carpet. Bowing sedately, corydalis flowers live out their entire annual life cycle in a couple of springtime weeks. Their competitors, the stronger summer plants, grant them a chance for public life only among the first flowers of spring. They share this fate with the cheery yellow star of Bethlehem, which vies with the corydalis in storing a year's supplies in its bulb before summer smothers its surface growth.

An elegant lungwort shows among the oaks. Seeming delicate, downright frail, it follows with its blossoms the ascent of the sun in the sky. The newly opened flowers glow pink; the older blooms on the stem have already darkened to violet, almost blue. The pollinating insects most important to the lungwort favor young flowers; these provide the best draughts of nectar, and at the same time fresh pats of pollen get shifted from blossom to blossom. After flowering fleetingly, the lungwort, instead of withering immediately, puts out large leaves over summer, using them to gather subterranean energy stores for winter dormancy and the following spring.

Ice thawed into splinters tinkles as waves generated by the spring wind break it up.

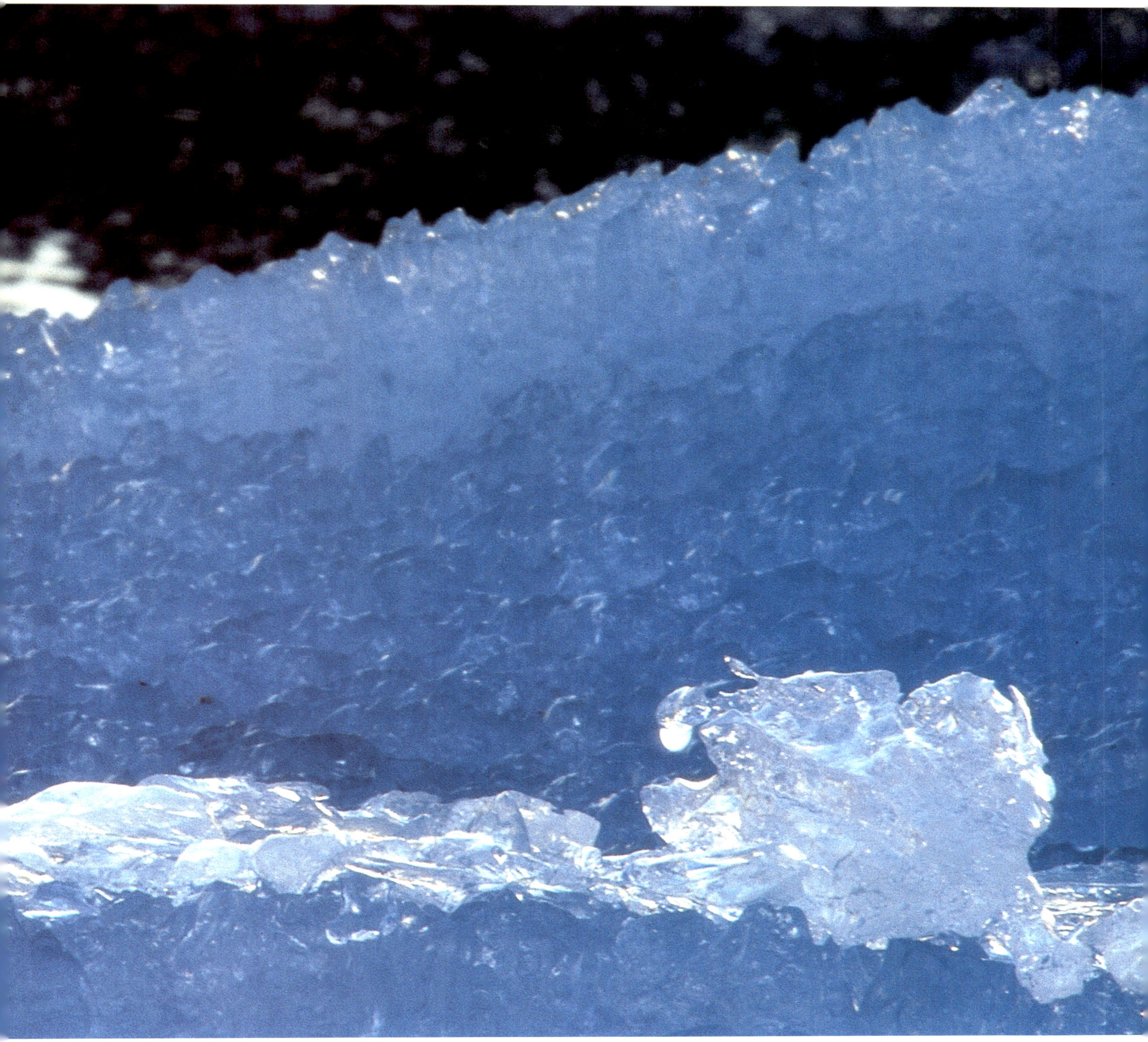

On the floor of the bright oak wood the green carpet is spangled with thousands of white eyes which meekly follow the sun from daybreak to gloaming. The wood anemone closes its petals and bows its head for the night, as if in slumber, waking again to a new morning, its gaze turned in the proper direction. The wood anemone flowers before the trees come into leaf. It also drops its seeds, which are coated in an oil attractive to ants, before the withering of its entire shoot by midsummer.

On a southern slope drier and somewhat more barren than its surroundings, hepatica already drops its petals as the sea of wood anemones undulates at its most bountiful. Only among shading spruces may brightly colored hepaticas still be found. With their yellow centers, they too follow the journey of light from morning to evening. Unlike other flowers of early spring, the hepatica has a full year-round capacity for photosynthesis: its leaves do not die until new ones develop after spring flowering.

Hepatica leaves can stand fairly cold temperatures and its root system is not damaged by light frost; its ant-borne seeds actually require chilling to germinate. By autumn its flower buds are ready for blossoming, and a mild Indian summer may mislead some specimens into opening the buds concealed within the forest litter. Despite its resilience, the hepatica is slow to reproduce, which is why picking it for bouquets does it so much harm. Hepatica development from germination to flowering adult takes a decade.

The prehistoric looking diver returns to its familiar nesting grounds as soon as the ice is out.

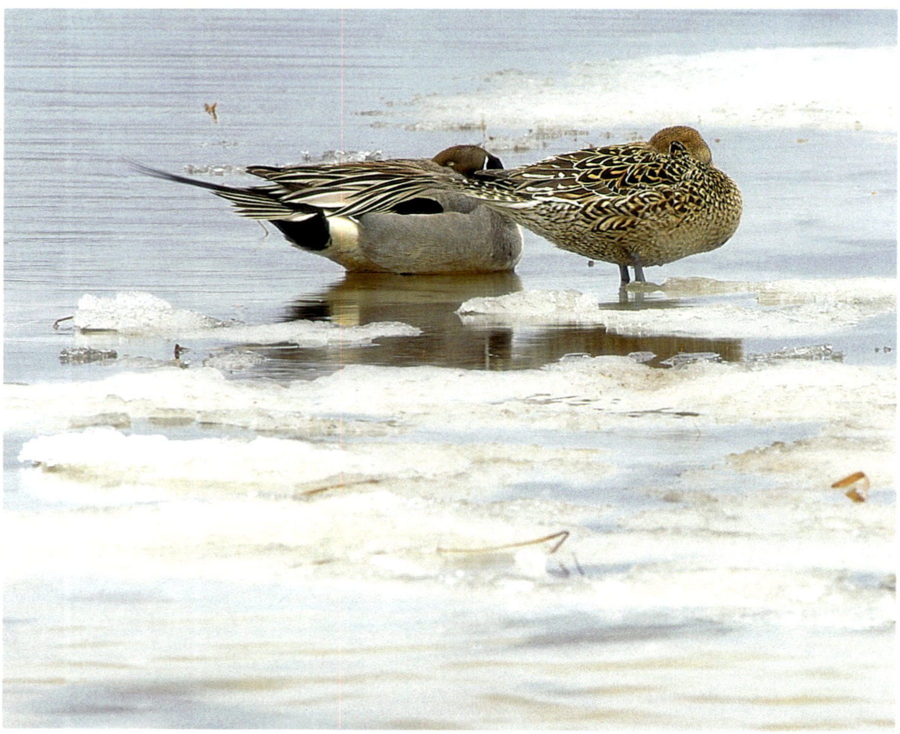

Pintails nap on their journey north.

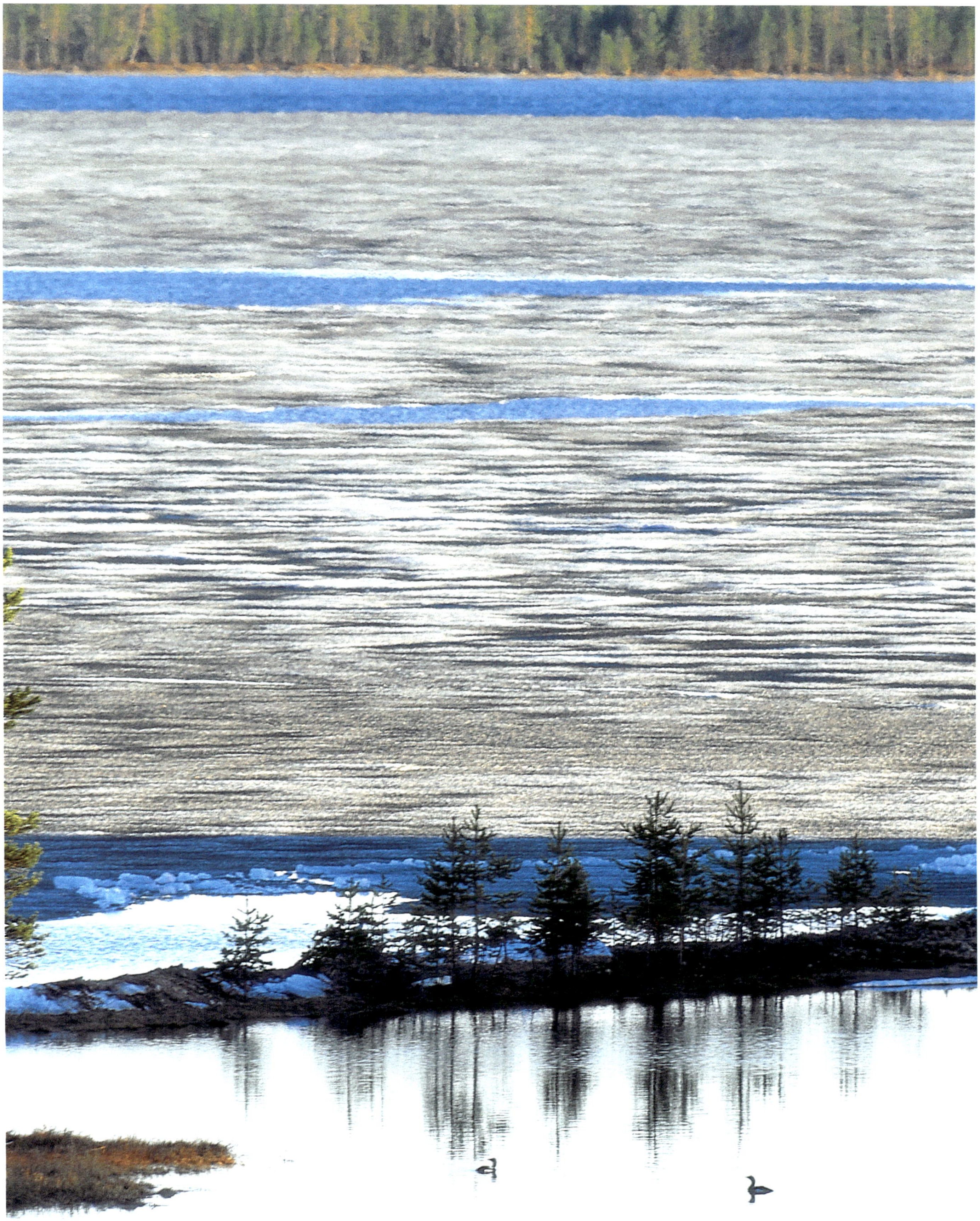

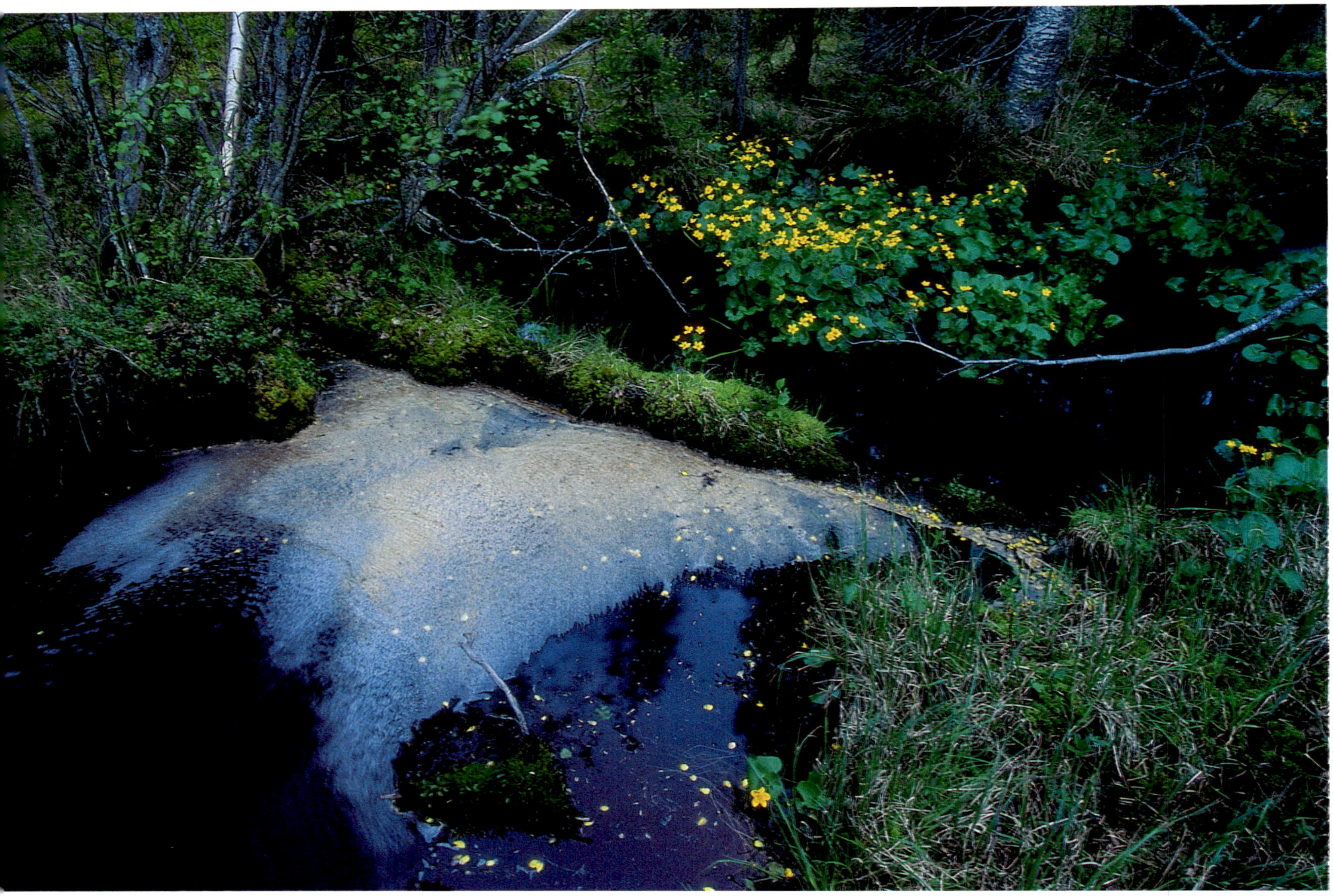

Nighttime quiet along a brook of marsh marigolds; a wood warbler chimes among spruces.

Unassuming hairy woodrushes may also be glimpsed in the shade of the spruces. Greenish-yellow alternate-leaved golden saxifrage flourishes in the silt of a wet ditch. The side of the ditch smells intoxicatingly of mezereon, its charming clumps of flowers open on twig-like, leafless stems. The scent, causing headache in those susceptible to it, is an invitation to pollinators. Without a care, butterflies lap up nectar from this plant, which is considered poisonous.

By the end of May, spring is in full blossom: floods bathe northern river valleys, along the southern coast summer is already at hand. The sea gives off cold, but the sun beaming through the long days warms the islands. Heat waves obscure the arching horizon of the Gulf of Finland. Gentle surf rolls ashore where a bustling wagtail stalks insects in a tier of seaweed. A heavy bumblebee drones in brush between some junipers. A lizard suns itself on the side of a rock.

The landscape teems with birds, and their cries fill the region in a mixed choir from which it is almost impossible to make out individual calls. The sounds billow in rhythm with the movements of the winged creatures journeying across the sky. Out of the distance there comes into view one swiftly advancing flock after another. Birds span the entire horizon: in skeins, strings, files and fronts, as lone navigators and in dense clusters.

The passing birds disappear beyond the eastern horizon as mysteriously as more appear in the west. The advancing voices are heard from afar; they gradually crescendo and form a more polyphonic choir than do the rapidly fading cries of those moving away. The rustle of wings augments the music of the flying orchestra; the flying gear of ducks and geese thrum the air currents in a different manner.

One of the birds travelling on the verge of summer to the Siberian tundra is unequalled: the long-tailed duck, a soulful yodeller rotund of body and long of wing. The drake's long tail feathers lighten its otherwise plump appearance. A single spring day sees thousands, tens of thousands, even hundred of thousands of long-tailed ducks winging it eastward. In addition to the drakes' repeated staccato, the nasal barking of the ducks also sounds from the flocks.

Having recharged themselves in the Baltic since early spring, the long-tailed ducks are in fine fettle; once on the move, they press on nearly non-stop to their nesting sites on the shores of the Arctic Ocean. The countless wedges and files can merge to form megaflocks of hundreds, even thousands of birds which, during the most intense migration phase, stream across the sky late into the night – and sometimes around the clock – in an uninterrupted flow. And when all the long-tailed ducks of spring are added together, the bottom line is seven significant figures: millions.

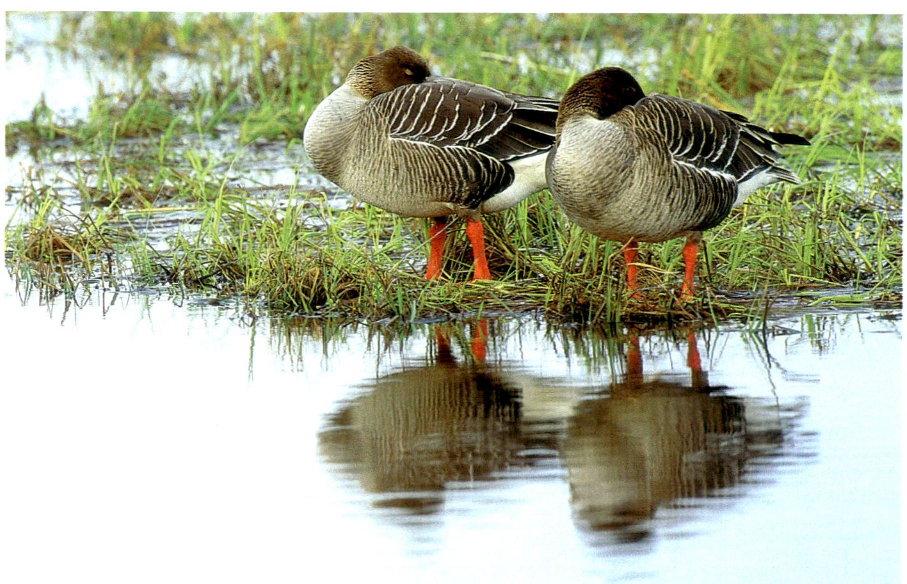

The peace of the wilds must remain undisturbed before a wary bean goose will close its eyes.

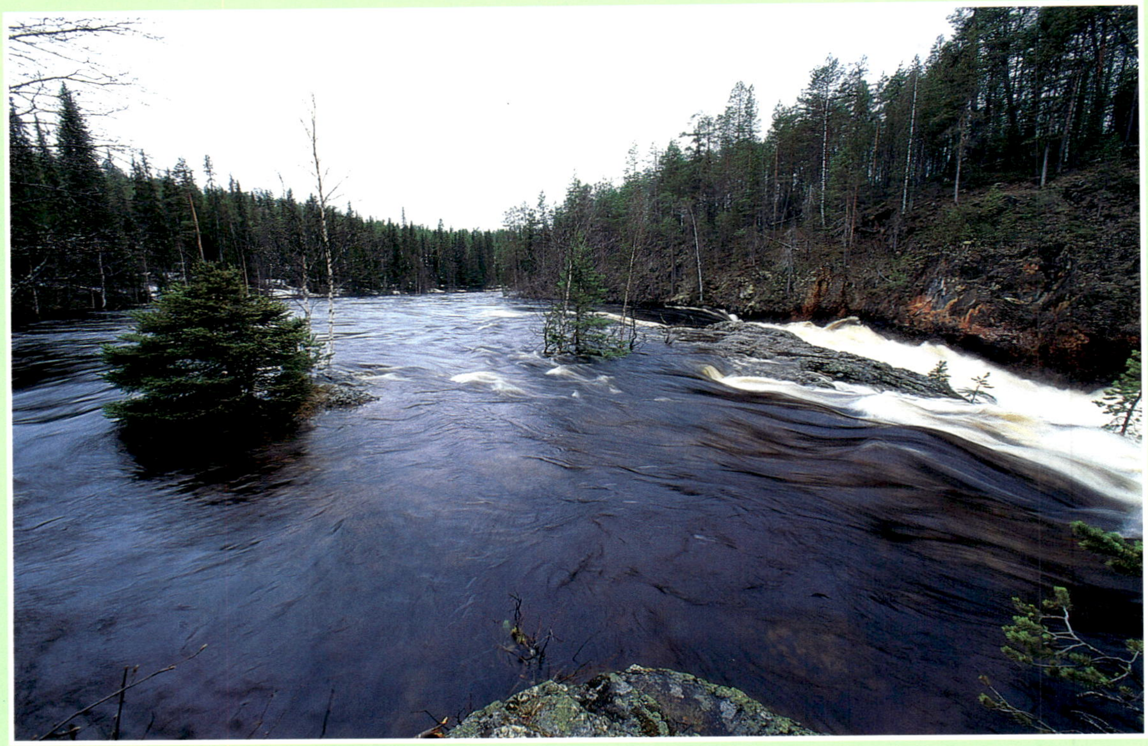

A rough shove from winter toward summer.
Runoff exceeds flood levels. Lakes even out the flooding rivers, but in areas of abundant snowfall there is nothing to keep the water from going where it likes. Along with the moving ice, the flood can create great material loss. In lowlands downriver it is often beneficial, however, as the water spreads fields with fertile silt.

Common scoters travel alongside the long-tailed ducks, in flocks that are club-shaped at the front end and trail off in long strands in the rear. The drakes' piping rings out in the landscape in short, melancholic whistles. This black duck's pace reaches fever pitch in late evening, but its voice also sounds in the darkness of spring nights. The ranks of arctic ducks include, in addition to these two dominant species, an abundance of velvet scoters and scaups.

Heavily built in appearance, the divers wing their way onward solo or in loosely formed assemblages of individuals bound in the same direction. It's not actually a matter of flocking when red-throated and black-throated divers migrate, for even when moving in formation they maintain a considerable distance from other travellers. Just as the odd Steller's eider and king eider will hitch a ride with ducks, a large, handsome white-billed diver will be seen among its companion species from time to time.

Arctic geese take over the skies once the duck migration begins to slacken. Lovely wedges of barnacle geese first fill the air space. The elegant birds announce their voyage with sounds reminiscent of the barking of a distant pack of dogs. And after the barnacle geese, it's the turn of the Brent goose, chortling and pottering as they hasten east in muddled aggregates. The vernal sum of geese also reaches the hundreds of thousands.

Only brief feeding breaks interrupt the devoted brooding of a mother hazelhen.

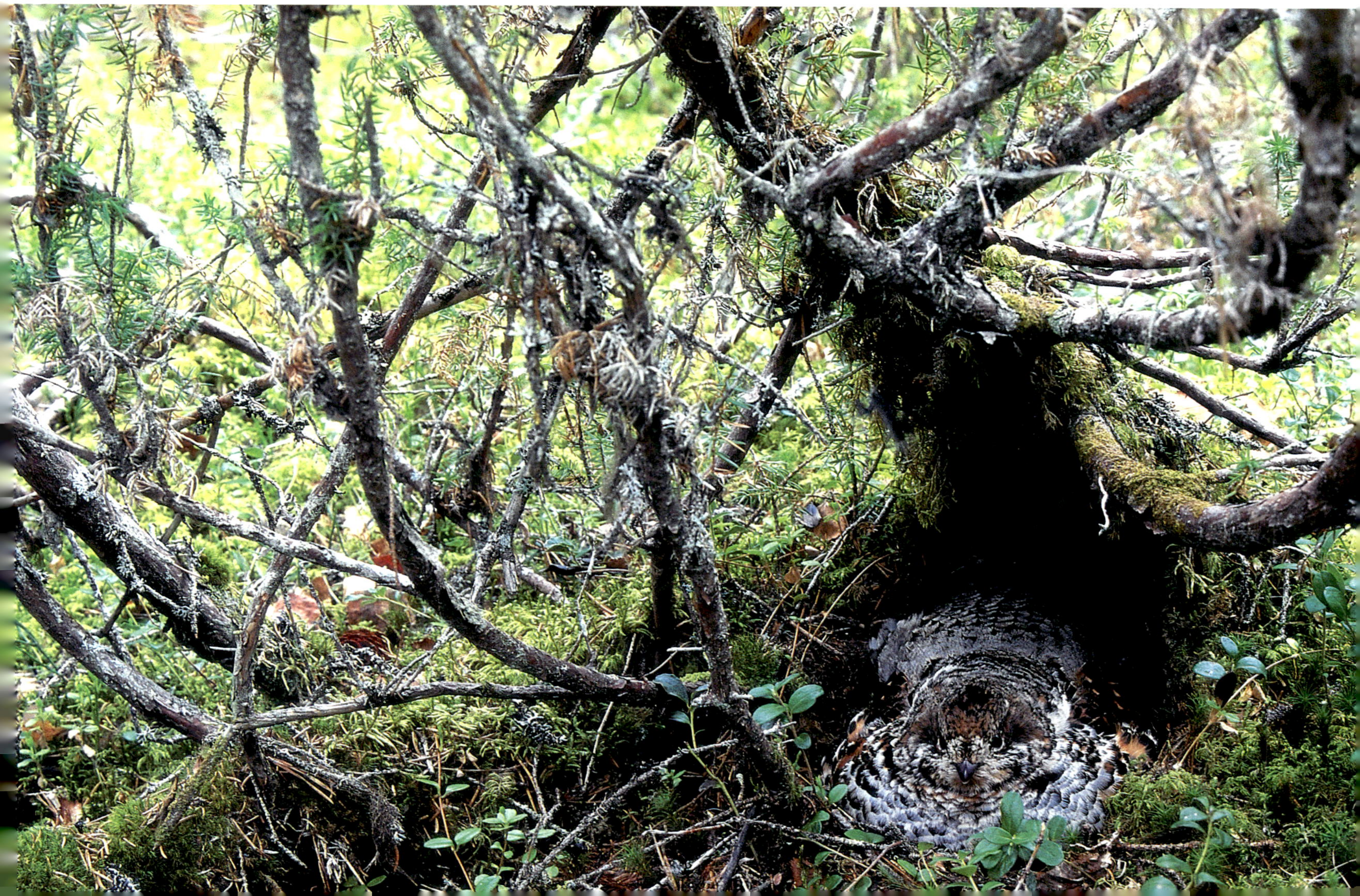

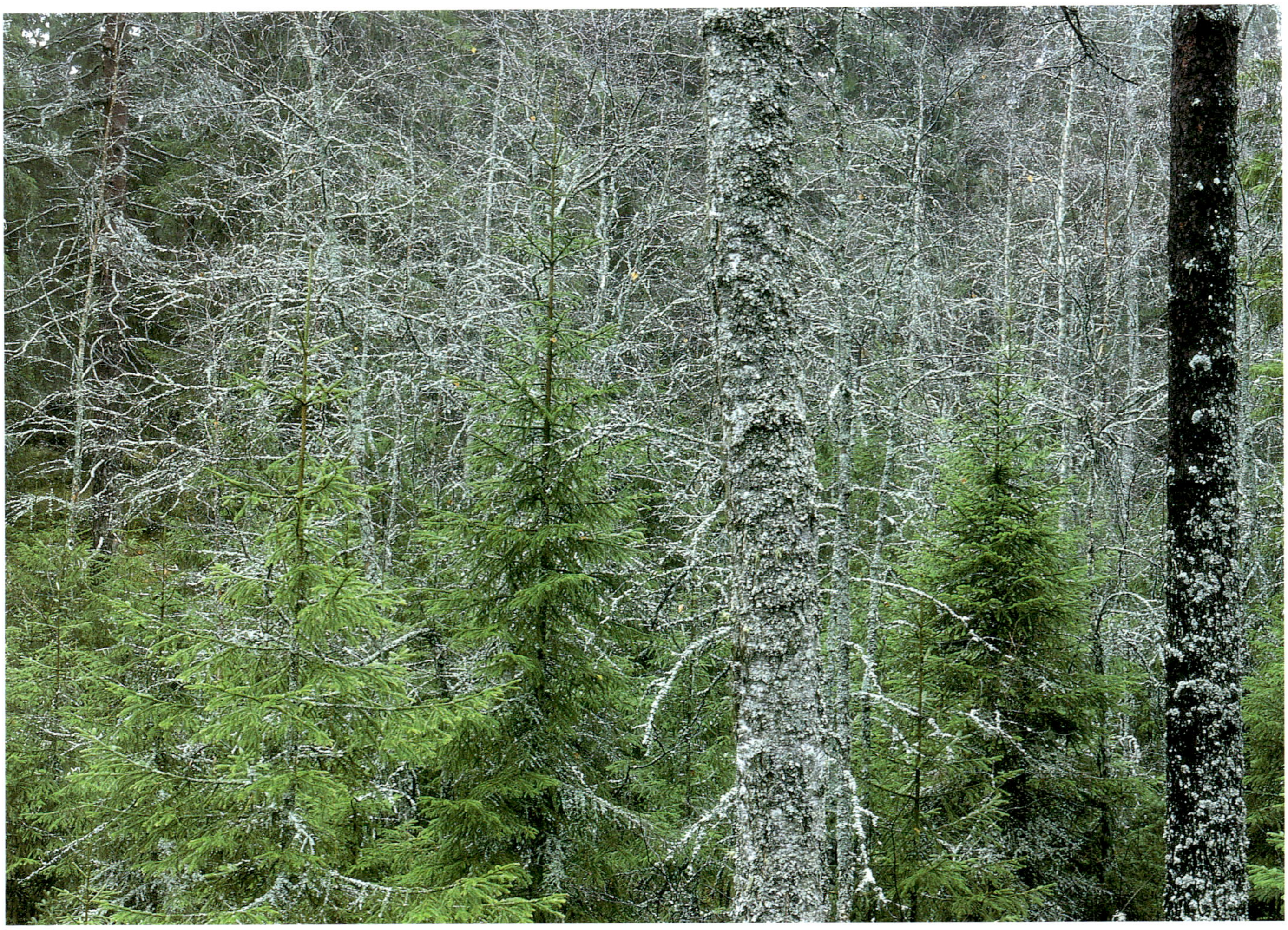

The hazelhen loves these woods. The silvery warbling of a dunnock chimes in the background; the shadow of a sparrow hawk sweeps by.

Arctic waders skim Finland in the same scramble: grey plovers, red knots, dunlins, bar-tailed godwits, oystercatchers and many more. Winterers on the Atlantic, the arctic skua and Pomarine skua also take part in northern migration; and now and again the alert observer descries as well a dainty long-tailed skua, which usually skirts Scandinavia entirely on its way to the lemming country of Siberia.

The mass arctic passage to Siberia of waterfowl is a phenomenon which may with complete certainty be compared to the migration of antelope on the African savannah or to any other world-class mass event. In one month the millions of birds that have spent the winter on the North Sea coast and the Baltic rim hasten via the fringes of the Gulf of Finland to their nesting sites.

At the peak of migration, the sky fills for days with flying carpets of birds travelling in an endless tide into the unknown, into an east which has preserved its mystery until the present. Somewhere out there on tundra freed from the clutches of a hard winter are vast food stores which will feed the birds and their young over the brief arctic summer. And it is from there that the birds will also return in the autumn as the wind strips the trees of their leaves. In the flutter of wings in autumn there is none of the rapture of spring.

Dense willows wreathe a water-logged meadow and border a wood dominated by large birches and young spruces. Their budding leaves are iridescent green. Something brown flits beyond a small knoll. A dunnock sings with a delicate brightness, its song chiming aimlessly through the woods. The modest accentor perches in a spruce crown giving voice to the joy of a spring dawn. The grey morning is warm and humid.

And something stirs again in the field of vision... All the senses are filled with birdsong; the formal chitchat of a song thrush dominates the dunnock's chiming. The horsetails on the forest floor are like funny, half-grown, bright green little firs. Pink bilberry buds glint like precious jewels in the undergrowth. Looking like stylized crosses, the new leaves of hepatica are lustrous with freshness, the old ones, withered brown and barely noticeable.

A path-like line runs from the meadow to the forest: bent sedge, trampled twigs, broken boughs. At the bottom of the furrow are distinct tracks, hoofprints splayed in the soft ground. A moose has come and gone, one and the same individual going to and fro. On a snapped spruce twig there is also a tuft of thick, dark grey hair. The moose smell is almost palpable, and the subconscious steadily makes it known that something is nigh...as if one were in the presence of a piercing gaze.

The springtime bustle of a fleet-footed capercaillie hen centers on nesting.

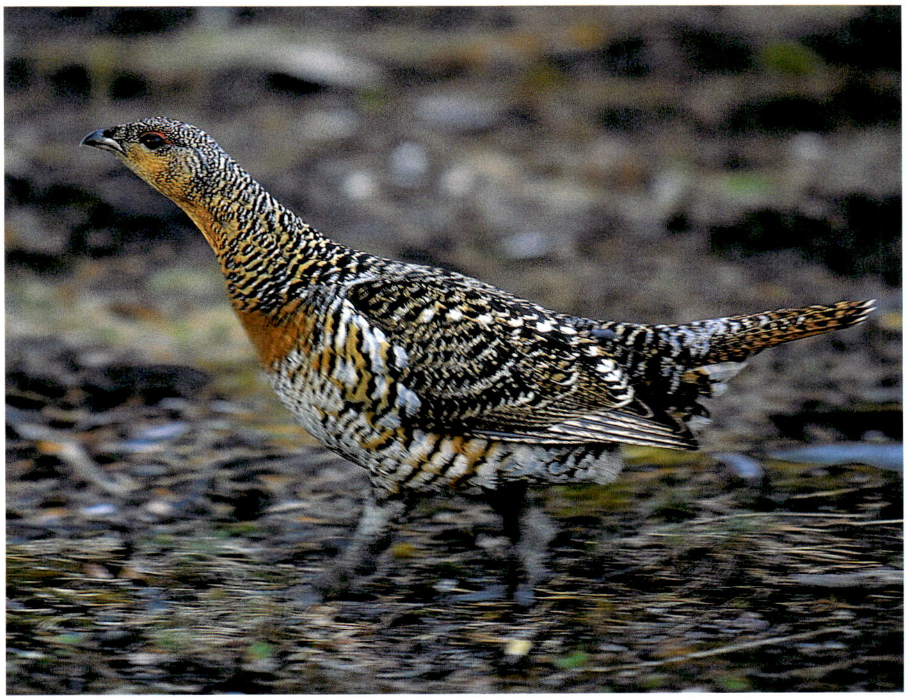

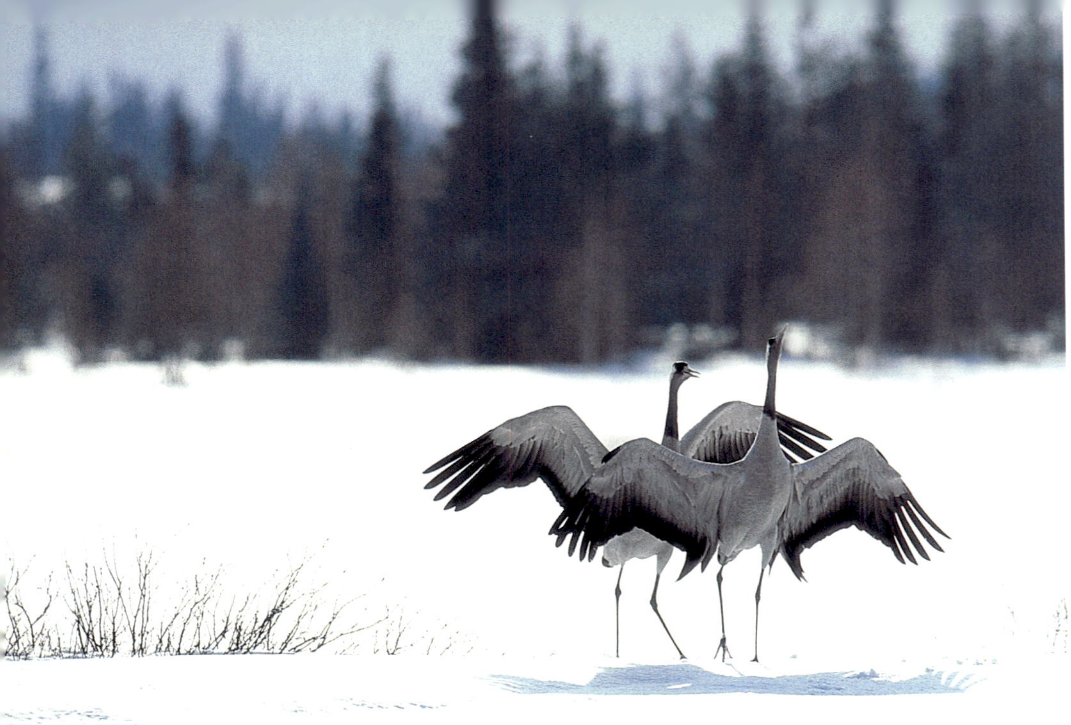

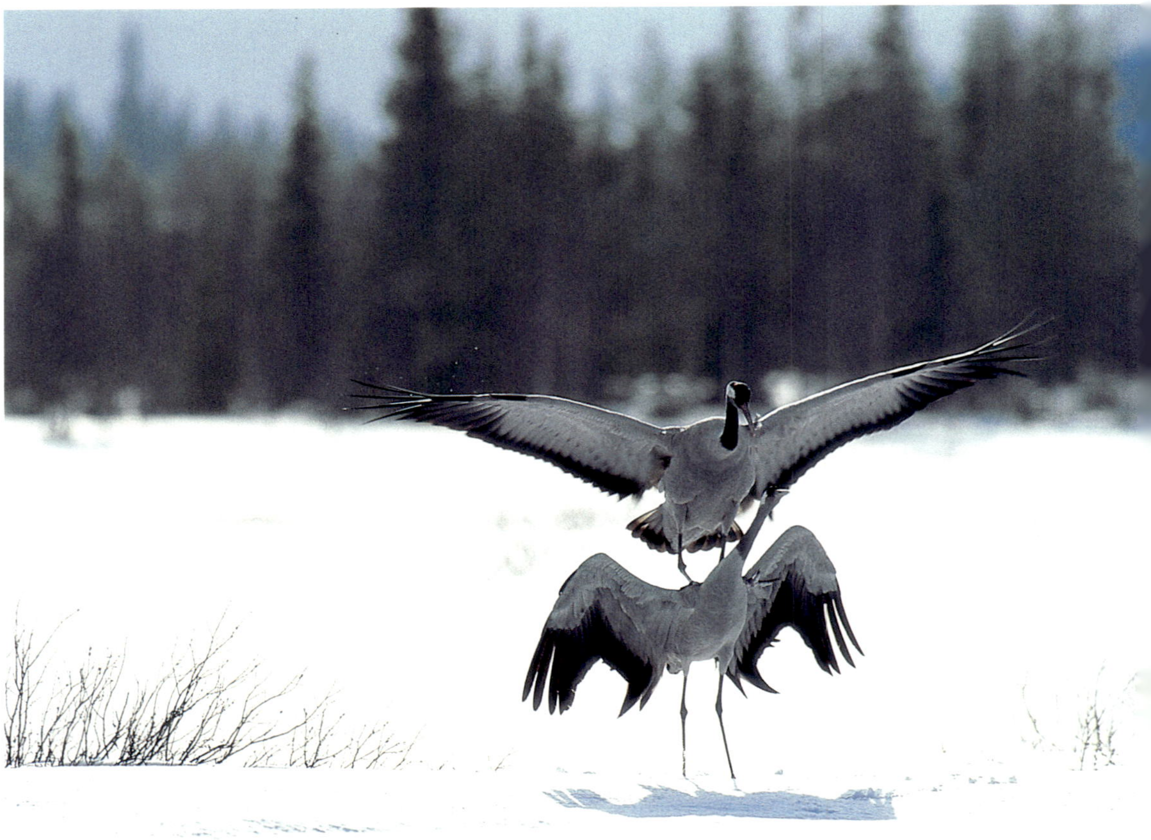

The dance of the cranes on
the last of the snow leads to vernal
consummation. It is time to
establish a home.

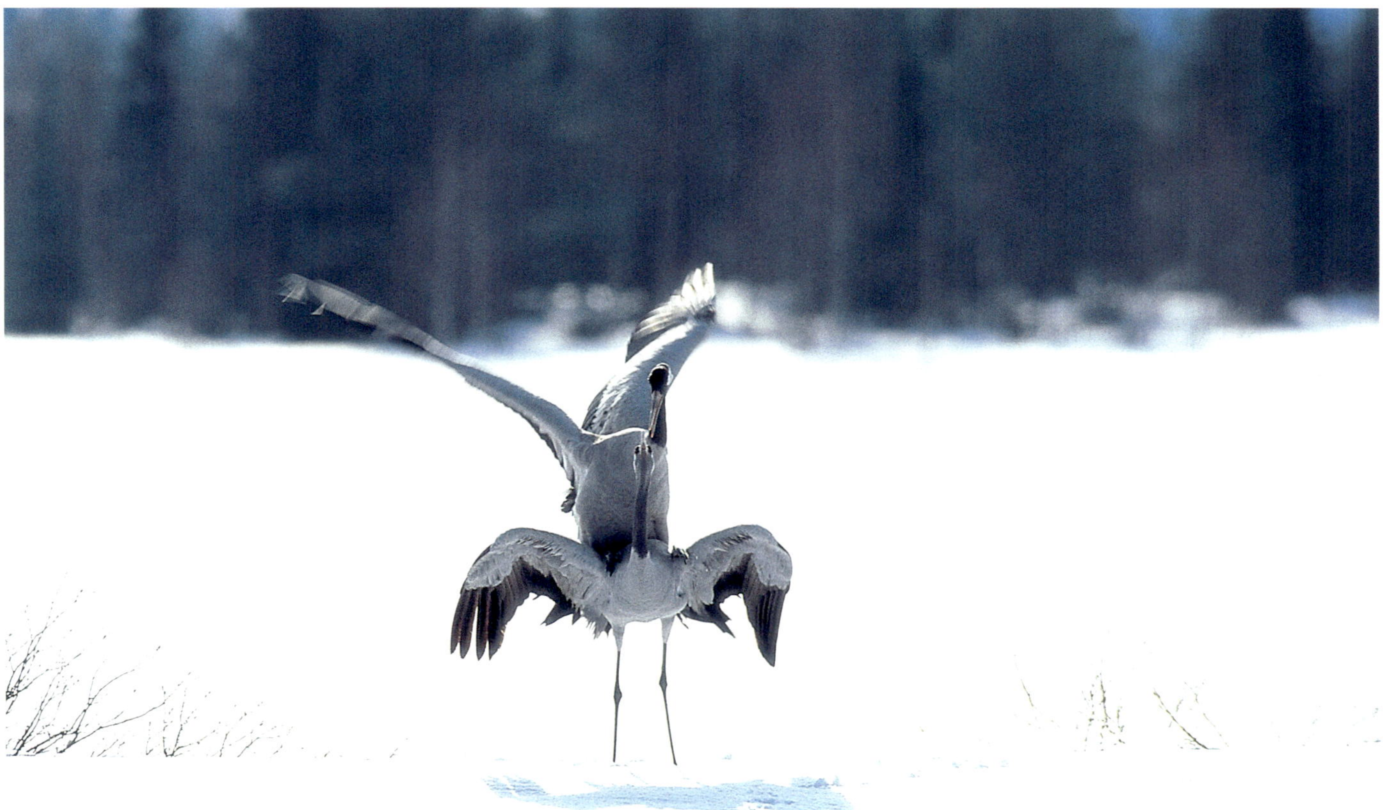

Eventually one's eyes find what they are seeking: a spruce branch stirs as the moose turns its massive head. Its eyes glint in the shadows, and its ears, like alert trumpets, are silhouetted against the green. The huge moose cow is attempting with evident resolve to determine what is up. The still air conveys no olfactory signals; its poor eyesight has yet to offer any clue as to the threat posed by the morning intruder.

The moose is loath to withdraw, for it recently gave birth to two calves in the gloom of the forest. This followed eight months of gestation; the youngsters, born as bundles a good ten kilograms each, are now shakily on their feet but not yet able to flee in the face of danger. This they cannot do until a week old. During the first days of their lives they are on their own when their mother goes off to feed, and they may even bond with some human who happens along and may in turn mistakenly assume the unattended calves to be orphans.

If the defenceless calves are threatened, the female may defend them very aggressively. And so powerful is its kick that confrontation is best avoided. Whether faced with a human or a wolf, a moose cow will defend its offspring and its usually drives off the troublemaker. This is one secret of the moose's success; another may be the scarcity of wolves and the regulation of the hunting done by humans.

The Finnish moose population is healthy and largely thriving, but the moose has not always had it so well. In the early 1900s it was still a severely endangered species. In the hinterlands of central Finland, a community of a few dozen, perhaps a hundred, endured. Elsewhere in the country the species had become extinct, with the exception perhaps of the easternmost border regions. With its protection and the subsequent determined regulation of hunting, the population began to grow. Preferring young forests, the moose has also benefited from intensive forestry.

The lesser black-blacked gull has declined to the verge of extinction.

June

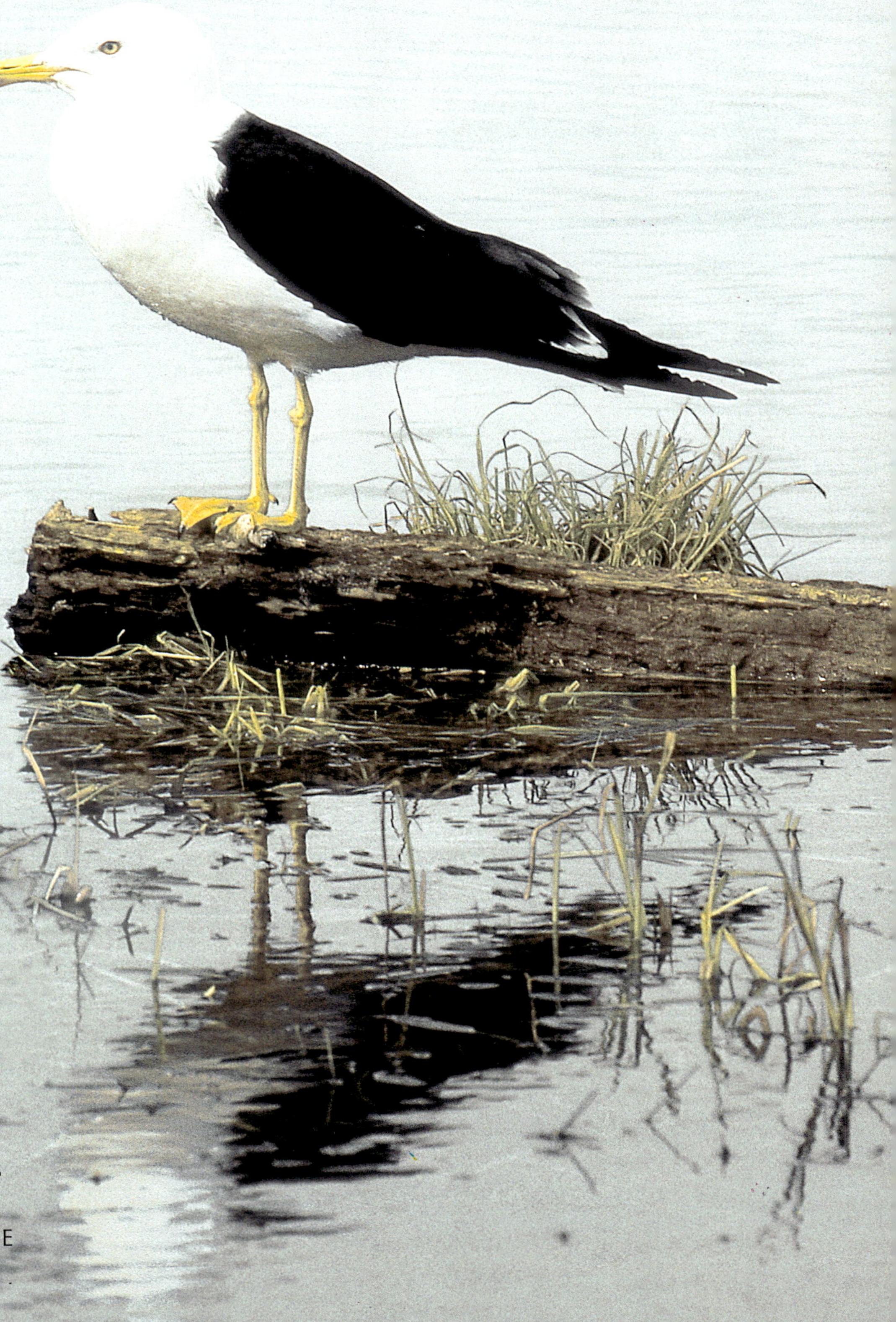

A convocation of grey seals on outlying skerries.

A marsh teeming with winged creatures.

The master singers perform at night.

The ice goes out of northern lakes.

The last birds of passage arrive.

The spruce and pine release their pollen.

Fjeld birches burst into leaf.

The autumn migration of the birds gets under way.

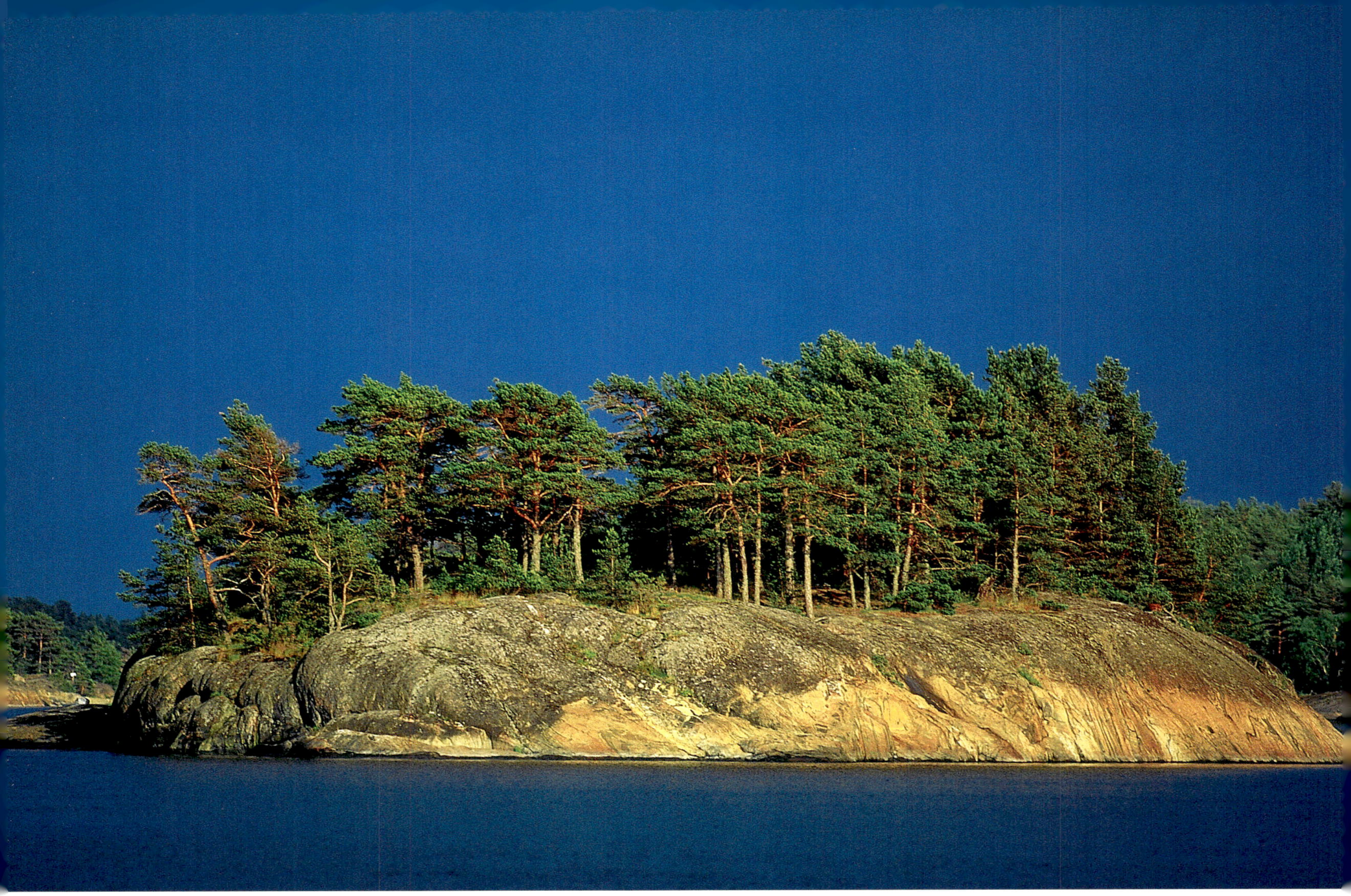

The Longest Day

The mist of a summer's night lies phantom-like over the outer archipelago. The sun has gone for a dip beneath the northern horizon and is now a bright silver coin beyond the grey veil of fog. Black guillemots shriek on the rocky shore, stretching their wings languidly before going off to fish.

It is dead calm. A female goosander takes its extended family farther offshore. Having been asleep in a nondescript bundle, the brood unwinds into a chain of twelve hatchlings and descends upon the fry of a cove. The goosander column efficiently trolls the local waters, the young birds popping to the surface here and there with three-spined sicklebacks in their bills.

But the fishing ends suddenly when the duck lets out a coarse warning call. The hatchlings scamper to their mother's side, and the entire troop closes ranks, those farther off literally running across the water to reach safety. The alarm sounds whenever the robust predatory form of a great black-backed gull or even a herring gull appears anywhere nearby. But when the coast is clear, the goosander family fans out to occupy themselves with fishing once more.

Arctic terns dart tirelessly about the sky. They bring the evening to a close by shrieking vociferously and, when darkness withdraws, they are among the first to take up their merry pranks again. The clear call of the common gull accompanies a fisherman making for his nets.

Ashore, the fragrant lesser butterfly orchid glows among junipers as if phosphorescent. Its roots delve what was once a littoral zone, where the lime from pulverized mussel shells provides an excellent substrate for this exquisite blossom. This tender woodland flower seems quite at home even in the seemingly harsh bleakness of the outer islands.

Between the island and the open sea lies a chain of skerries, an infamous shoal whose whiteness on sea charts marks unsounded water. Low skerries, reefs, underwater ledges. Boats have no business there. In calm weather it is a region of pleasant primordial vistas, but even a very light wind brings the sea up enough to send waves spilling over the skerries and breaking above the ledges. In stiff winds and in gales these parts are in the grip of awesome forces, the effect underscored by the rumble of surf.

Following a thunderstorm, the landscape exudes freshness.

This area, which employs the forces of nature and unnavigable waters for self-protection, is the habitat of the grey seal. From within the dispersing mist sounds a hollow dog-like barking. The still weather allows the rare song of the seal to carry for kilometers. Out there somewhere on the furthermost skerry a molting pod of seals lolls, jabbering boisterously. The gathering may consist of ten, a hundred, easily five hundred, but not a thousand, seals. Idle loafers, scratching themselves. Some minor internecine scuffling.

The tender new green on a spruce is cold-sensitive. Frost can destroy a year's growth.

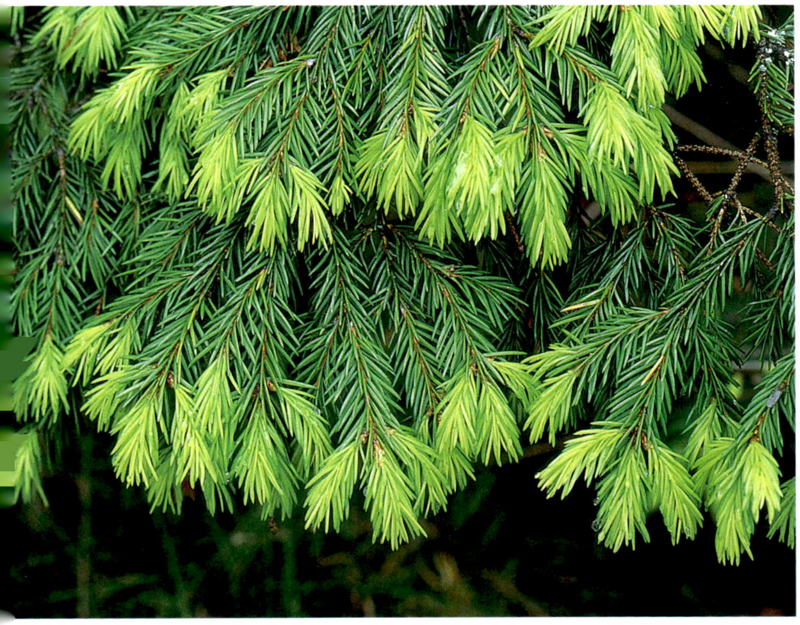

The rare beauty of copses and marshland, the lady's slipper, is the most singular of northern orchids.

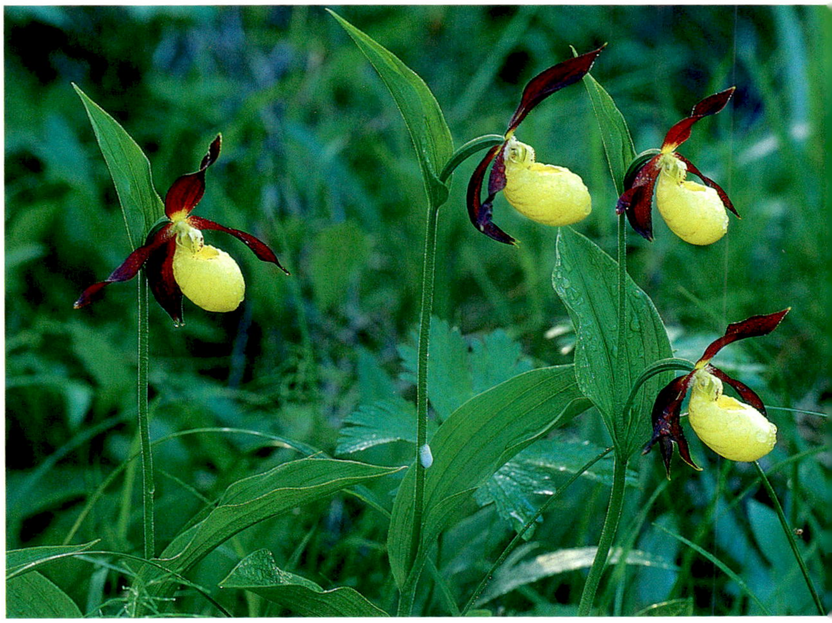

The grey seal is an excellent example of a species which has been saved through determined conservation efforts. According to some estimates, about one-hundred thousand grey seals swam the Baltic in the early 20th century. Heavy hunting, abetted by bounties, sent the animal into a decline that steepened even further from the effects of environmental toxins. At its lowest in the early 1980s, the number of grey seals in the Baltic was counted at a measly 2500 individuals.

Protection and the reduction of toxin-induced stress have resulted in population growth. The five-thousand-specimen threshold was crossed in the mid-1990s, but it is still a long way to a state which may be considered normal. The food chain still contains toxic residues which have weakened the reproductive capacity of older seals in particular. An unacceptably high number of young die in fishnets and traps. Finland's grey seals do not yet have protected basking skerries. There are also Finns who are whetting their knives in anticipation of the reintroduction of seal hunting.

The air is thick with mosquitoes; along the river summer's first horseflies have already appeared, sanguivors the size of plum pits. On the banks grow gaunt, taper-shaped Lapland spruces beyond which is a gloomy wilderness of horsetail ferns. Clumps of sedge hem black

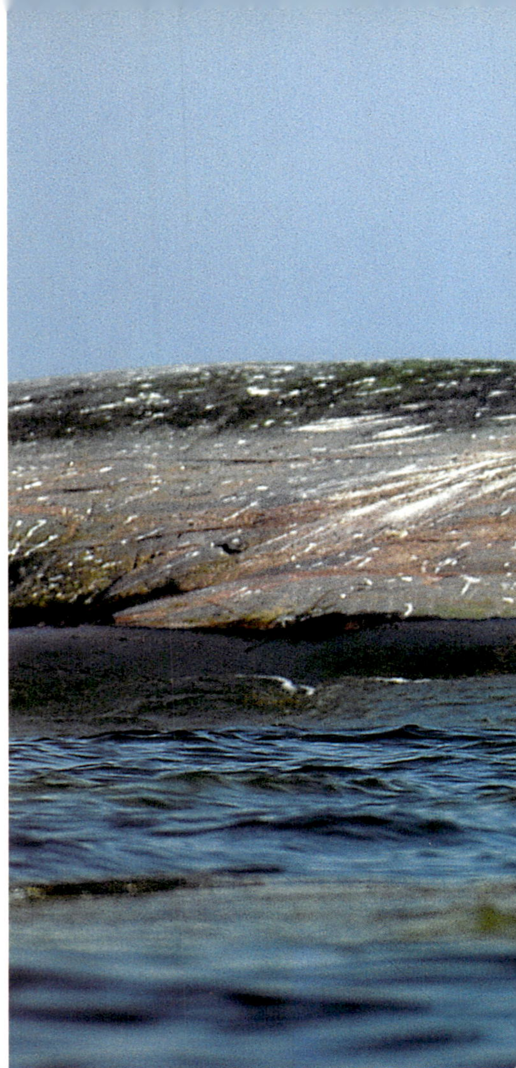

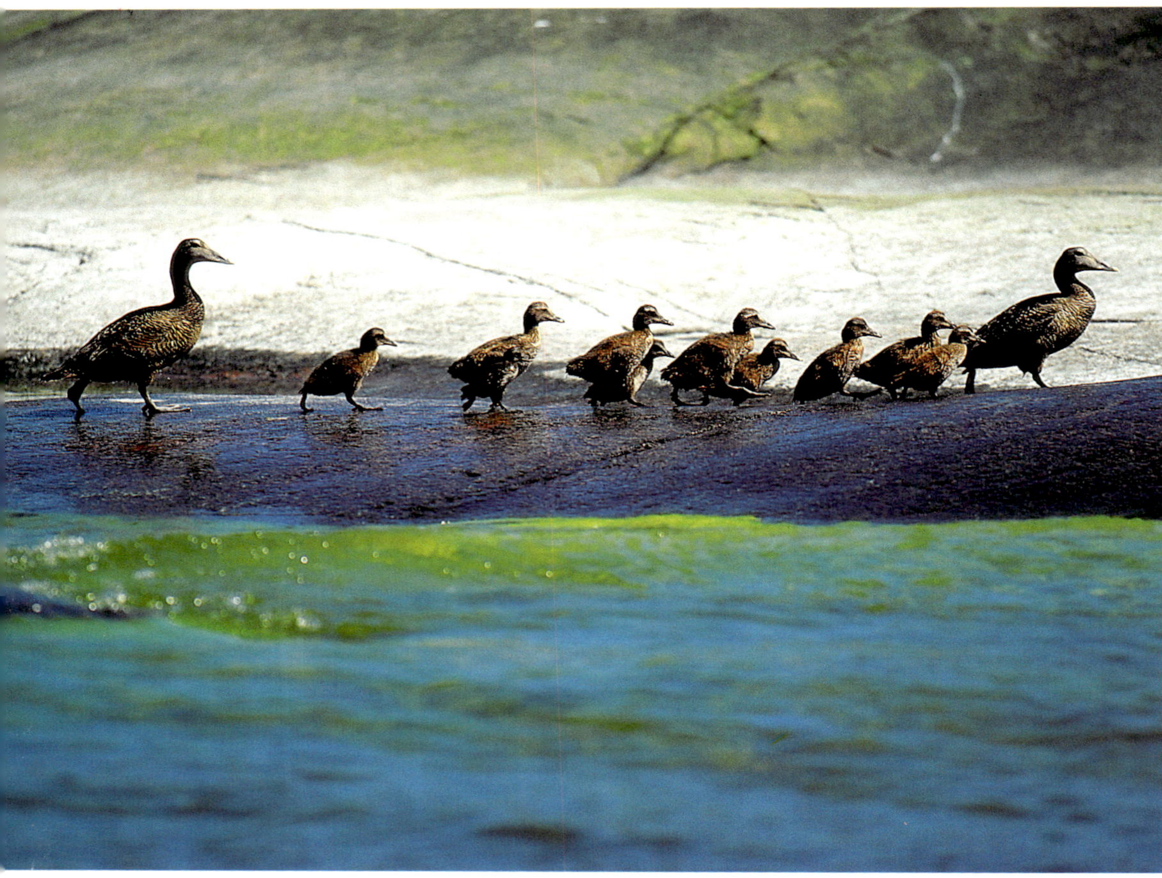

Eider broods join in extended families tended by nestless females.

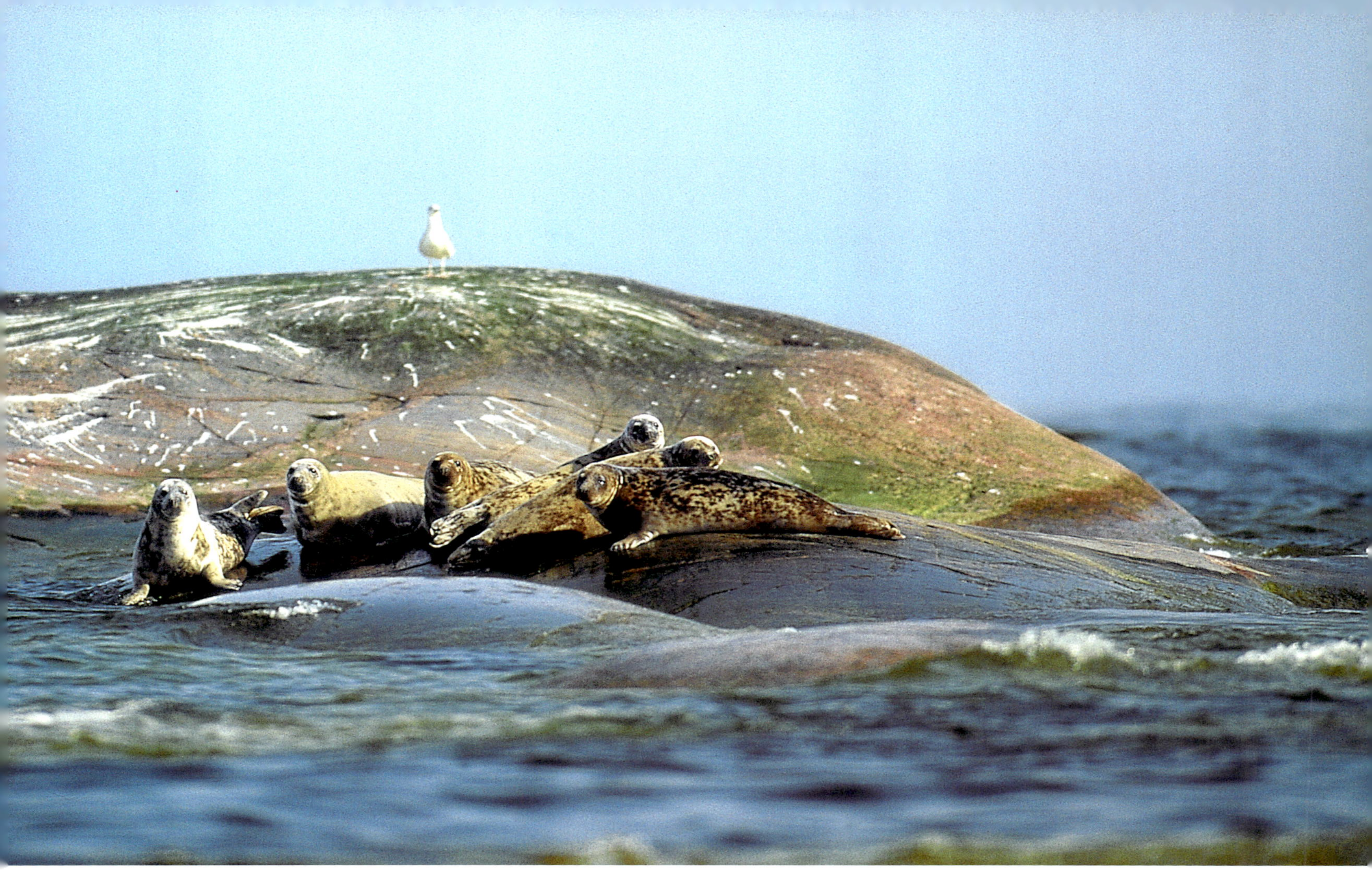

Brothers-in-arms... Juvenile grey seals, born on the winter ice, loll on a skerry.

mires aswarm with hatching mosquitoes. A large bird flits across the far edge of vision, a great grey owl, and vanishes at once into the greenery.

The wilderness opens out into a marsh dominated by stunted pines. Cotton grass stretches in glossy tufts as far as the eye can see. A few lush patches sustain broad-leaved cotton grass. A tree pipit sings fervently, mounts to the heights on its wings and descends, twittering, to stiffen comically atop a wetland pine.

On solid sphagnum hummocks there grows the intoxicatingly fragrant Labrador tea, the rhododendron of the North. Running beneath the plants are ant trails, all of them leading to a stout mound. The workers haul needles and small lengths of twig, scraps of bark; flattened by winter, the hill is the object of endless repairs. A caterpillar caught as quarry is borne along by an entire procession.

The ground gives beneath one's feet. Boots make a sucking sound with each step. And, as if by surprise, the pine-clad marsh extends into an open, virtually boundless bog. The channels between hummocks cover hectares, pools thick with bogbean. From the hummocks jut occasional stunted pines, bleaching boughs. The desolation is tangible.

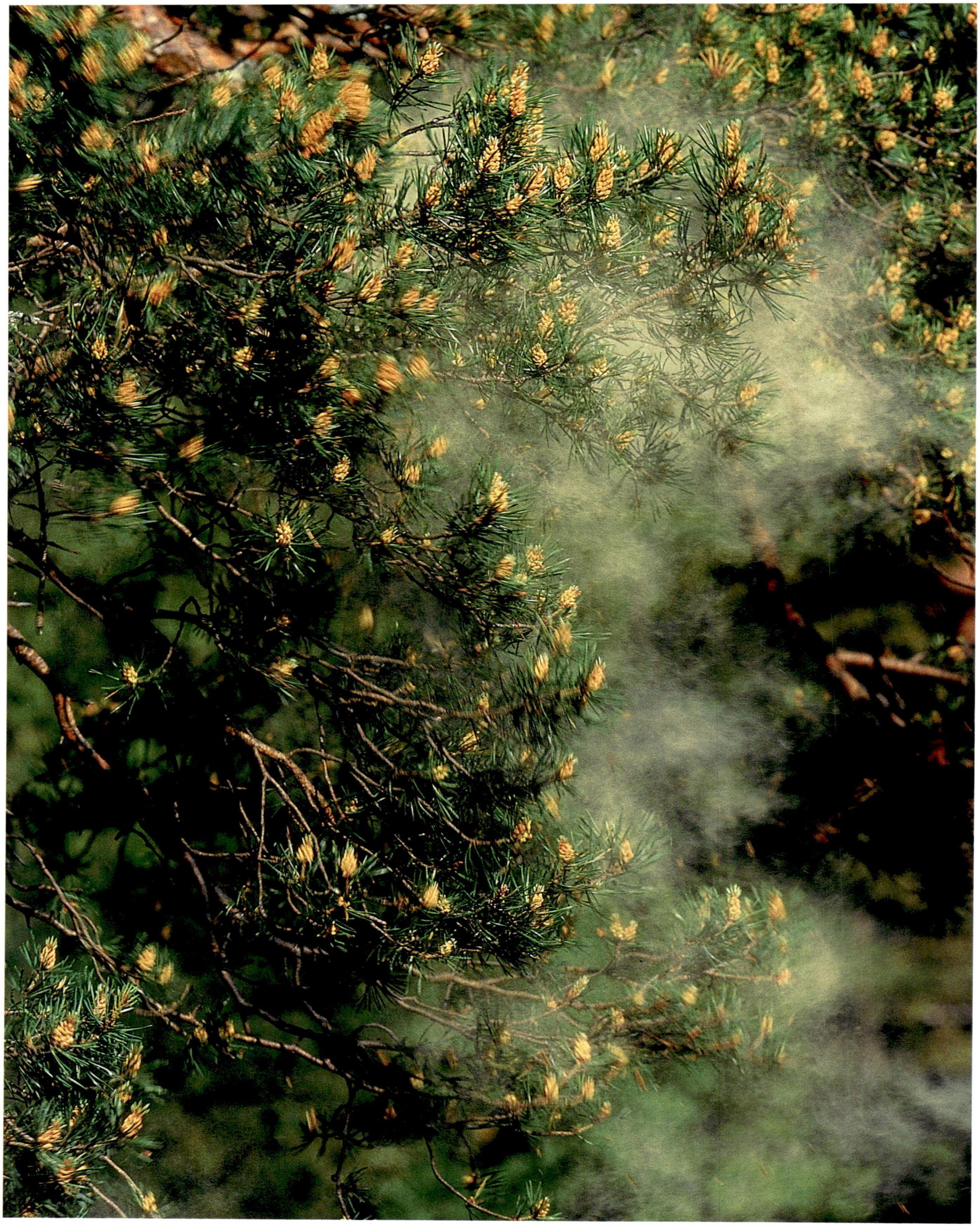

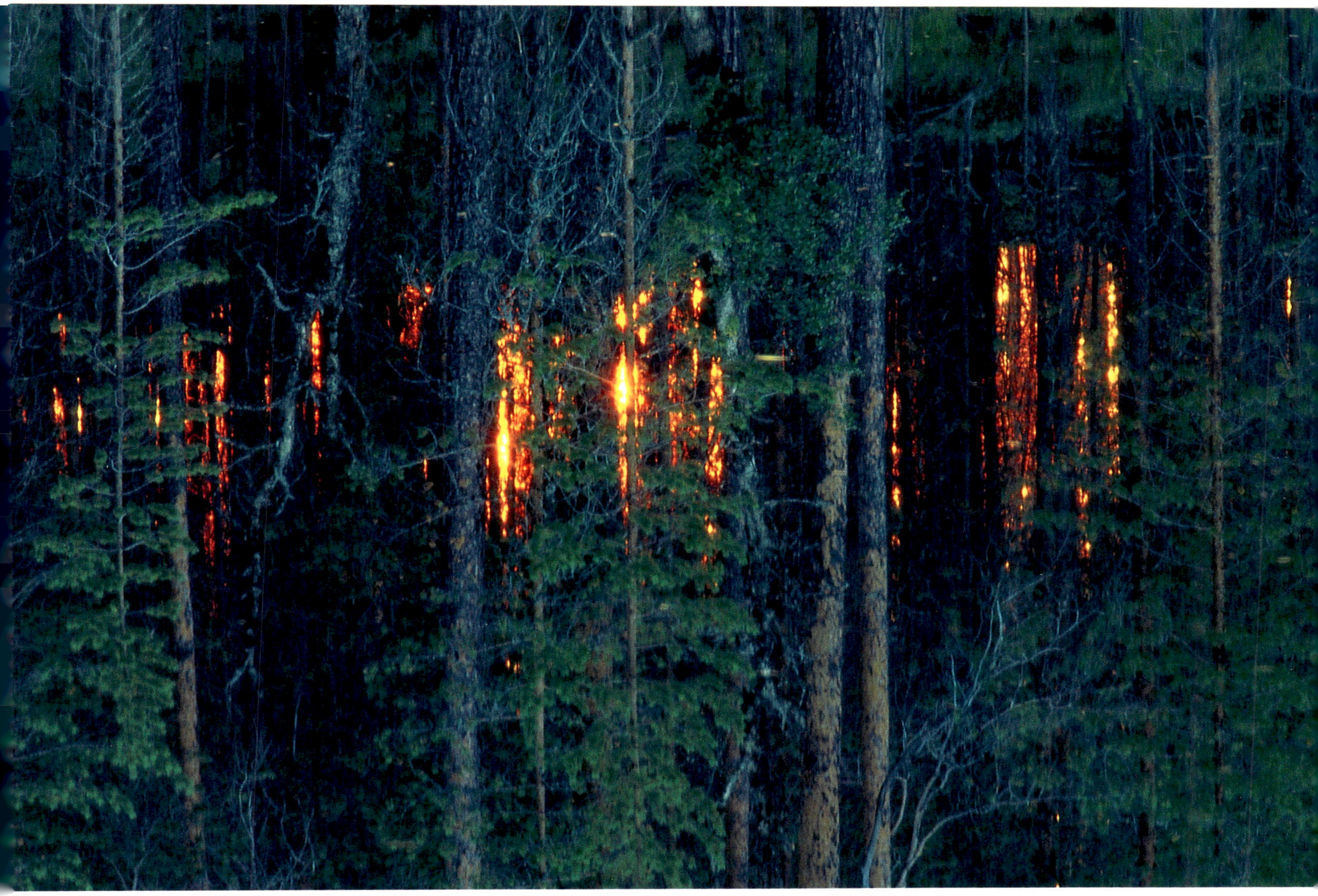

A cuckoo calls. Somewhere on the moor a lynx stalks a hare.

Who sows the wind… the pollen from a blossoming pine fills the air and covers the water.

In the sunlit night the bog is filled with activity. A jack snipe hurtles across the sky, displaying. Its unusual voice, reminiscent of the clatter of horse's hooves, comes from so uncertain a direction that spotting the little wader is difficult. The thrumming a common snipe produced by means of an current through is splayed tail feathers is more clearly discernible. Alighting stiff-winged among some clumps of sedge, this squawker continues to express its feelings on the ground. A tinkling rasp reveals the whereabouts of a bird otherwise so clever at camouflage that it goes unnoticed until, huffing, it breaks cover right beside one's boot.

The thin courtship psalm of a broad-billed sandpiper is barely audible at all; the attention literally drains away under the attack of a swarming string-section of mosquitoes. The small, unassuming sandpiper performing in the sky above the bog is also extremely adept at concealing itself on the ground, its habitat the wettest shores of fens.

Highest up a wood sandpiper jeers. Its warnings have sounded ever since the wooded marsh, and there's no escaping its metallic clangor even on the most open of bogs. It is the most common alarm system among marshland birds. No stranger branded as enemy can prowl about the marsh unobserved by this sentinel; and after its warning, anything with feathers knows it had best beware.

The cranes suddenly come to attention as the wood sandpiper sounds the alarm. They move away from their nesting places and make themselves known only when the trespasser nears the nest or hiding young. Even then, instead of jeering on the nest, they draw the visitor's attention to themselves, elsewhere. They seem to know that they must try to lure the stranger their way.

On a mound of moss in the wettest depression in the middle of the open bog there dwells a peregrine falcon. It too reads the wood sandpiper's warning. Sitting in its lookout tree, the tercel observes events on the marsh and launches into flight when the intruder comes too near. Shrieking implacably, it shoots through the sky, drawing along a strapping female that also proceeds to cry out a warning. They attack in a rush of wings.

Threatened and driven to the verge of extinction by environmental toxins, the peregrine fiercely defends its offspring. And there are now beginning to be offspring to defend, for the effect of the poisons is diminishing. Peregrine falcons are producing viable young. Such was not the case in the 1960s and 70s, when toxins rendered the females sterile. Eggs broke during brooding, hatchlings died prematurely, even females succumbed, and nests became deserted. The steadfast peregrine is making a comeback, though still a fairly tenuous one.

The silhouette of this raptor sows terror among marshland birds. Waders and ducks are the hawk's preferred provender; and, being a tireless and accomplished hunter, it catches them at a steady pace. The feathers, down and bones of its prey accumulate in heaps at its nesting site. Carrion beetles scurry about, polishing off the scraps left by the powerful predator.

The peregrine doesn't disturb the red-necked phalaropes flitting about the pond in the marsh. They are too small to top this robust raptor's menu. They swim about the water creating eddies which lift small creatures to the surface. Dibbling incessantly, they stuff themselves with insect larvae and plankton from the pond's surface waters.

The warm day gradually darkens into evening as moisture given off by the ground dances as sylphs of mist in dells and the river channel. The water glints steely grey, insects hovering on its surface. With a quick strike, a brown trout bolts a caddis fly floating in an eddy. A few bubbles linger on the mirror-smooth surface, until they too even out into the unruffled current.

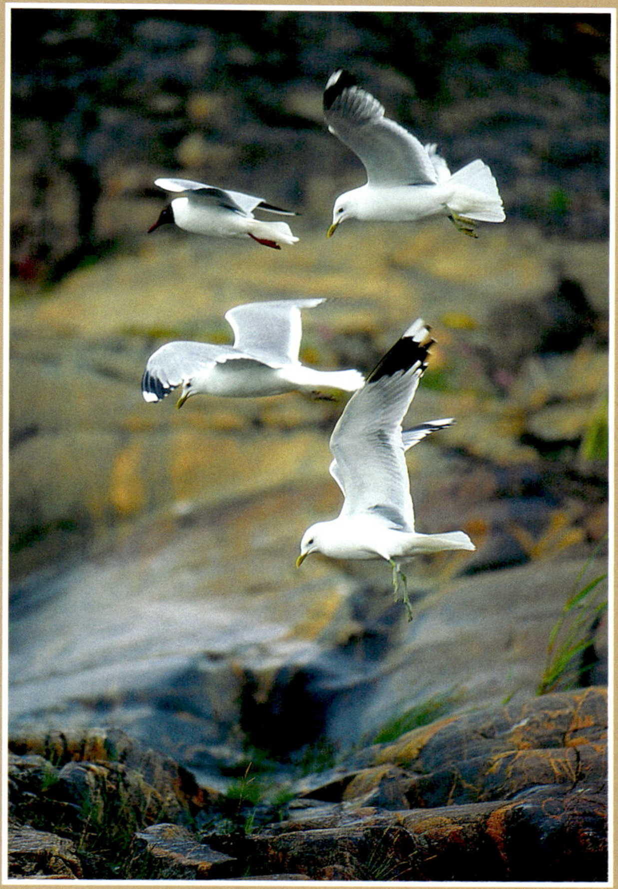

Gulls are the principal birds of shorelands.
The black-headed gull, with its brown hood, has declined in recent years, but the common gull is thriving and probably more widespread than ever. The elegant lesser black-backed gull, on the other hand, is now rare and threatened. The stout herring gull and sturdy great black-backed gull have simultaneously increased in number – possibly at the expense of the lesser black-blacked gull and with human aid.

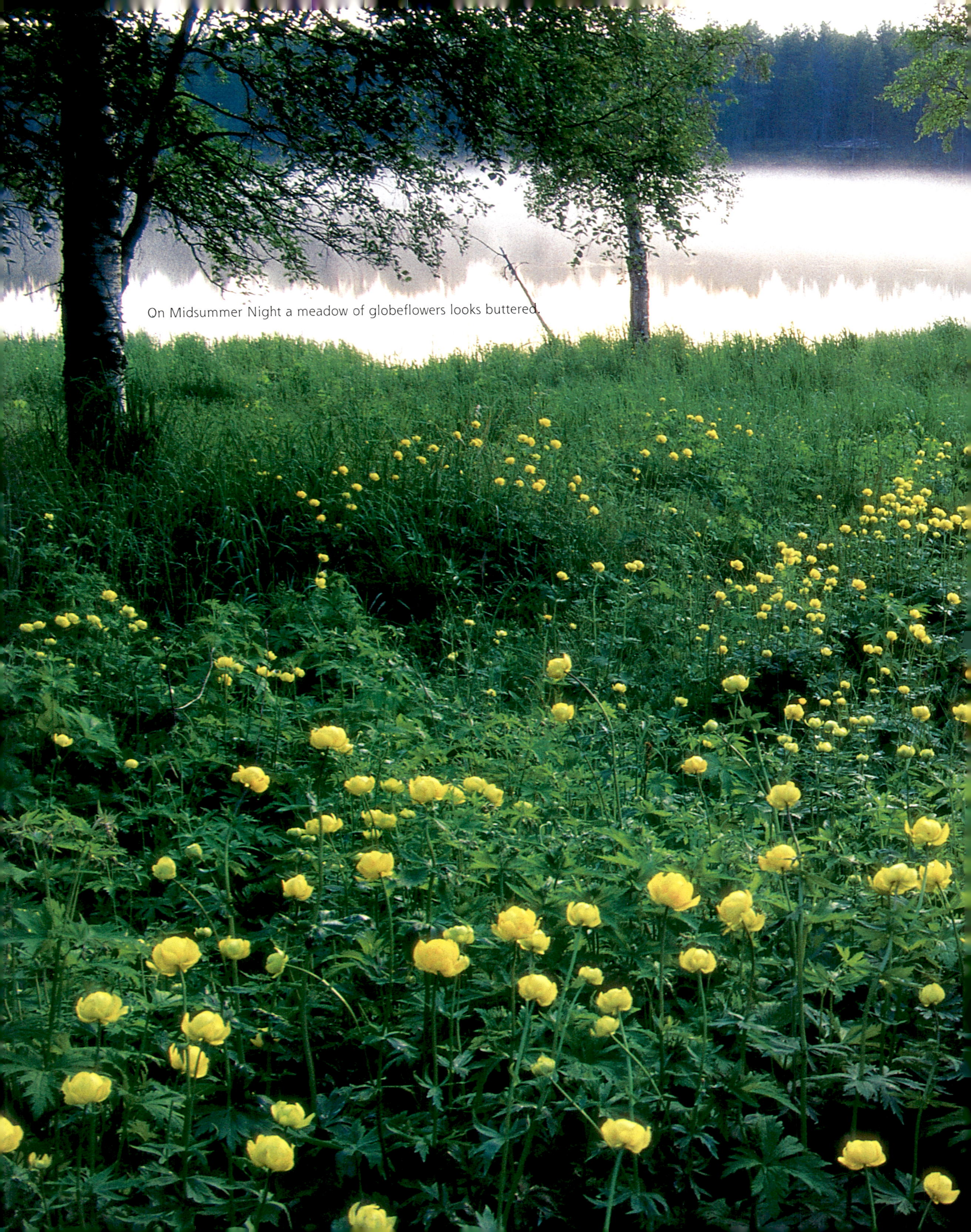

On Midsummer Night a meadow of globeflowers looks buttered.

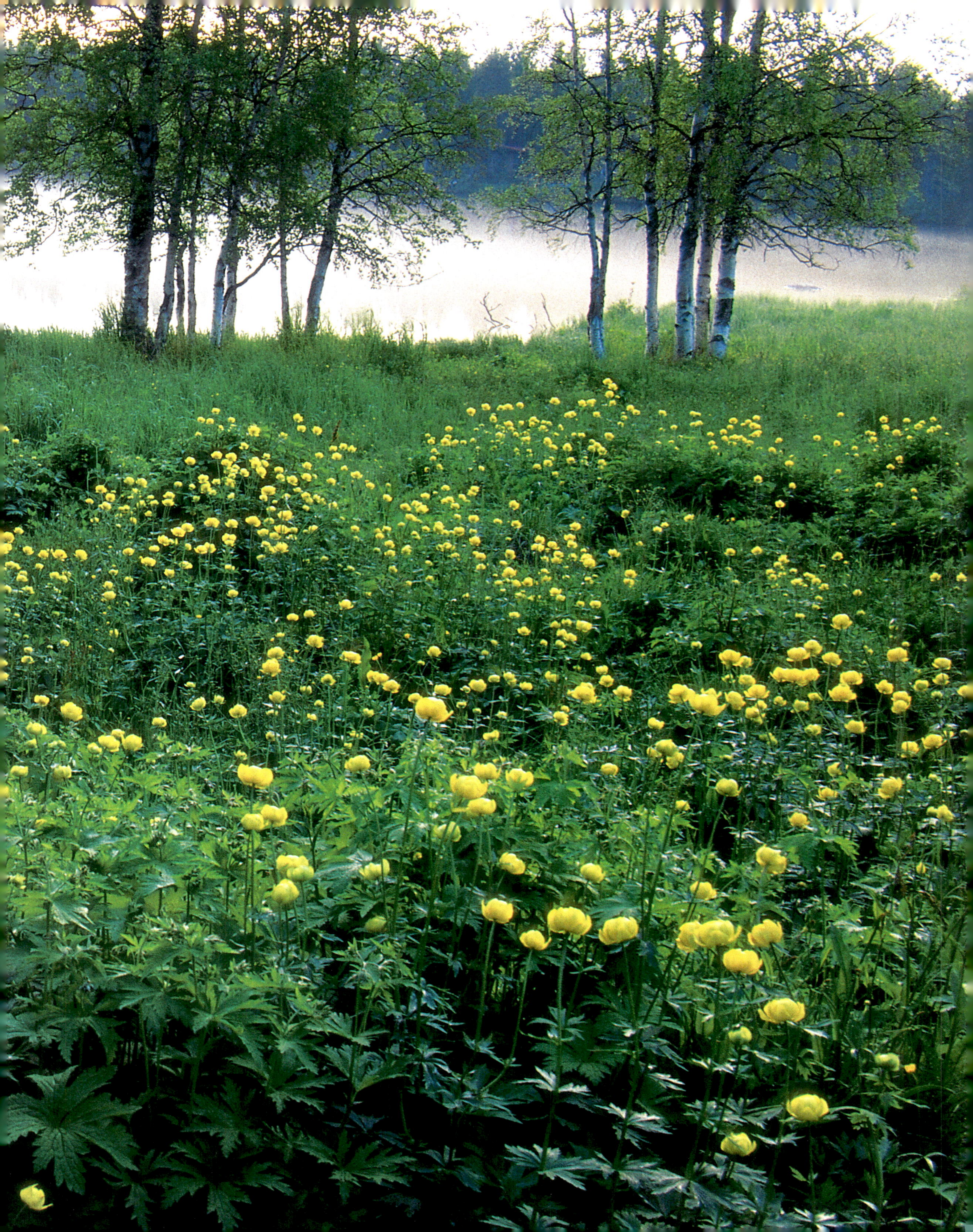

A flock of sheep wanders a riverbank meadow chomping its evening snack in a broad front which advances slowly downstream toward familiar overnight lodging. The animals mouths are in motion, the whole crew bowed, heads in the grass. One of them bleats, inspiring its companions to say something too. Lanky lambs suckle feverishly, almost belligerently, but the ewes remain composed. The sheep at the head of the formation trots a few paces and the entire lot does the same in a slightly lagging wave. Hooves click.

The opposite bank looks buttered: the globeflowers are in bloom. The lush meadow glows yellow. The sheep don't care for globeflowers, for as a relative of the buttercups it is poisonous and thus avoided. The blossoms attract flies, mining bees, and beetles; and the most conscientious of these may grope among the petals for days on end.

In the thickening mist the slightly sweet scent of cow parsley wafts from a fallow field. Its corymbose flowers teem with flies drunk with nectar and beetles flat on their faces and entirely coated in pollen. Its white lacy flower blossoming earlier only on narrow berms, cow parsley now dominates abandoned fields and wasteland. Utilizing the nitrogen in air pollution, it gains ground over smaller and weaker competing meadow plants.

The distant harping of nightingales is heard on every quarter. In lush stands of bird cherry along fields in Karelia, a region fabled for its song, these master singers dwell a few hundred meters apart. High fluting and rhythmic warbling blend in charming concert. The birds seem actually to incite one another into feverish bouts of song, and the loudest salvos from near at hand set the teeth on edge. The beaus have time yet to sing: their mates do the incubating, and the parental responsibilities of a paterfamilias begin only when the eggs hatch and tiny gaping gullets demand bugs to eat.

Two woodcocks flit on fluttering wings over the forest. A frog-like croaking and sharp exclamations accompany the patrolling flight of this funny looking woodland wader, which hour after hour, from one evening to the next, travels an identical territorial borderline etched on the air. Their routes run parallel for a moment, and then each swerves off in its own direction.

Also playing in the main orchestra for the concert of nocturnal songsters are the robin and song thrush; the soulful tune of a redwing is also included, as is the amusing cackle of a fieldfare. From shoreline reed beds comes the squabble of black-headed gulls frightened by a raccoon dog, along with the jeering of a common sandpiper. A lapwing meows a few times and a small flock of ducks flies overhead. Their wings whistle in the darkness.

In the reed bed a tireless sedge warbler emits its impassioned song: abundant whistling, a carolling climaxing in a rattling glissando. The singer emphasizes its message by lifting into flight while singing, then descending, wings stiff, to concealment among the reeds - only to begin over and over. At night the insistent tune of the reed warbler doesn't seem to get off the ground, and the rasping of the great reed warbler doesn't appear to gain momentum until first light.

But the agitated marsh warbler in a shoreline willow copse is another story. This master singer hides not its light under a bushel. The themes tumbling from this little bird sound familiar, but joined through the warbler's skill they form a wholly unique entity. The compilation includes a bit of swallow, a few measures of chaffinch, the fluting of a blackbird, a magpie's laughter, and a series of unrecognizable whistling sounds that probably originate in its tropical wintering grounds. The quick-tempoed medley builds in a jumble of rasping and rattling sounds.

The intoxicating scent of Labrador tea wafts through the summer night.

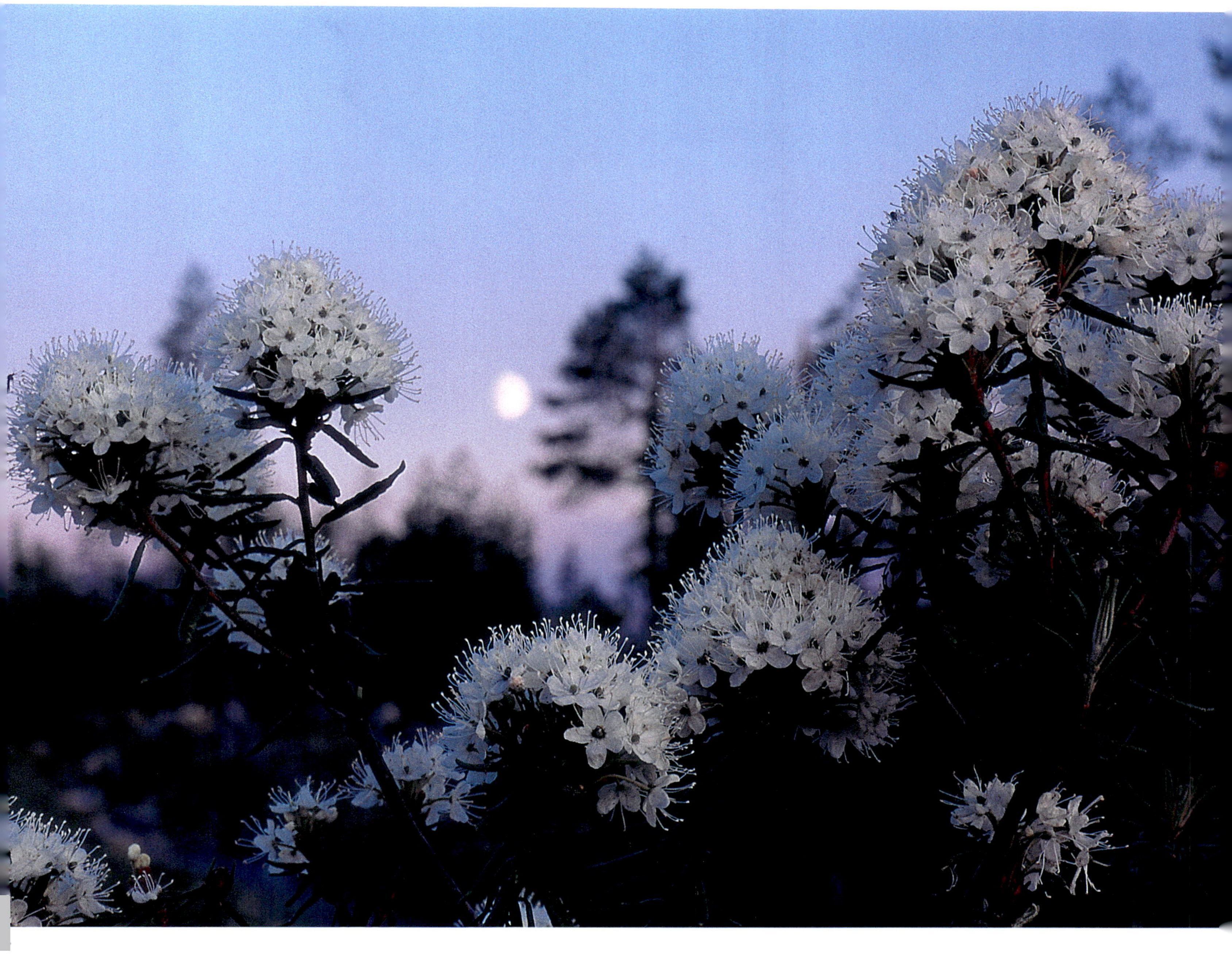

And after only a moment's silence, the soloist bursts into a fresh mélange.

Coming from a willow copse in a low-lying field, the shy churr of a grasshopper warbler contrasts perfectly with the marsh warbler. This unassuming bird tirelessly repeats its simple love song from dusk till dawn. The monotonous whirring resembles somewhat that produced by a grasshopper's organs of stridulation. But this bird is the singer of limpid early summer and the dark, whereas the grasshopper performs during the hot days of high summer.

In a manor-house yard the sweetness of the cow parsley blends with the cloying fragrance of a lilac hedge. A privet hawkmoth flits like a hummingbird among the lilac blossoms. The large butterfly imbibes nectar with its long proboscis and hovers skilfully before its lovely chalice.

From within a cow parsley corymb, which resembles a parachute frozen in place, there sounds what may be the most stylish solo of the summer's night. A Blyth's reed warbler pours forth is piping with deliberation, masterfully imitating other crack singers and diligently repeating its favorite tunes. This concert master links its themes with a few juicy sounds and brings its performance to a conclusion with a lovely, descending whistle.

On a pine-dotted heath the eerie churring of a nightjar fills the dark landscape. In a field adjoining some cow pens a corncrake repeats its trifling message. Only a poet could call it a song, but it has its mysterious appeal as well. There is no need to envision the moon over a field of corn. Two crakes may even maintain their monologues from evening to dawn, week in and week out, for a month.

A trout leaps falls on its way to spawning in tributary waters.

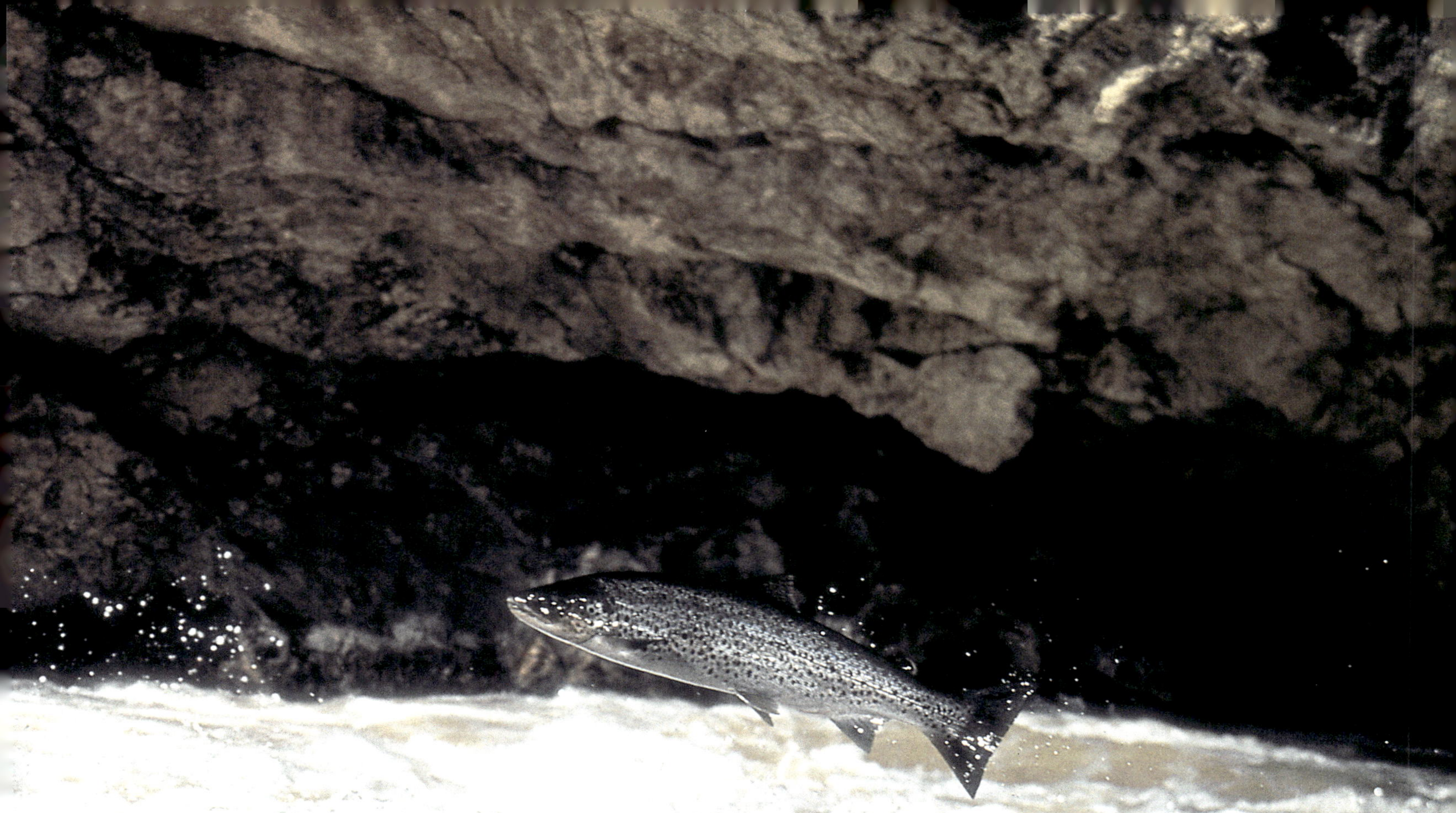

July

Dragonflies and damselflies hatch at the water's edge.

Adult waders populate the shores.

Pressures mount in lemming country.

Ants swarm.

Time for geese, swans and ducks to moult.

A grass snake lays its eggs.

Meadows blaze with blossom.

Berries and mushrooms begin to ripen.

Algae rafts in eutrophic waters.

The Joys of High Summer

It is hot at midday. A crow perches motionless atop a pole, panting. It is hunched, its shoulders drooping and beak ajar, its blue-grey nictitating membrane covering its eyes and its wings hanging slightly akimbo.

The heat is sweltering, the sky cloudless, the air muggy. The thirsty vegetation droops but insects buzz about the blossoms: bumblebees, honeybees and other Apidae, flies and all manner of beetles gorge on nectar and pollen from the meadow flowers. In thanks for their meal, they get to transport from blossom to blossom the pollen essential for plant reproduction.

Between the meadow and lake grows a thick forest in which even the birches look wilted with drought. Their leaves hang limp, the verdure of late spring gone; and, though summer is in its prime, there are even splashes of yellow among the leaves. Some have stopped photosynthesizing and sent the building materials of chlorophyll off to winter storage ahead of time. Not a leaf stirs in the woods, except for those jostled by a redwing fussing over its young.

A billowing sea of cottongrass also serves as swings for damselflies.

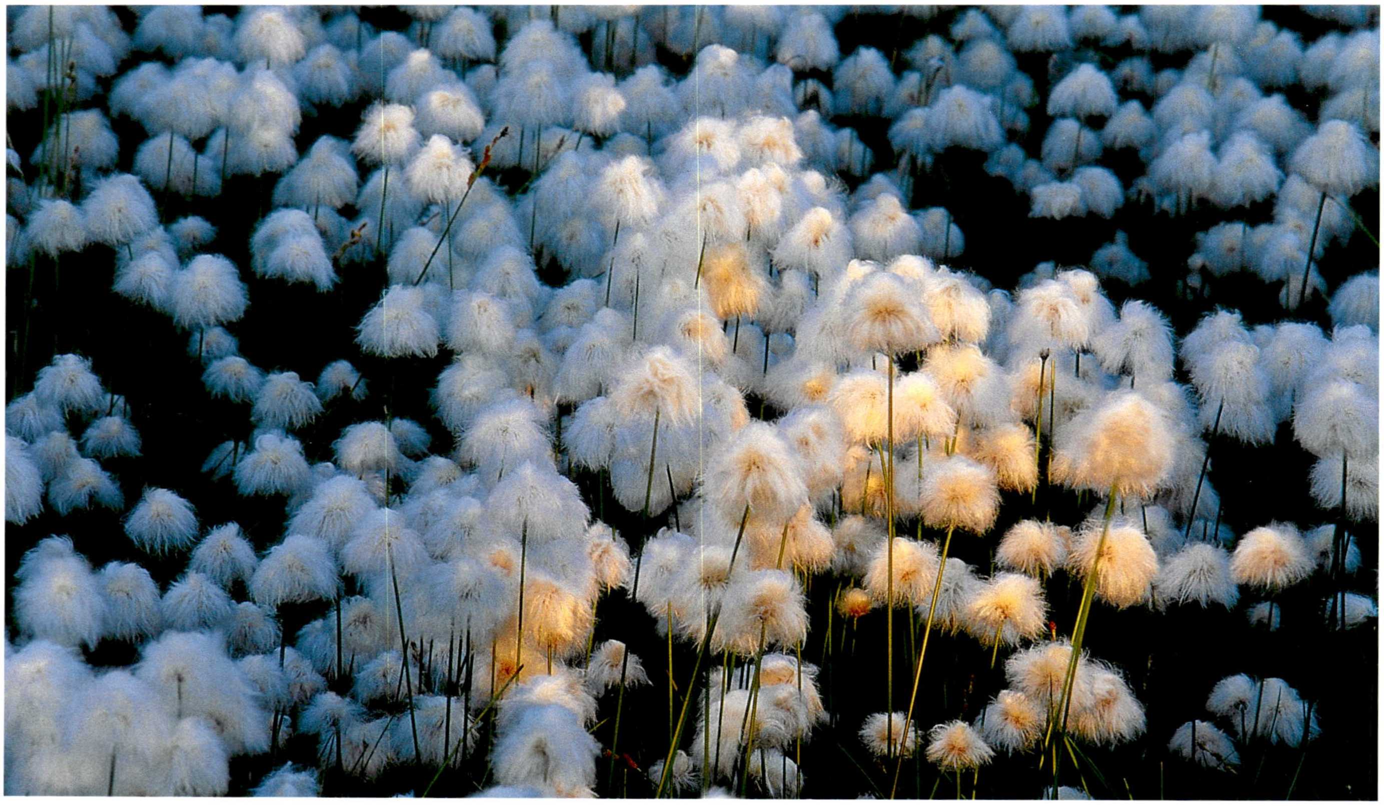

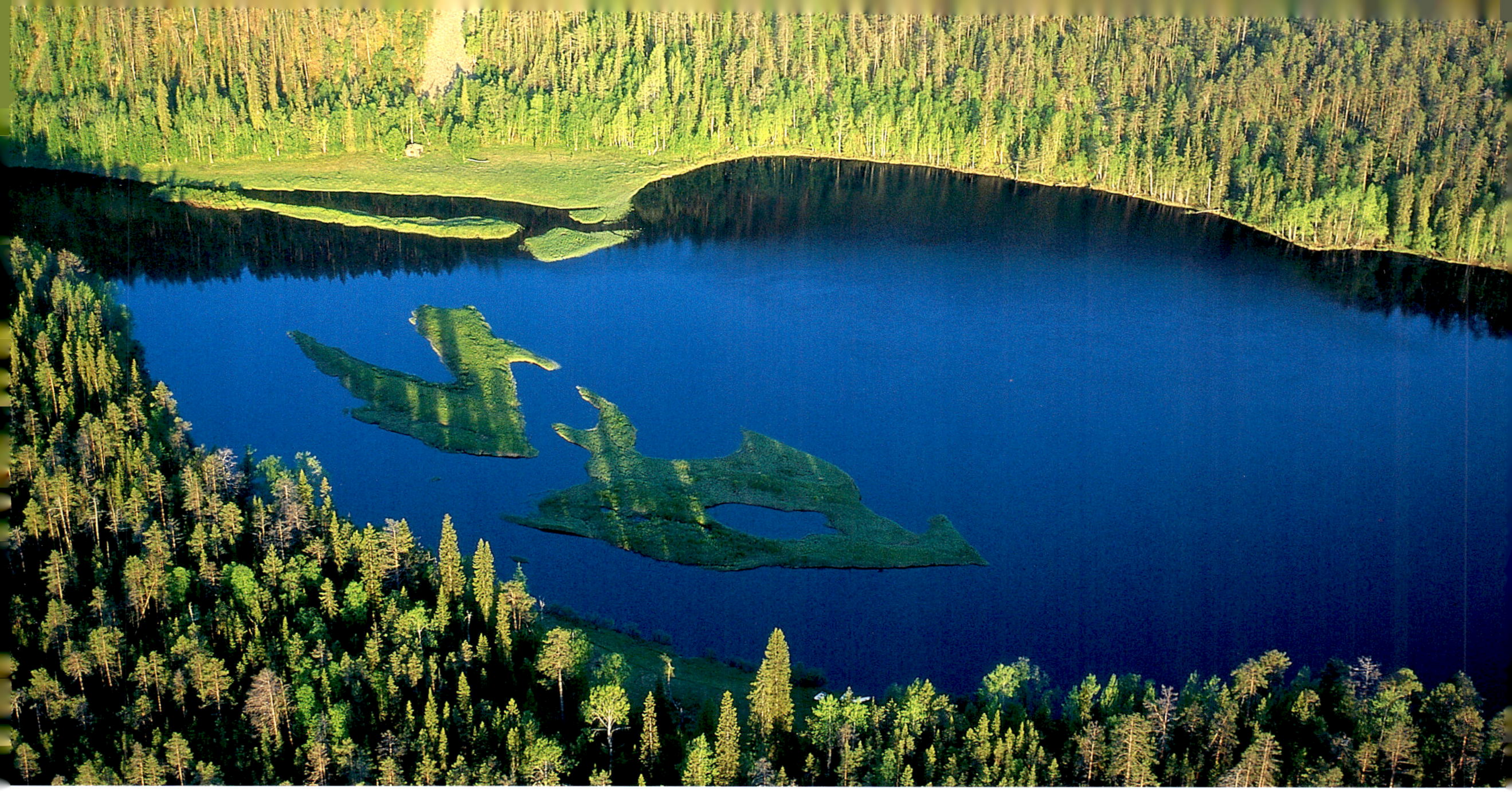

The long shadows of a summer's morning.

Something brilliant green and dazzling yellow flashes by the shore. A dense growth of yellow irises blossoms brightly. The handsome flowers look toward the sun, their leaves spread in all directions like symmetrical fans. The plant suffers no thirst as the horsetail-choked lake is within reaching distance. When high water prevails, the irises are actually awash in waves. The heat has subdued the swarms of whining mosquitoes, but heaven help us when, come evening, the air cools slightly.

A scurrying and rustling comes from the underbrush. Wee creatures scramble about branches from which flying animals shoot into the air. Transparent wings flash in the sunshine. Disregard scale for a moment and it's easy to imagine that the sky is filled with helicopters, the cruel roar replaced by near silence. The rustle of dragonfly wings is no assault on the ears.

Out of the water into a shoreline willow crawls a small six-footed creature. Its head seems large, its abdomen tapers evenly, its limbs are somewhat crooked though sturdy looking. The animal climbs a willow cane with determination, positions itself at the tip of a bough arching over the water, and gets a good purchase. It seems to freeze in place, but soon there appears on its back a small rent from which something living issues.

Having lived under water until now, the nymph now climbs out under the free sky to shed its skin and become an adult dragonfly. The teneral squirming from the nymphal skin is a pitiful, bedraggled excuse for a dragonfly. Its wings are small and crumpled, its abdomen has but a hint of the helicopter shape it is known for. But the animal matures before one's eyes. Once hatched, it begins to pump liquid into its wings; and in an hour or two, beside the empty, lifeless shell there is a noble, full-fledged dragonfly.

Day dispels summer morning mists.
A female Ural owl returns home after
its night shift.

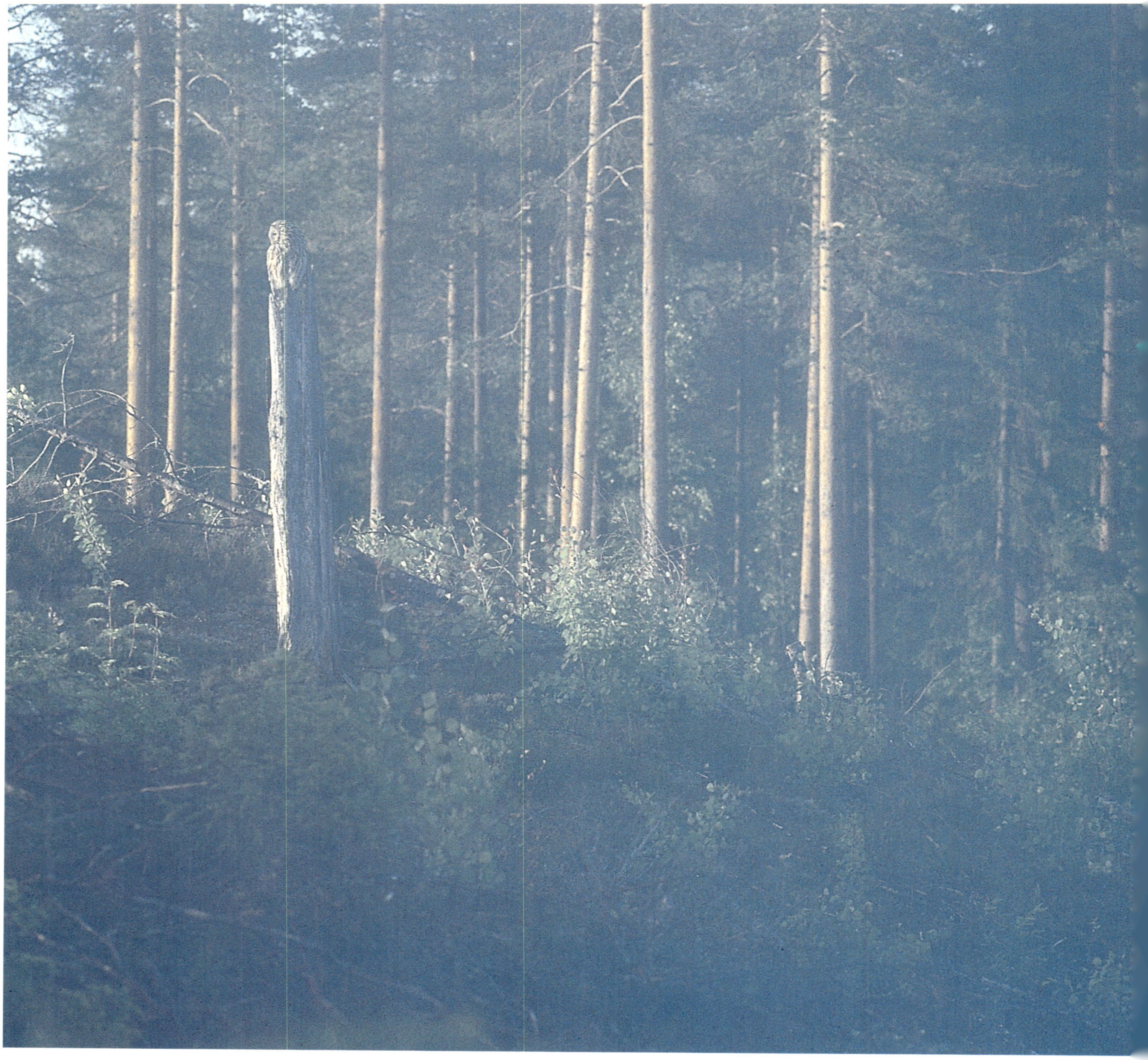

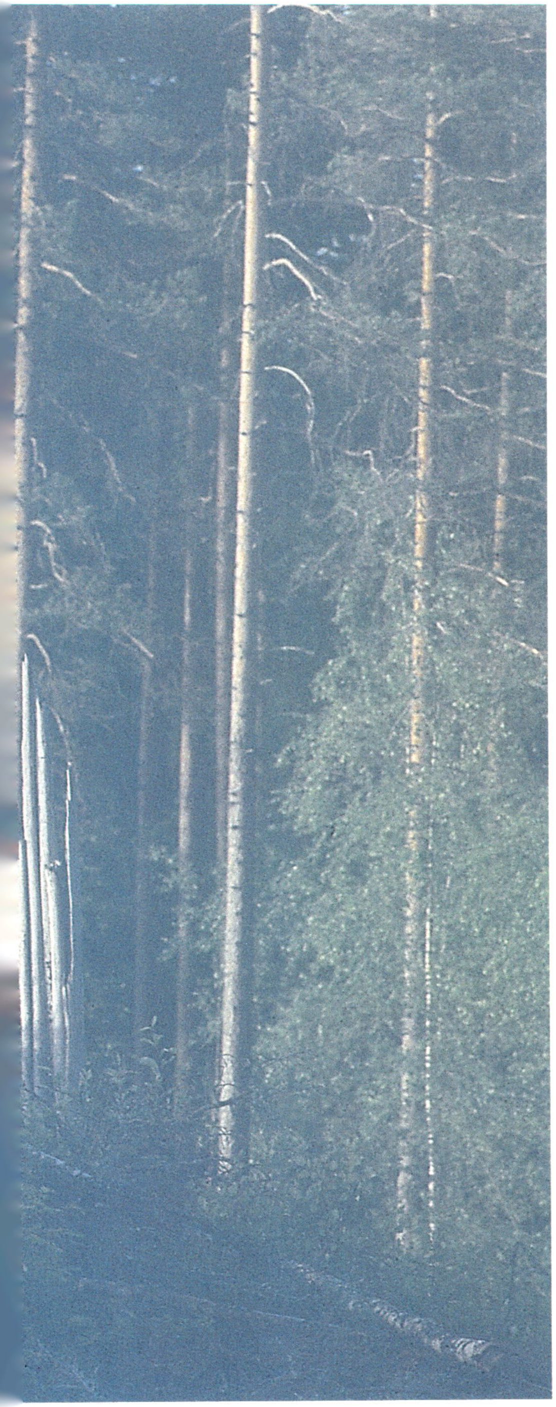

There are eyes everywhere in the forest. A Ural owlet surveys the world. To see without being seen is a most crucial lesson in survival for this little creature.

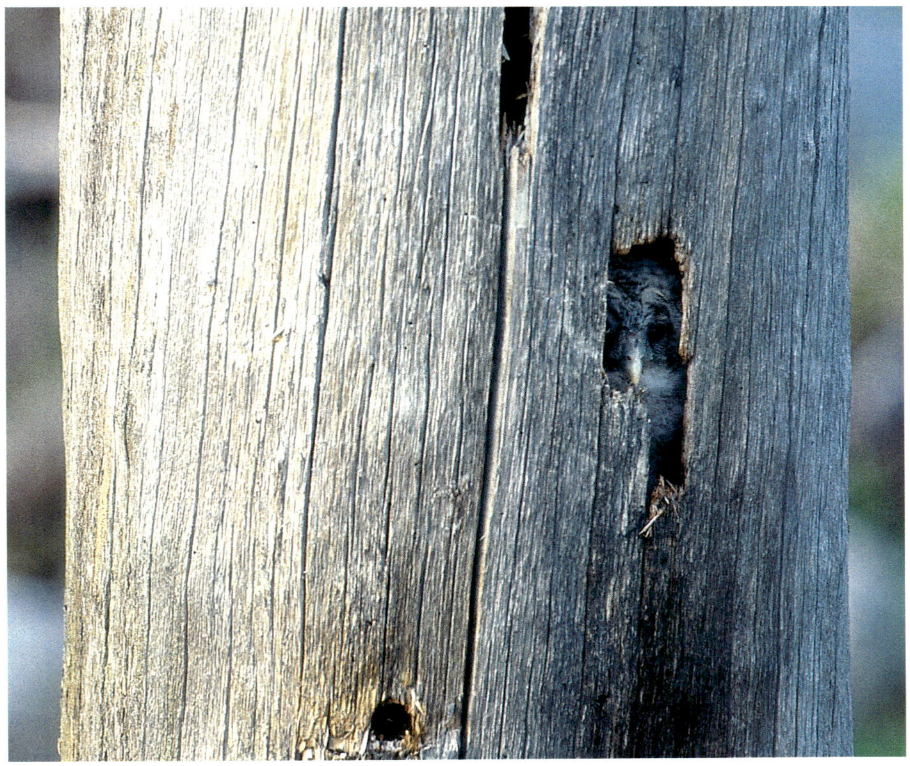

A large head and large compound eyes are the hallmark of the dragonfly; its little frontal eyes are rarely noticed. Its thorax is also large, while its abdomen is long and thin. Its long, powerful legs are at the front of the thorax, highlighting the dragonfly's forward center of gravity. The long, narrow wings are probably its best known feature.

The dragonfly, of which 51 species are found in Finland, is exclusively a lover of daylight, a true creature of warmth. As a skilled flyer, it can remain hovering in place for long stretches. It can fly backwards if necessary, as well as straight up or down, and flits from place to place in the wink of an eye. These aerial acrobatics are possible because the animal uses each pair of wings independently.

Upon reaching sexual maturity at the age of a few days, the male dragonfly takes possession of a territory from which it expels other males. A female, of course, is welcome and does, in fact, visit when it is time for reproduction. Dragonflies can mate in flight, or on a solid surface, a twig or a piling. The female lays its eggs on aquatic plants, a rotting tree at the water's edge, or straight into the water. Born after two or three weeks of maturing, the nymph sinks to the bottom, where is sheds its skin repeatedly before climbing back to the surface.

The dragonfly is a predator. Adults hunt insects, from flies to butterflies; the large Aeshnidae sometimes even snatch little damselflies. Nymphs hunt other larvae on the bottom, larger ones even tadpoles and minnows. Poor swimmers, they hunt by lying in ambush; pursuit is a hopeless waste of energy.

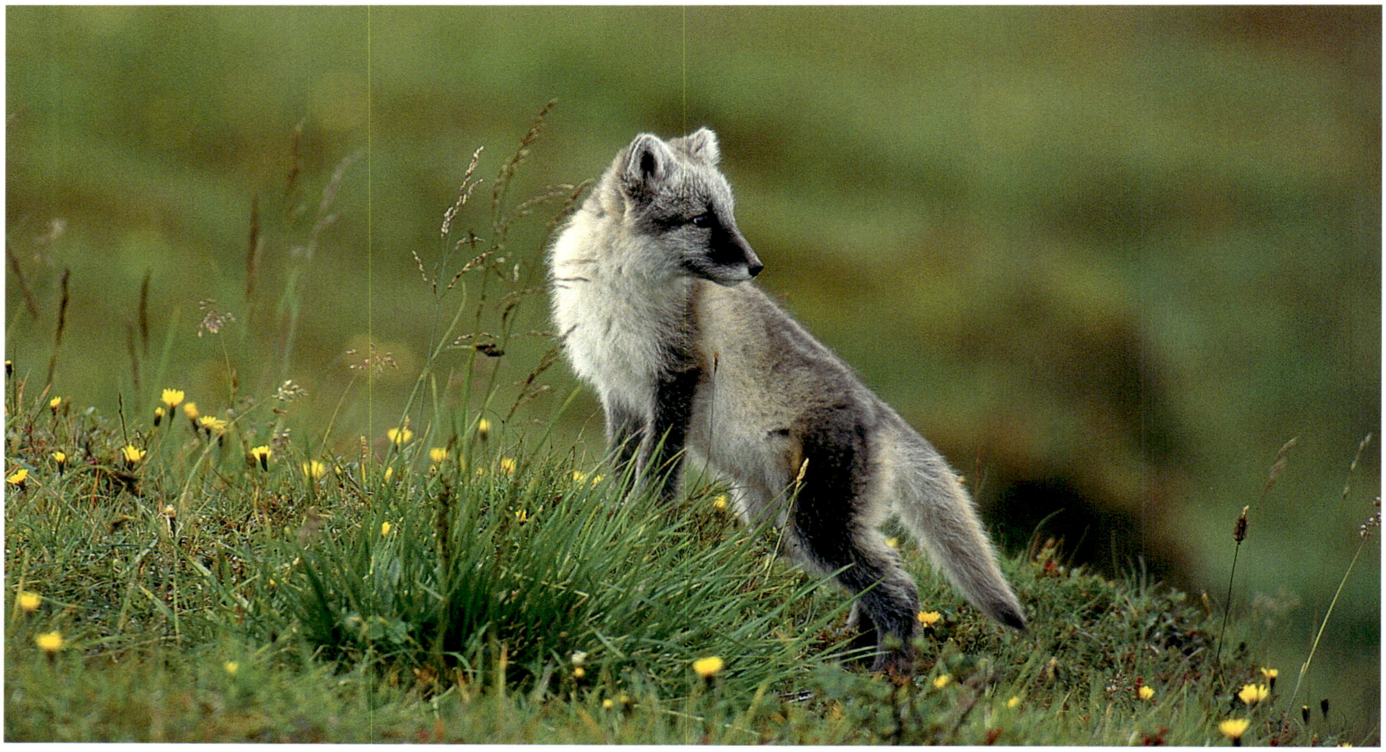

Driven to the verge of extinction. Harried by humans, the arctic fox threatens to vanish as the climate changes.

But the dragonfly is also preyed upon. Dippers dive for nymphs even in winter. In summer, as the host of nymphs crawls out to shed their skins, songbirds may take to feasting on them.

And, as adults, flying dragonflies are a staple of the hobby's summer diet. Patrolling the wetlands, the slender, sickle-winged and extremely fast hobby strikes at dragonflies like an arrow. It skilfully seizes the prey in its talons and shifts it to its beak in mid-flight. A shorefront grove echoes with the joyous shrieks of a hungry brood of hawks as the female brings the crunchy food to the nest of twigs. Dragonfly wings spiral through the air as the nestling hawks scrap over the snack.

Putting pay to the joys of the hot spell, a low-pressure zone brings intervals of drizzle; and, approaching the force of a summer storm, the wind flings the raindrops to the ground at a slight angle. The sand dunes are dark brown, the crests of waves break white, leaden clouds sweep the horizon from view. And though the rain occasionally eases, the bellows of the wind show no signs of letting up.

The waves give out before reaching shore, the water is shallow, and the beach, reaching as far as the eye can see, slopes very gently westward. The shoreline shifts with the water level some tens of meters, even more than a hundred meters. The land, depressed under the burdens of the Ice Age, uplifts steadily but imperceptibly: just under a centimeter per year. Even this rate shifts the shoreline enough to make the changes evident within a human lifespan. Shorefront sheds and docks are gradually left impossibly far from open water.

A covey of small, rotund birds skitters along the low-lying beach created by gradual isostatic adjustment. Bowed, they advance in a group at the water's edge, probing the boggy silt. They grub for invertebrates stewing in the muck: worms and larvae. The rufous brown and black mottled back and the white belly with a black patch indicate that the birds are adult dunlins which already have the annual task of reproduction behind them. They are en route from the tundra to the alluvial zones of Europe and from there onward to winter along the African coast.

When this flock of waders takes to wing, the wind flings the whole lot hundreds of meters away. They fly very close together, the entire flock in a tight ball. As if by consensus, they all turn simultaneously in the same direction, then immediately in another, and very soon in a third. Not a single bird breaks ranks. The sounds, the distinctive markings and streaked wings serve as signals which companions of the same species can quickly interpret.

Sandpipers protect themselves against predators by rapid flock movement. A hawk on duty at the migrating waders' feeding place will not attack a whole flock, but any poor bird separated from it will suddenly wind up on the raptor's menu unless it succeeds in returning to the cover of its kind.

In addition to the dunlins along the shoreline there are other birds of a related feather: Temminck's stints, little stints, curlew sandpipers and red knots. Now and then the skilled observer also picks out rarities which have come from the far eastern regions of Siberia or even America. The familiar ringed plover also scurries along with the flocks.

Long-legged and -necked sandpipers wade in deep water: the late spring arrival, the spotted redshank, is among the first to depart in the fall. Soon the greenshanks and wood sandpipers are on the move, not to mention the green sandpipers. Curlews, ruffs, common sandpipers, lapwings... waders from throughout the north are in autumn passage by midsummer, especially adult birds. Among many species, female birds set off as soon as they have laid their eggs or, at the latest, once the young have hatched. Among some species, the female's familial responsibilities last longer than the male's.

Eventually the wader progeny are left behind at the nesting sites to follow along in their own good time. By following coastlines they end up approximately where their mothers are without having to compete with their parents for sustenance during the difficult migratory journey. Nature has arranged things sensibly: the chances of survival increase when uneven competition decreases. For little waders, migration is a perilously stressful adventure in and of itself.

In good weather the migration of the waders progresses quickly from the tundra to the coasts of the North Sea. The numbers pausing to rest in Finland during hot spells are usually few, but when the sky sheds tears and clouds hang on the horizon, flock after flock settles on the mud flats. The beaches positively teem with intriguing life then.

The wing-borne life of damselflies is brief. They are true children of the summer.

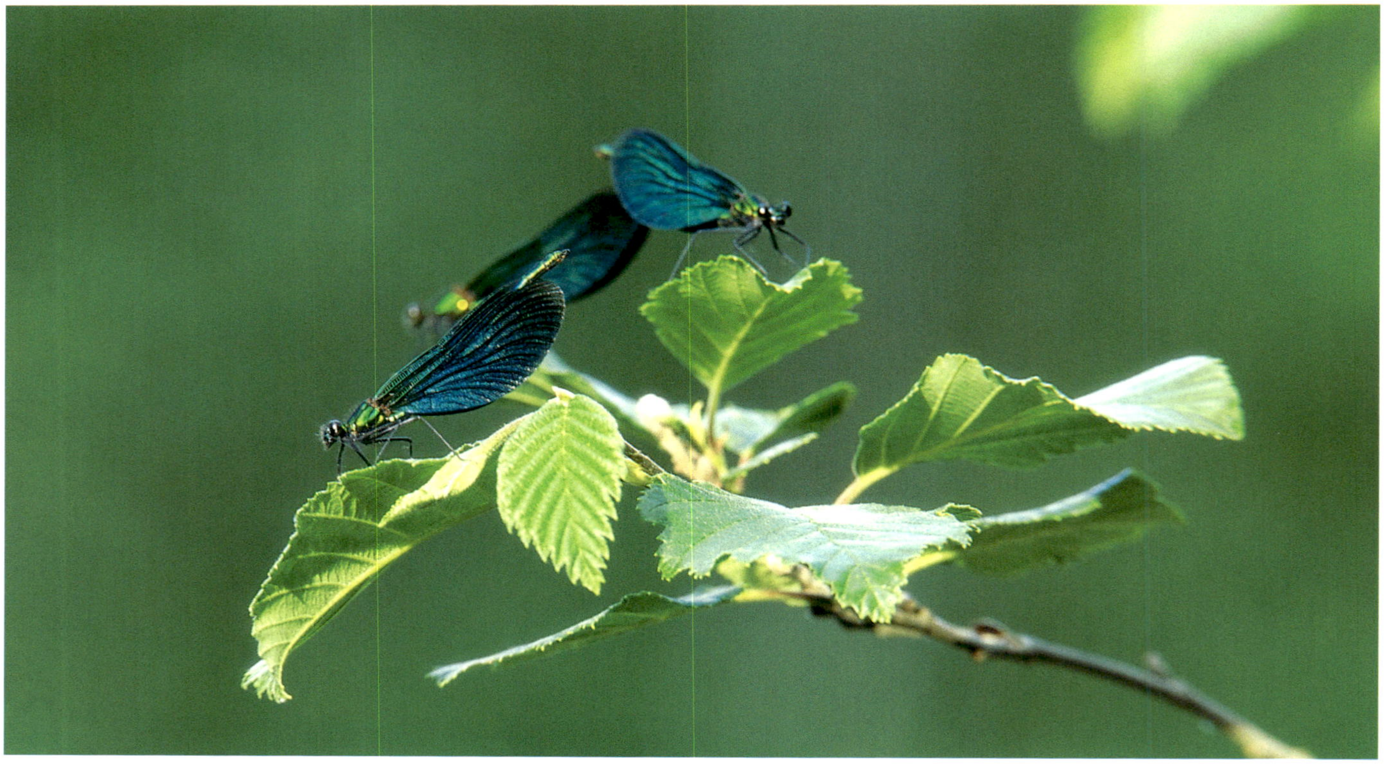

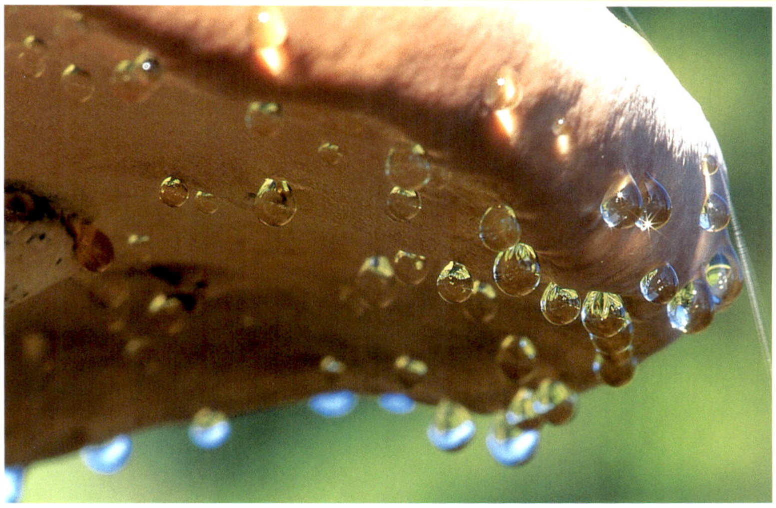

Bracket fungi strike when a tree weakens.
Their fruiting bodies are but the tip of the iceberg, as is the case with all parts of fungi visible to the human eye. Invading a frost cleft or other wound in the tree, the bracket fungus extends its rot-inducing hyphae into the trunk. In the tubes of the fruiting body of *Fomitopsis pinicola* tear-like drops bead during the season of most intense growth. The bracket fungus perspires as it exercises its powers.

In the openness of the fjelds human smallness is emphasized. Beneath a sky adrift with cumulus clouds there lies a blue-hazed wilderness in which the gentle contours of treeless uplands are drawn across the entire expanse of the vista. In low-lying areas the light green of birches prevails; the odd pine grows here and there, venerable northern veteran of a grim lot, solitary survivor of extreme conditions. The birches mount the fjeld slopes in clumps, like tufts of hair on a clown's bald pate. The summits belong to low-growing scrub, mosses and scant lichens. Beds of stones, raw humus.

A lemming scampers about a bare summit, a furry fist dappled yellow and brown. The lemming population explosion which began beneath the snow in the dark of winter has quietly gone into decline. Their mass swarming has halted. Disease and predators have killed vast numbers of these creatures, which where still milling about everywhere in early summer. The chirping and spitting that marked the sojourners' advance have ceased. Only the occasional specimen darts into view, and even these have more than enough takers.

Barnstorming, a long-tailed skua etches its slender silhouette against the sky, gaining altitude and then launching into a glide accelerated with a few wingstrokes. As if in fun, it swoops over the lemming's head and into the sky, repeats the mock attack, and finally settles on a rock to keep watch. The wind bends the long middle feathers of its tail. Soon another skua arrives on the scene. The couple has a nest on an adjacent hillock; beside it is a pile of lemmings and two strapping youngsters.

Home as castle: the nest of a rough-legged buzzard is often a front-row seat on the landscape.

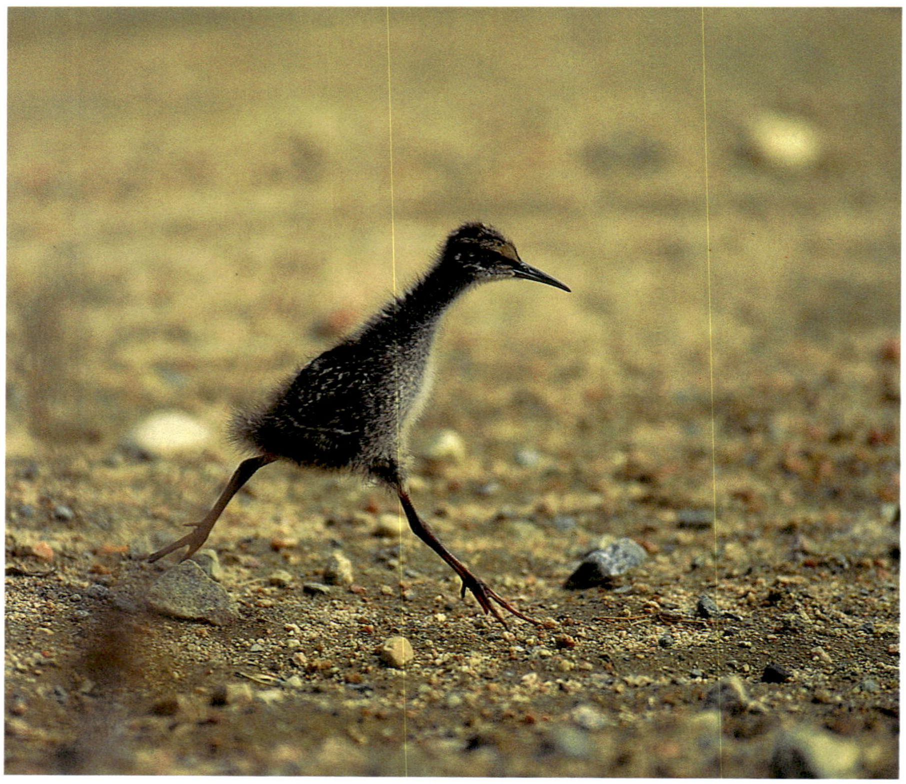

With their long legs, spotted redshank progeny are born to run.

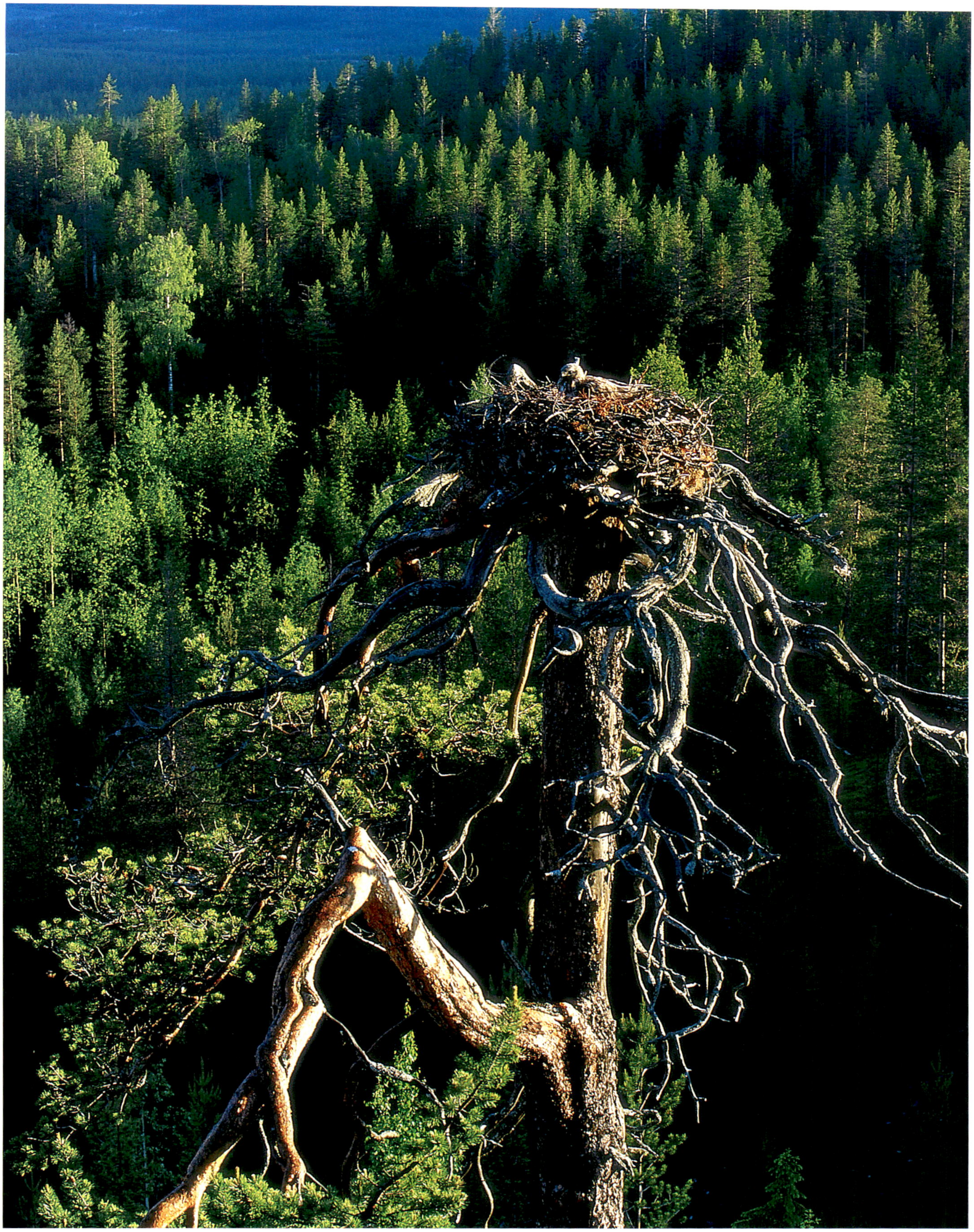

The fearless skuas will attack an approaching human relentlessly. Almost silent in flight, the birds at first attempt to instil fear by flying close, but if necessary they will dive on hissing wings and snatch the intruder's hat. They will emphasize their message by striking with their beaks, like terns.

The scruffy shape of a rough-legged buzzard also floats over the fjeldscape. Mournful cries echoing from all sides indicate that nesting has succeeded. The handsome raptor's young have already fledged, though they still return to the nest for food; and the heaped hoard of slaughtered lemmings is at least as impressive as the skuas'. Hovering in place with a flick of its wings, the buzzard focuses on some quarry, but the satiated bird lacks any real will. The lemming readily escapes into a cranny among the rocks.

A great, white-winged creature glides far off, keeping a respectful distance from humans. The immense bird flies with a steady beating of its wings, the dark speckling visible in its white plumage. The snowy owl, legendary wanderer of arctic climes, ever seeks out places in which the small mammals it favors as food are on offer.

Its yellow eyes stare steadily at the intruder, but the solitary bird is probably a juvenile with no nest. No mate is visible anywhere, and the bird shows no signs of returning to a possible nesting site. The piercing, tensed warning of the snowy owl does not sound; there is no snow-white male whose fine suit is tinted blood-red by a surfeit of lemmings.

On a sand ridge along the flank of a fjeld the ground is riddled with holes; the courtyard of an arctic fox is also covered with bits of lemming fur. The residents of these recesses are careful to stay hidden, but tracks in the sand reveal that a vixen and two tiny-pawed kits inhabit the place. From a distance the fox earth looks more animated: the adult appears briefly near it and eventually the cubs too appear to wrestle at its entrance.

An extremely endangered species, the arctic fox is now rarer in Finland than ever before. In recent years no young have been born, and adults have sought refuge for long periods in Norway. In principal the arctic fox is a survivor: it lives in harsher conditions than any other animal its size. The small ears, short muzzle and tail, and very thick fur coat so reduce heat loss that, as long as a reasonable amount of food is available, winter poses no problem to the arctic fox.

Nature is no threat to it, but humans are. Once pushed to the brink of extinction by fur hunting, it now suffers from other spin-offs of human activity. With the aid of humans, the common fox has spread every further northward: the warming of the climate and lax waste management have improved the sly beast's living conditions. And wherever the two species end up facing off, the snowy coated arctic fox is forced to give ground. If it doesn't, it may have to pay for its obstinacy with its life.

This engaged swan couple will not face nesting cares until next year.

August

Morning mist veils the fjelds.

Dew glistens on a spider's web.

Bats flit through the velvet night.

Hawk fledglings in flying school.

A viper, a lizard and a blindworm give birth.

Crickets chirp in the daytime, bush-crickets at night.

Insectivorous birds during autumn migration.

Duck hunting gets under way.

Mists and Velvet Nights

A brisk climb up the flank of a fjeld gets one's heart pounding. Sweat breaks to the surface and one's breath comes quicker. After the night, the path is wet; the surface roots and clefts in the rocks are slick. Moisture has condensed on spider webs to form silvery beads that shower to the ground when a passer-by jostles the twig supporting the snare.

A still misty morning. Somewhere a family of spotted flycatchers tweedles, heading south; a startled robin suddenly scolds, nearly underfoot; a silent chaffinch bustles about its business among spruce boughs. At the bottom of a saddle-shaped gully a mezereon displays its red berries. The bush, with its intoxicating scent and pink flowers in spring, now offers its crop of berries for the birds to pluck. To mammals, humans included, they are poisonous.

The swift, which nests in southern buildings, is a true bird of the wilds in the north, where it occupies the same woodpecker hole year after year.

The pioneers of a felling vie in showiness. Following willowherb, meadowsweet colonizes fertile ground.

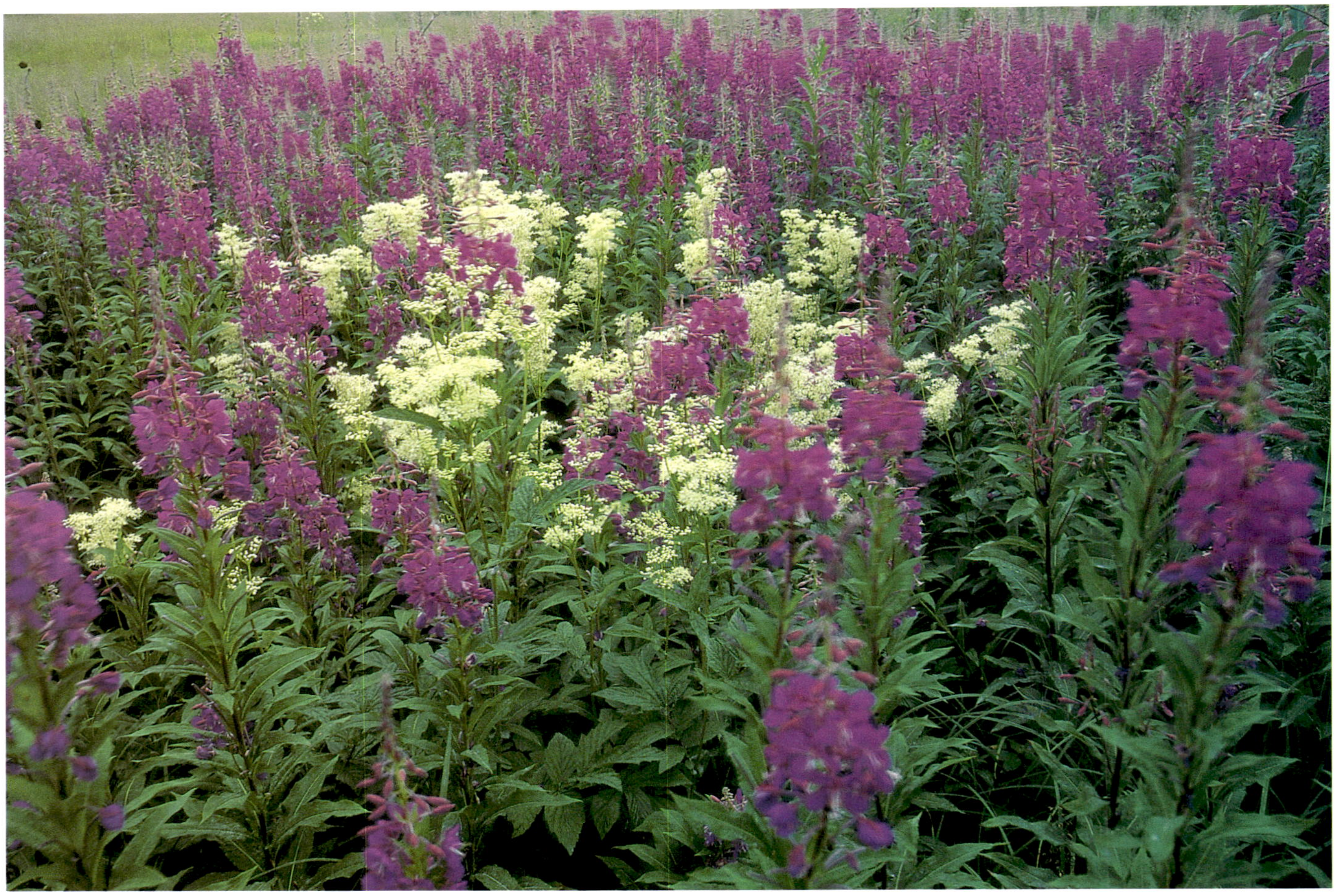

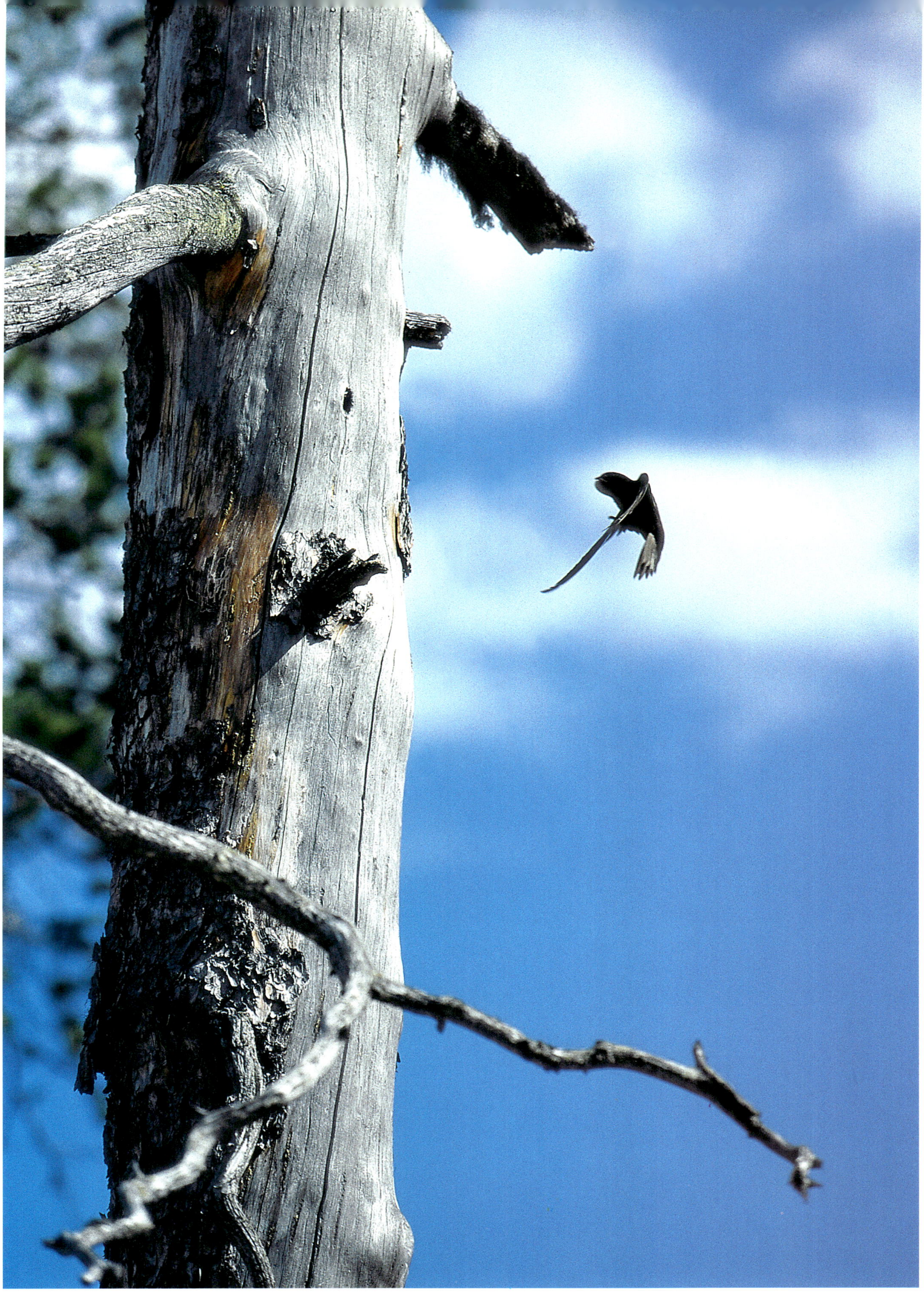

The panorama opening out from the fjeld is enveloped in thick gauze. A softly shaped greyness dominates as great peaks of fog which the day, ascending to the zenith, shapes with heavy hands. The summits of the celestial range erode quickly. All that remains are wisps in the lowest ravines, a vast fog serpent in a meandering river gorge, a small patch hanging in the air space over a shoreline meadow. Until the sun chases them away as well.

The fog emanating from the clear, starlit night lasts but a few hours. The earth and the air above it cool in the chill of the long night, and the cooling causes invisible water vapor to condense into fog, which forms a veil of steam a few hundred meters thick across the landscape. The fog arises in low-lying, wet ground; it is usually a local phenomenon, best viewed in all its splendor from the highlands thrusting above their surroundings, the fens and fjelds.

A flock of titmice bustles about a hardwood thicket beside a lake. A peevish great tit, a crested tit that seems to be laughing at it, an absent-minded looking willow tit, and a bevy of delicately twittering goldcrests. The distant croaking of a raven sounds. Something dark flits through the thicket, the grass stirs and sapling spruces tremble; here and there is a glimpse of black. The tits go on about their business, disappearing out of earshot with the goldcrests; but the dark creature goes on loping through the landscape.

The mink advances in a few determined bounds, then immediately leaps aside once or twice. Soon it retraces a few of its steps, springs across its trail and then dashes furiously on again. Thrusting out its little snout energetically, it sniffs the odors in the vicinity, its sharp eyes glancing about incessantly: forward, backward, to the side, up to where the titmice are, its ears pricked.

Its glossy coat glints in the bright light as the mink streaks along the shore. It thoroughly inspects any gaps among roots, any heaps of stones or holes it comes across. Before long it will happen on a vole, a cold-numbed lizard or eventually, in the gravel-bedded pool of a stream, a brown trout: food. This is what it seeks, as fuel for the day's needs and to lay down fat beneath its skin for the hard winter.

The feral mink, so similar to the European mink now extinct in Finland, divides opinions. For some this mustelid is vermin at its worst, for others it has the same right to exist as any animal. Whatever the case, the feral mink, originating in North America, is an established element of Finnish nature. It lives on its own, without human assistance, and, being a predator, consumes nature's other creatures as food.

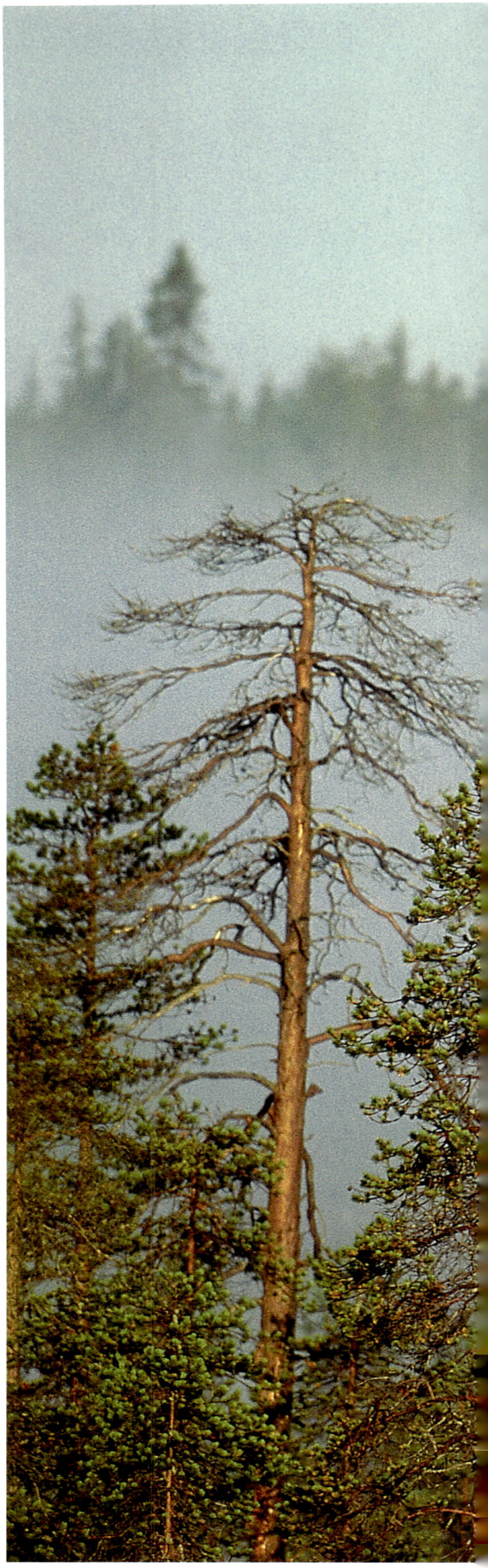

The sentry post of a female osprey. The osprey couple maintains a clear-cut distribution of labor: the male fishes, the female does guard duty near the nest and apportions the quarry to their young.

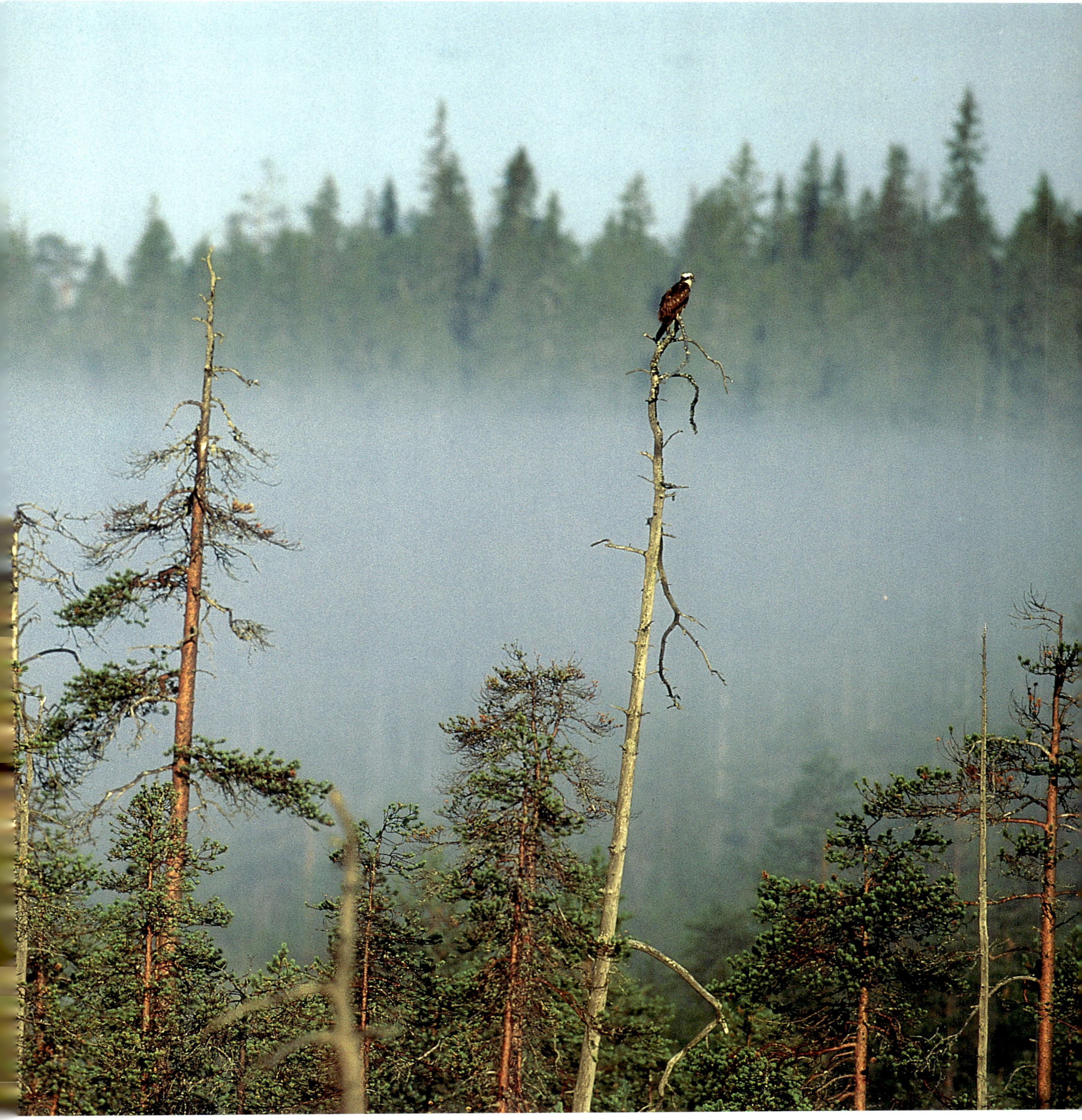

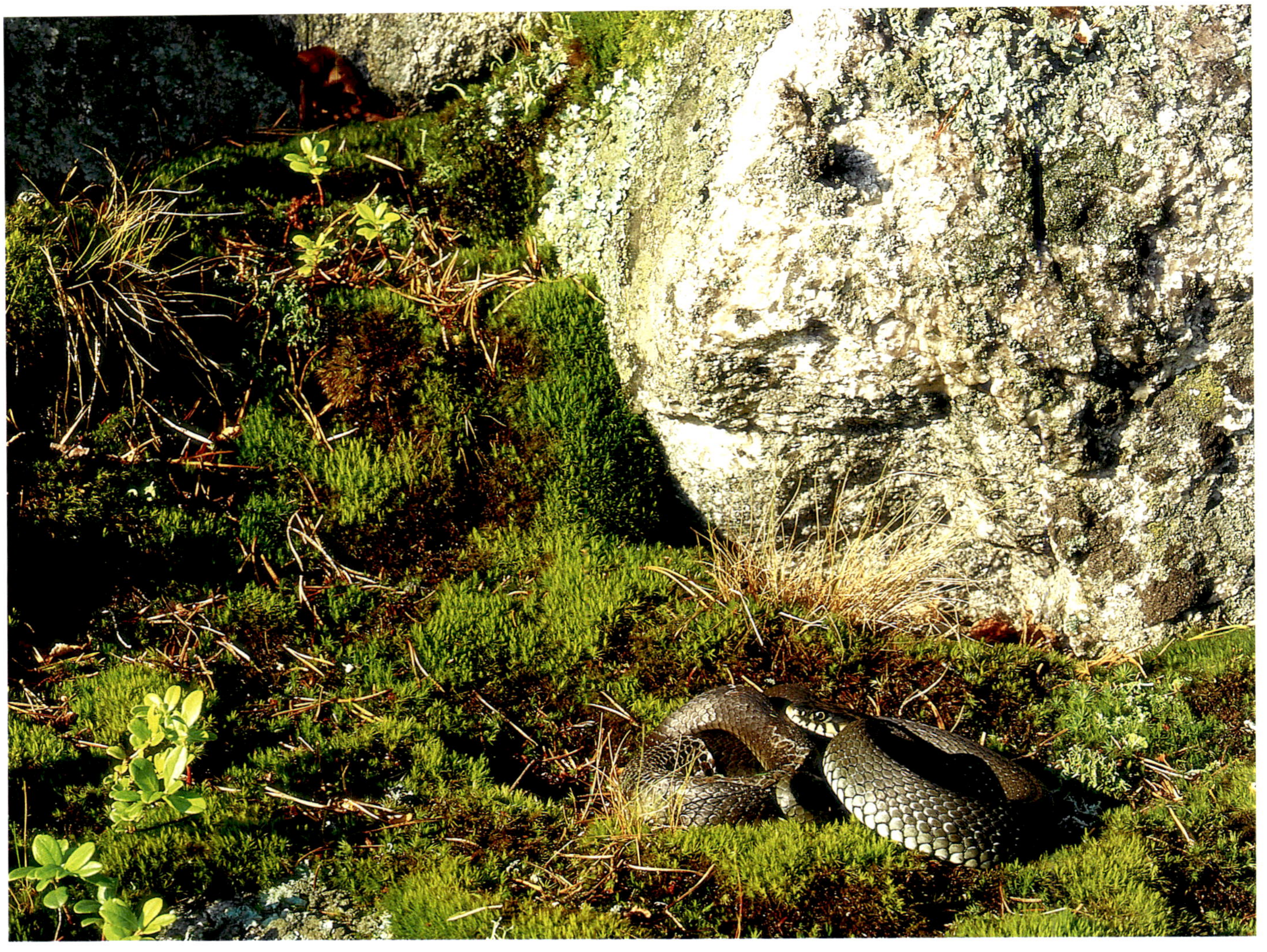

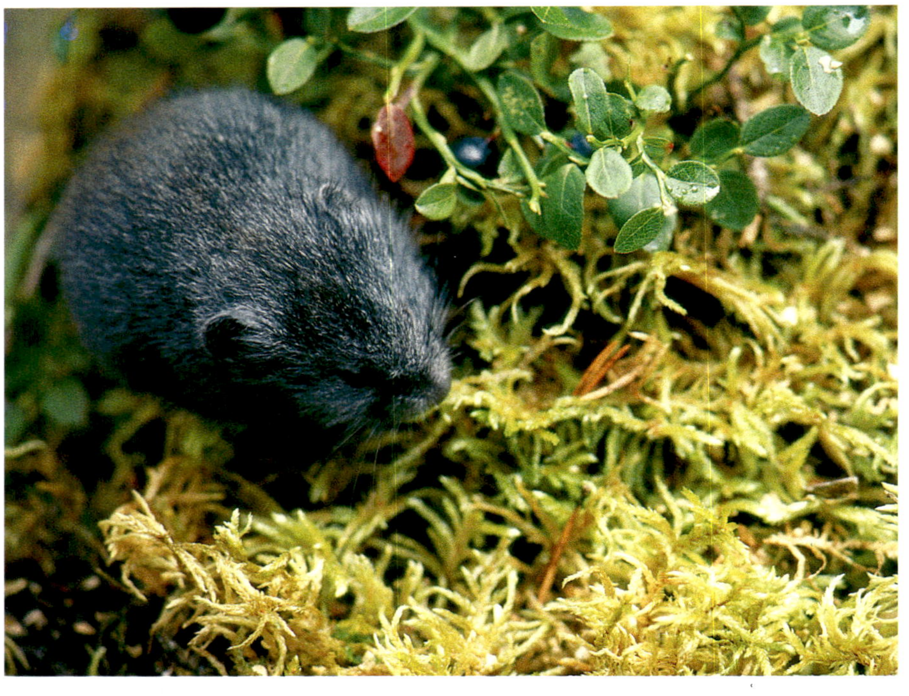

The terror of the frog world at rest. A ringed or grass-snake is a genuine sun worshiper.

The nibbler of moss in ancient spruce forests, the wood lemming.

The strong, adaptable mink has often been sited as the cause of the European mink's extinction. The two species are alike in appearance and habits, the American mink being merely somewhat larger. Both are adapted to living near water. However, they are not closely related; genetically the American mink more closely resembles the sable of Siberian coniferous forests than its does the European mink.

The feral mink population originated with escapees from fur farms and specimens intentionally released into the wild. Experiments with mink farming began in Finland in the 1920s, but it did not become widespread until after the second world war, when the European mink had already vanished from extensive areas.

An adaptable beast, the mink has colonized the whole of Finland as its habitat, and there is no denying the annoying manner in which it has specialized in exploiting the food reserves offered by bird communities. Toward autumn, when bird hunting becomes more difficult, fish and voles become ever more conspicuous on the mink's bill of fare. Any surplus stores are also to its taste. During the most severe winter weather, the mink conserves energy by resting; if need be, though, it will slip through a crack to fish beneath the ice.

But no matter how one feels about the mink's role, the animal itself is perky, attractive and energetic to a downright enviable degree. If one sits quietly on a rock near water and suitably downwind, a patrolling mink may come loping right up to one's feet. Its eyes do not reveal the human as anything stranger than a peculiar lump, and the mink finds no sure scent upwind. But one careless move or excess utterance, and the mink disappears. In an instant the animal is gone, vanished.

A warm, velvet night; the bush-crickets churr and a few mosquitoes whine, but otherwise it is quiet. On the verge of a meadow the light of the glowworm shines and stars spangle the sky. The human eye can only see a few meters. A bat flits past close by, silently, like a premonition. A vole shuffles dry leaves.

Suddenly a fresh breeze fans one's cheek, one's hair stirs almost imperceptibly. And again it falls eerily silent, until something whisks the air anew. There is a glimpse of something grey each time a breath of air caresses one's cheeks. In their hankering after a meal of blood, the mosquitoes themselves have attracted predators. A colony of Daubenton's bats earns its daily bread. The small bats race through the air, mouths agape, scooping insect quarry down their gullets.

The silence, in fact, is an illusion, for the inadequate human ear cannot hear the bats' unrelenting babble. A bat flying in the dark creates an image of its environment with sound: it emits from its mouth high-frequency sound pulses and listens to the echoes returning to its ears. An air-borne insect reflects an echo different from that made by an obstacle ahead: the hunter speeds after prey, but adroitly avoids obstructions.

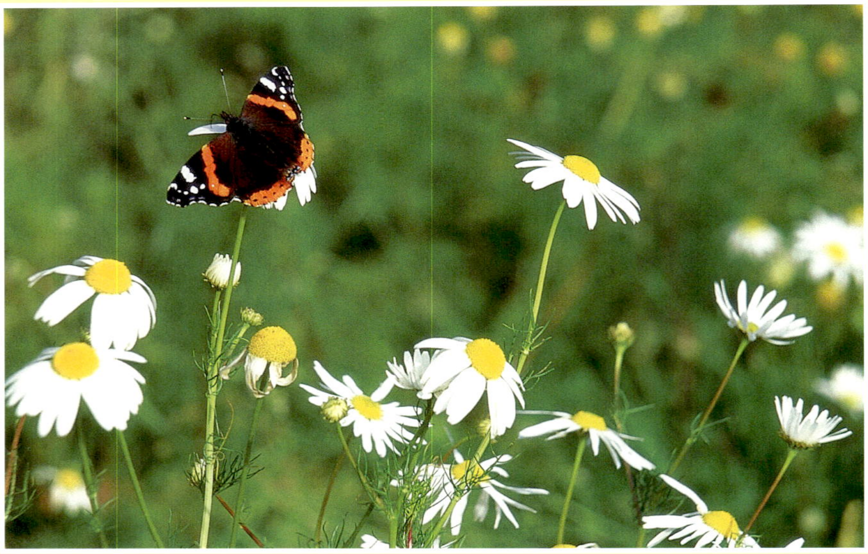

The darkly-clad butterfly, the red admiral, is a summer visitor to Finland's natural environment. The individuals appearing in early summer are migrants from the south. They reproduce normally, and by high summer meadows are aflutter with the wanderers' Finnish-born offspring, which then expire at the approach of winter. The intensification of the greenhouse effect may so change conditions that the admiral will succeed in wintering over at these northern latitudes.

This high-precision echolocation system has opened to the bats a world in which they have few competitors. During the day many birds and dragonflies hunt flying insects, but bats are the sole monarchs of the nighttime sky. At dusk the Chiroptera set off to hunt, each to a site typical of its kind, so there is little competition between species. Daubenton's bats often flit about near water, many of them even skimming the surface, and each one cruising the same flight path at regular intervals. Naturally there are exceptions to the rule, particularly when appetizing insect prey is on offer.

For bats living on the northernmost extreme of their range, the velvet nights of high summer are of crucial importance in terms of both physical condition and reproduction. By gorging on insects the bats are building fatty energy reserves in their bodies in order to properly survive the long winter hibernation. Asleep for up to eight months, they lower their body temperature to around freezing and slow their metabolism to the minimum.

In the darkness of the velvet nights the bats also frolic with intent to multiply. Copulation does not lead to immediate fertilization of the ovum: the female stores the male's sperm in her womb and conception does not occur until spring. Thus, the growing foetus does not stress the wintering mother. If a harsh winter taxes a female's health, fertilization may be postponed or abandoned altogether. Also, if food supplies are poor due to cold weather, a female bat may put off a midsummer birth by sinking into dormancy.

The most common of the bat species whisking about Finnish skies is the northern bat, the only one in the world to be found as far north as the Arctic Circle. The common long-eared bat of southern woodlands is also abundant, as is Daubenton's bat. The whiskered bat and Brandt's bat are also common, whereas other species are encountered more or less occasionally in Finland.

Spotted flycatchers twitter in the woods. In piercing voices the young beg food of their mothers, who diligently hunt insects. The brood is mobilized, their native region long since left behind; and bit by bit the true migratory instinct grips the birds and launches them on their far-flung travels. For a few days, even a week, the journey is halted at a good feeding site, but there comes a day when one notices that the familiar sound has ceased and the flycatchers have fled.

No birdsong has been heard in the land for a good while. Sharp contact calls and the frantic begging of hungry nestlings reach the ear from all quarters. The random whoops of migrating waders are as much a part of the aural environment of a summer hastening toward autumn as are the colloquies of greylag geese converging on their meeting places and the croaking of cranes gradually preparing to depart. For an instant the air churns with a passing flock of starlings.

A vendace net filled with bright silver.
(following pages)

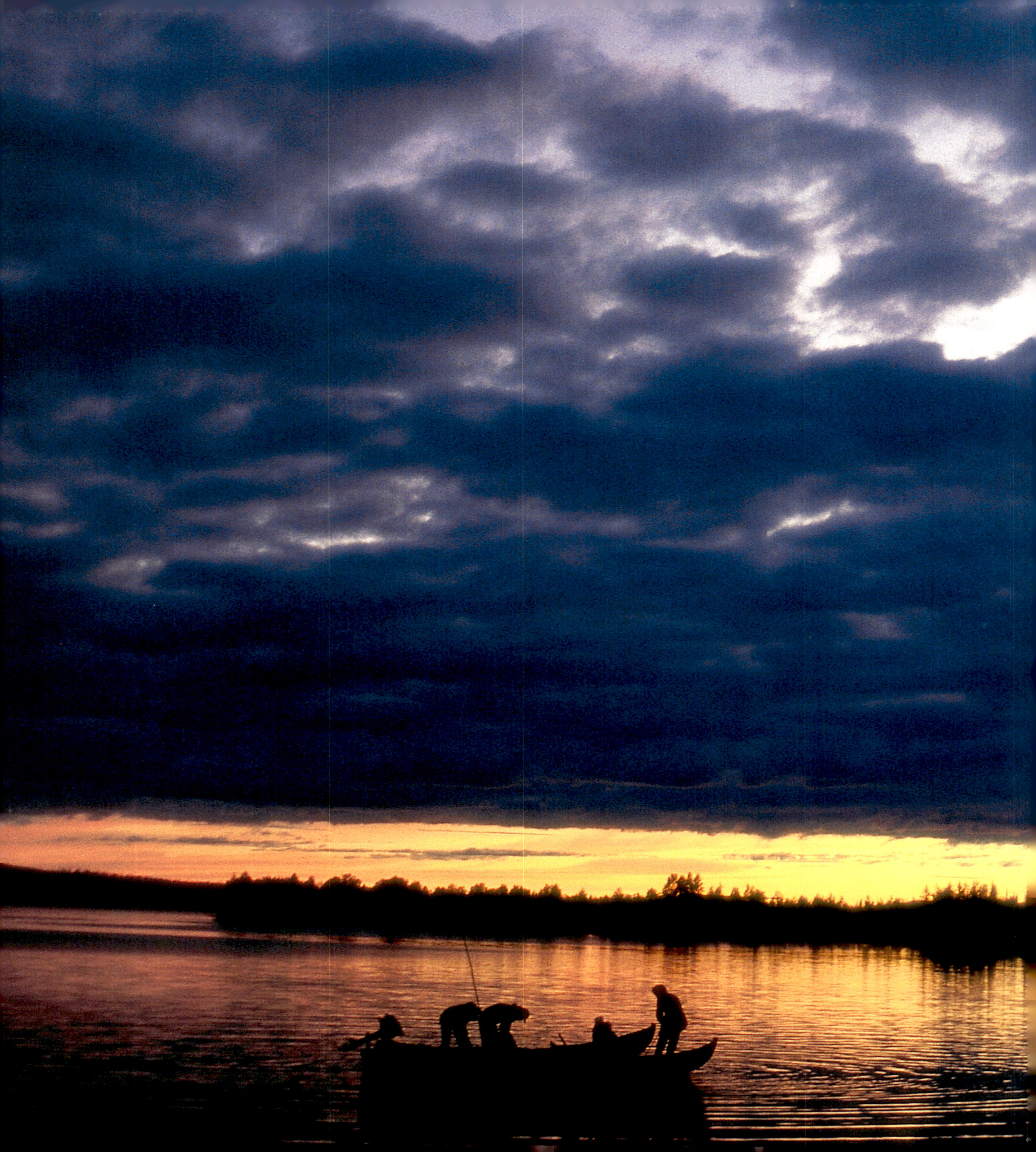

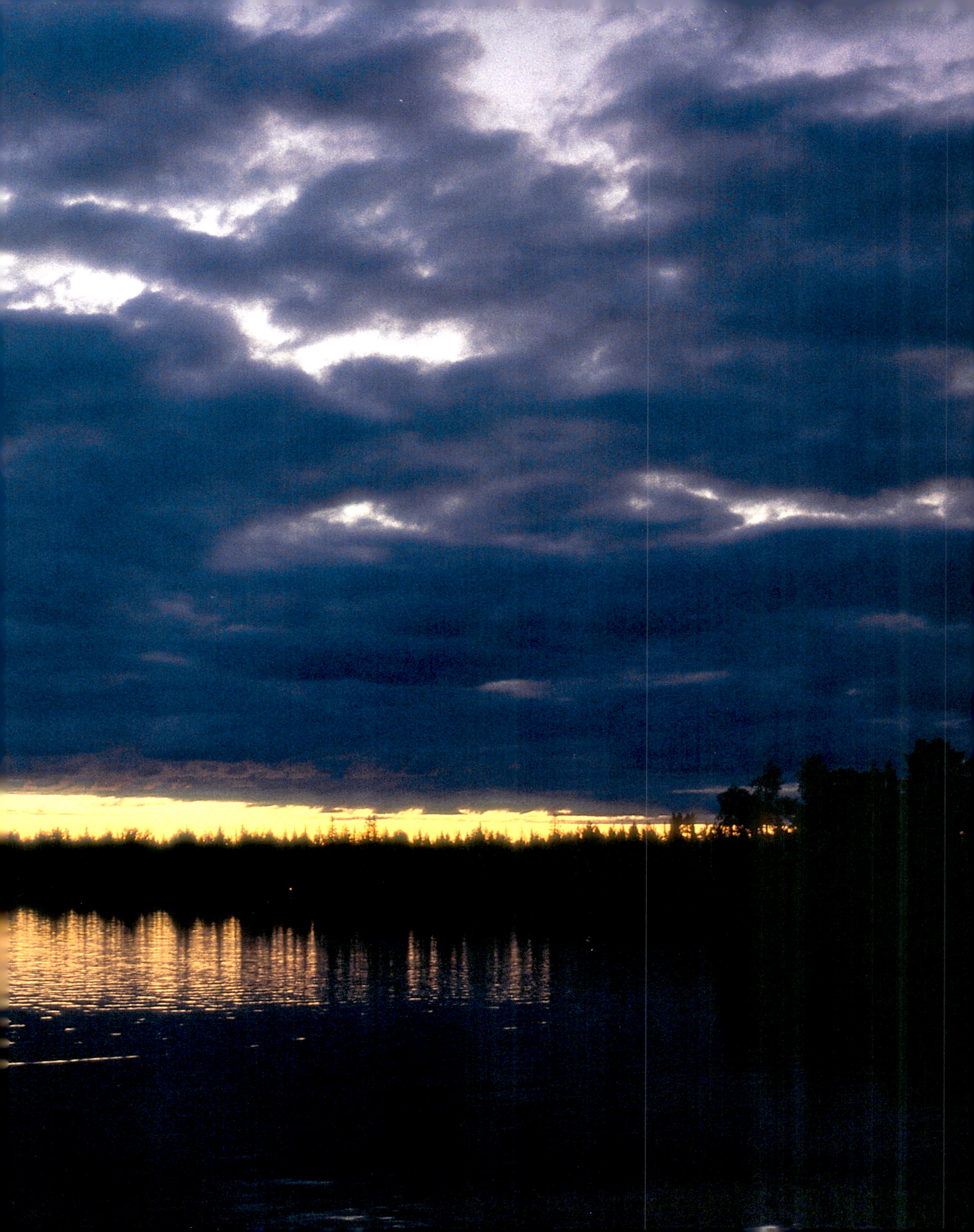

The tireless whistler of hot, sleepy days may be found in a twig aerie atop an outcrop pine. Osprey young shriek the daylight hours through, and not even the fish delivered by their mother silences them for more than a few ravening moments. Having shot to adult size, and even over, the osprey offspring flail the air with their wings and hop up and down on the nesting deck. And all the while their beaks emit a strident whistling. This noble bird has an almost pitiable excuse for a voice.

Juvenile ospreys attend flying school for a long while, strengthening their wing muscles with constant practice, until suddenly, almost by accident, the bird lifts into the air, accompanied by a suitable puff of wind – only to drop back again immediately to the edge of the nest, or to an upper branch beside it. It soon gives it another try. With each attempt, it gets more air beneath its wings.

Haven't I posed enough? Mademoiselle moose is both curious and timid.

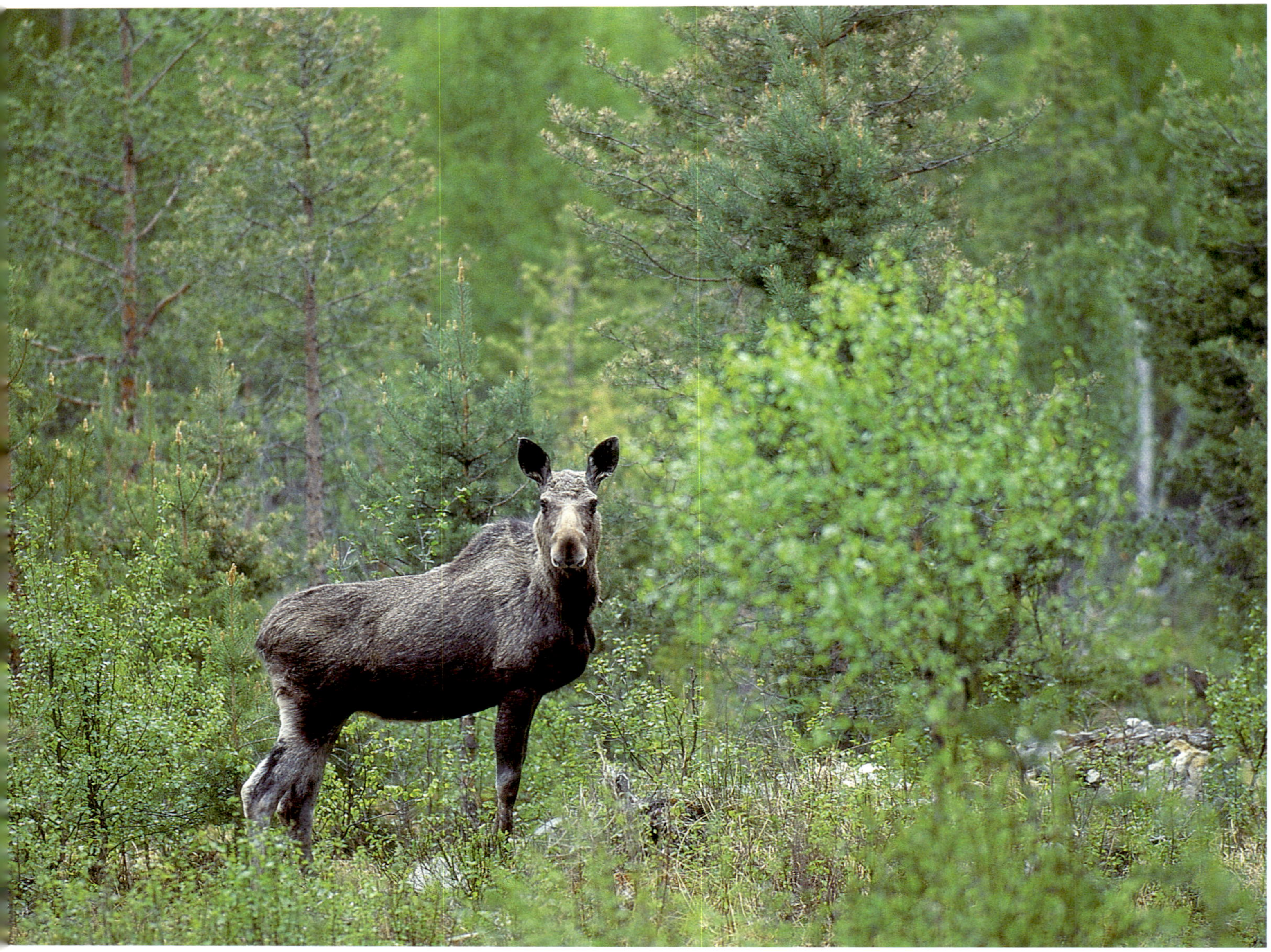

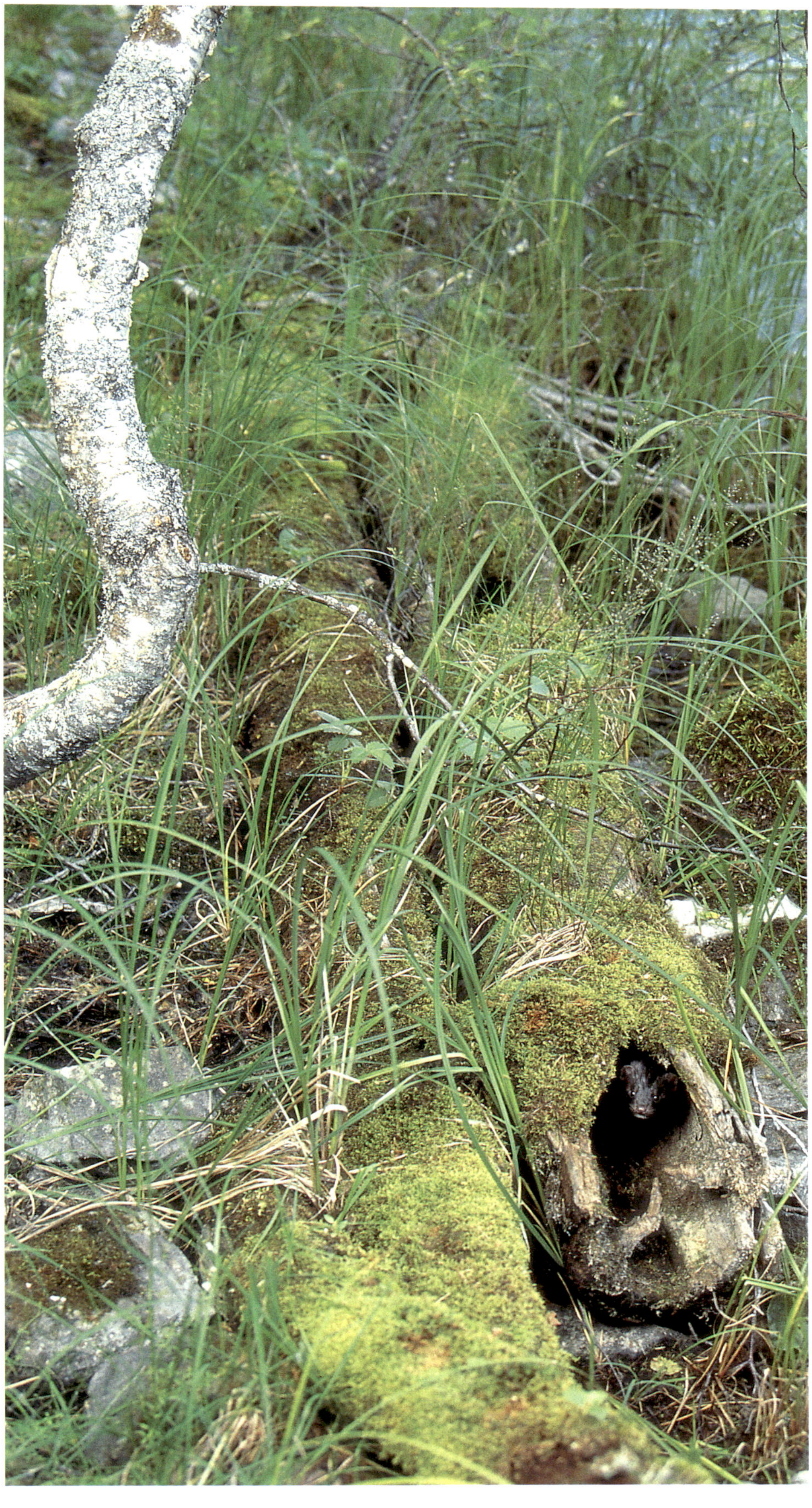

That immigrant, the lissome mink, has settled in near water.

In the end the young bird makes some brief circuits around the nest. Sometimes the return flight is successful, sometimes not. It may flop to a branch instead of the nest. It might overshoot the runway, in which case the poor thing may fall to the ground. A suitable gust may bring it up on just one foot. A buffeting wind may cause it to loop the loop on a limb. Such acrobatics usually conclude with the bird temporarily hanging upside down. Eventually it finds the courage to let go and tries to turn the fall into a glide before reaching solid ground.

With these aviation lessons the expert fisher trains to become an able flier, and skill is of the essence. As the osprey hunts its prey from water, it truly requires more strength and ability than is ordinary: it must be able to rise from the water straight into the air on wet wings, often with a large fish wriggling in its talons. It does not have the webbed feet that gulls and aquatic birds do for running on water to provide lift.

As their skills improve, juvenile ospreys set out with their mothers for the west coast of Africa, where the whistling of the osprey echoes through wetlands when ice chills its native fishing waters and snow covers its aerie. They do not return home until of breeding age, two years old or more.

The grey heron is a newcomer among birds breeding in Finland.

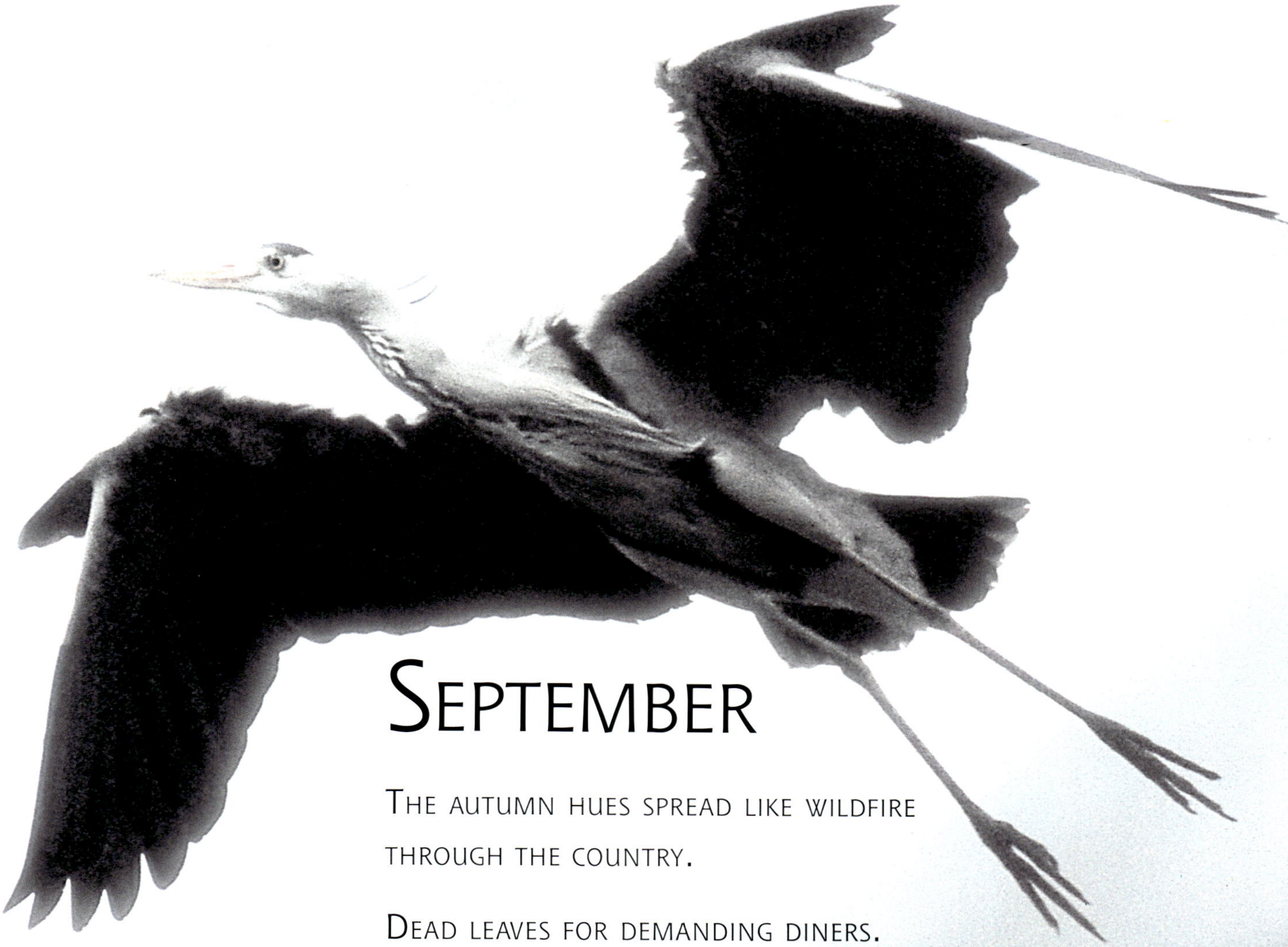

September

The autumn hues spread like wildfire through the country.

Dead leaves for demanding diners.

The flight of migratory birds intensifies.

Salmon make for their spawning grounds.

Snakes disappear into their winter holes.

Frogs burrow into their winter quarters.

A bull moose in rut seeks a mate.

Deer flies pester mushroom pickers.

First snowfall on the northern fjelds.

The intensity of the autumn colors varies with the year.

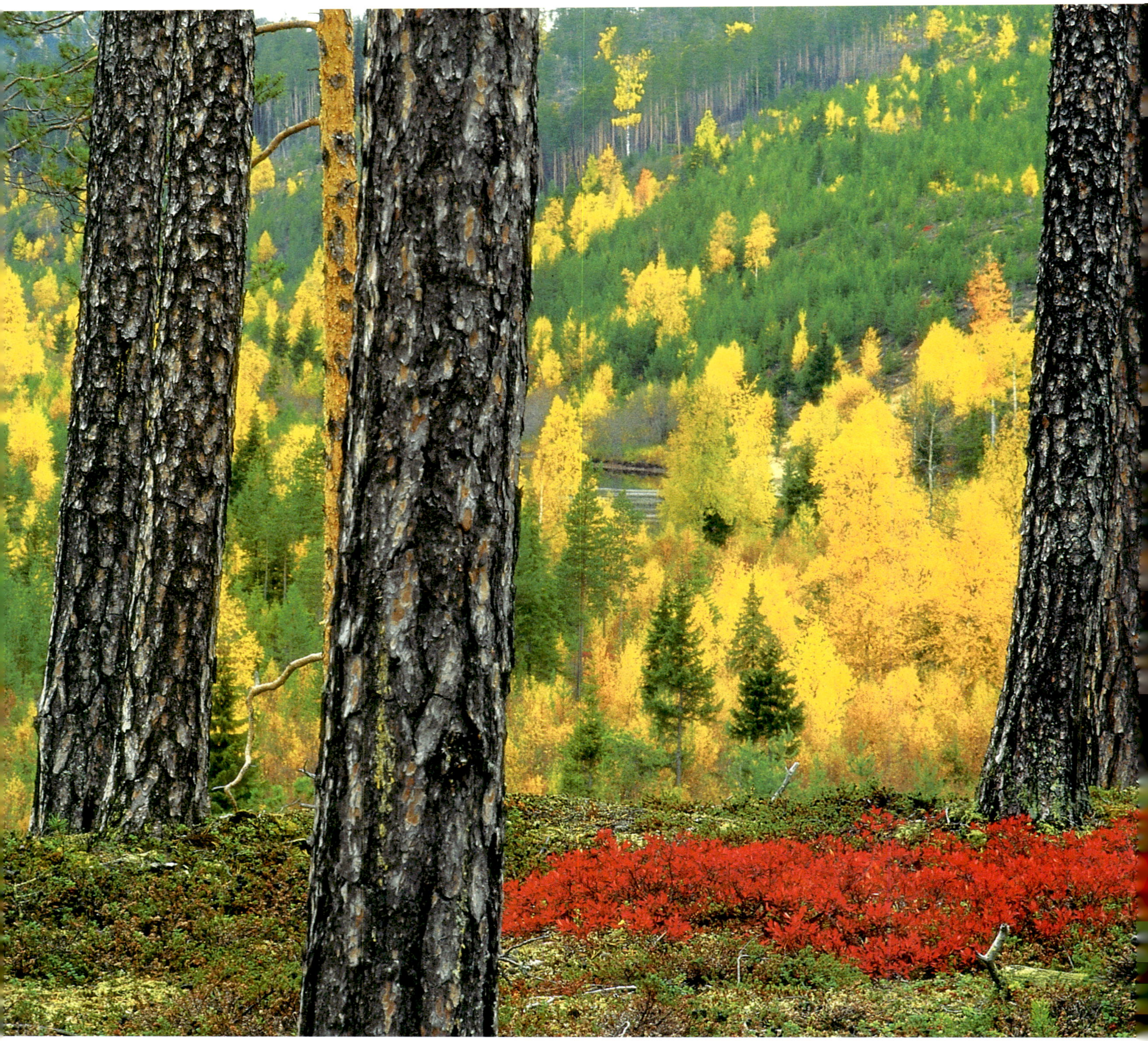

A NATIONWIDE BLAZE

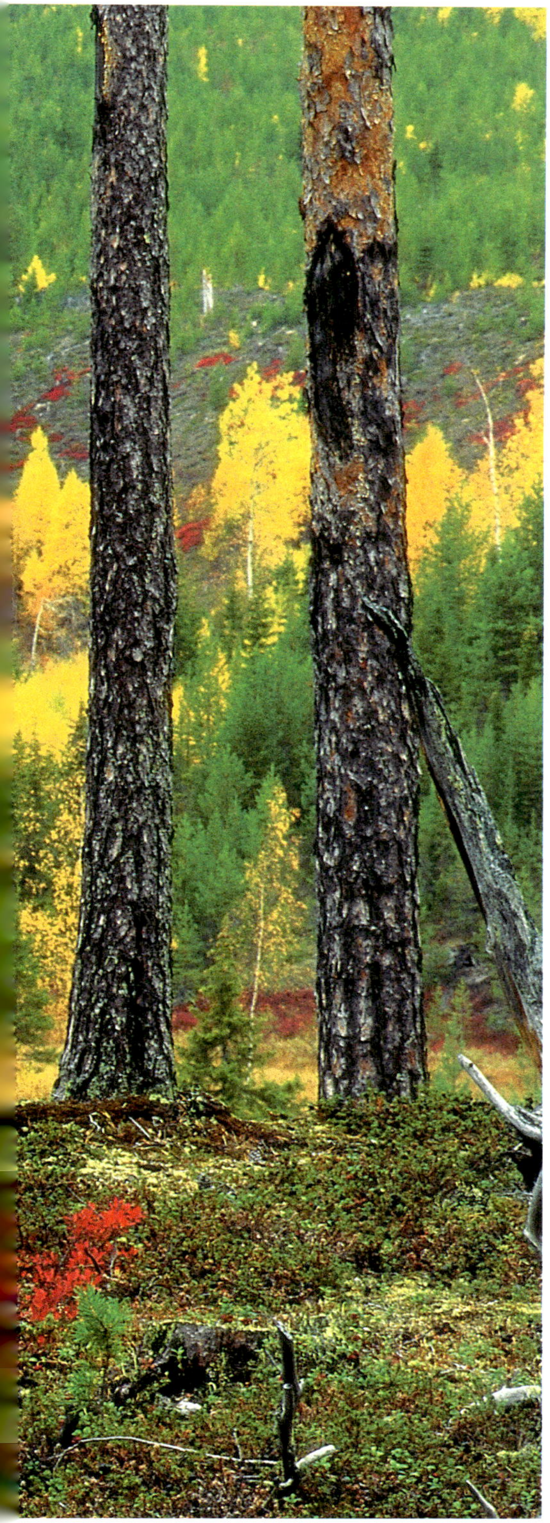

A limpid light bathes the area. Distended clouds wander the sky at speed, the dazzling sun flashing between them. The light of the sky casts the shadows of clouds onto field, marsh and the needle-green verdure of the forests, where the occasional hardwood blazes like a great bonfire. The play of shadow seasons the autumn colors, which, seen from afar, seem like splashes painted freehand, generously, like beauty spots tastefully arranged about the landscape.

A robin ticks in a thicket, in its voice a note of farewell. A large garden spider bumbles along a rock, the golden yellow cross bright on its red abdomen, as if this eight-footed creature too had dressed in autumn colors to seek winter shelter.

A thicket in a wet ravine smolders red: the bilberry-blue fruit of bog whortleberries has already lost its taste but the leaves are all the richer crimson. The grasses in a small sphagnum bog hollow are also at their most decorative. Like yellow tufts of hair, they project from the dark mire like the illuminated trails of fireworks frozen in place.

A stiffly moving toad plods resolutely forward. In autumn's honor, the nocturnal beast is out during the day, for it is time to dig in for hibernation in scree along a slope, adjacent, if not among, the vipers. It has no cause for concern with vipers for neighbors, for they are poikilothermal and do not hunt in winter; and in spring each species, to get its metabolism started, goes its own way in its own good time.

The red and yellow splashes of undergrowth in pine forests are faint flickers compared to the incandescence of the aspen groves. The tall trees positively blaze with yellow, their leaves rustling lightly in the mild breeze. The leaves of saplings growing on the verge of the aspen wood are blood-red, almost purple. The first night frost of fall has nipped them harder than it has the crown leaves billowing in holdover trees.

The laid-back boughs of the white-trunked birches are elegantly cloaked in yellow; on the slopes of fjelds, the birches glow orange, even a vivid red. The colors creep into the trees gradually. One day the green begins to fade, the first yellow autumn leaf appears clandestinely on the tip of a branch. Initially it is like a stigma. A few days later the end of the bough glows yellow, soon the entire tree is ablaze, and before long the whole forest flares splendidly before disrobing.

The change in colors moves north to south in a few weeks' time. The countrywide blaze is the trees' way of preparing for winter. They shift the precious components of chlorophyll into storage, beyond reach of the cold; by doffing their leafy mantle they reduce their evaporative surface area and increase their ability to survive the rigors of winter. Their cells expel water, distilling their protoplasm into a cold-resistant anti-freeze agent.

The tree stores in its roots, trunk and buds the precious elements of chlorophyll: nitrogen and phosphorus, along with starch, minerals, sugars and fats. As the tree shuts down its biological production machinery for the winter, it reveals during the short fall season the colors that chlorophyll concealed in summer. The predominantly yellow carotenes and xanthophylls may go on show only at the change of seasons.

The red colors of autumn do not originate in the chloroplasts but rather in concentrated protoplasm. The more acid the color, the more intense. The red anthocyanins enhance a tree's cold-tolerance; early frosts intensify the florid hues of red.

It is the shortening days that initiates the yellowing of trees, not the cold. So a mountain ash, matured from seed brought by a migrating bird from the north to the south, will live in keeping with its pedigree and burst into color earlier than members of its species sown in their own native region. Of course, the weather has an effect of the length and quality of the season of colors, but not very much on the timing.

The trees have strewn their parti-colored billets'-doux on the ground. The wind-tattered leaves fade quickly. Bacteria, algae and moulds attack them at once, but countless tiny beasts also play their part. An incredible scurrying goes on under the feet of someone out for mushrooms: one step can trample as many as a hundred thousand animals. Among them are herbivores and those that prey on them.

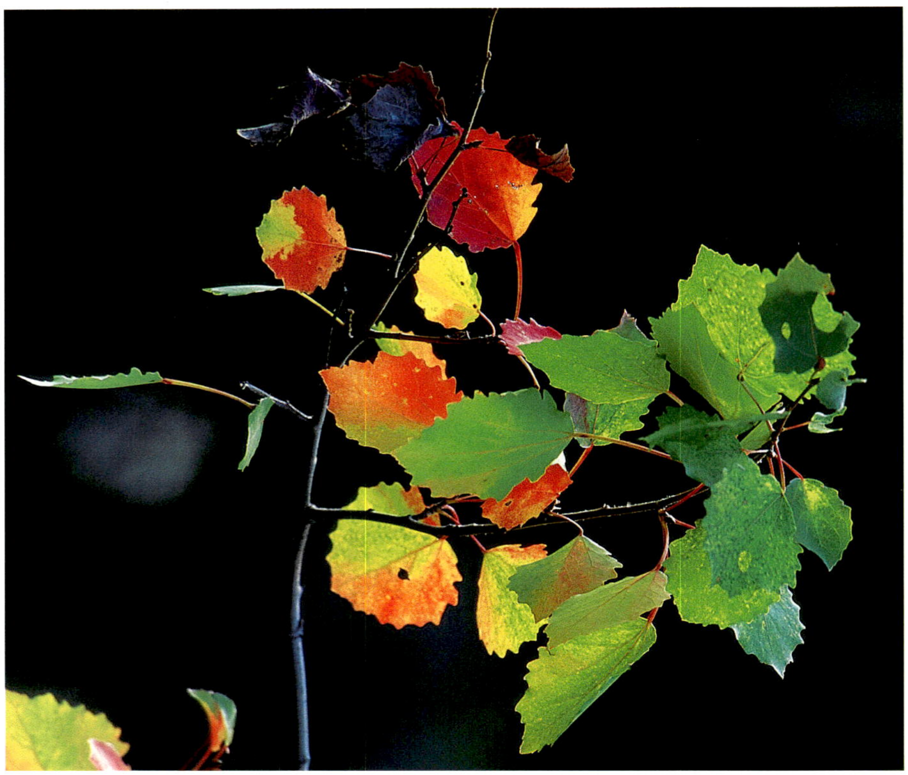

A stately aspen stores its essential components with flare. Autumn winds and frost eventually cause the leaves to fall.

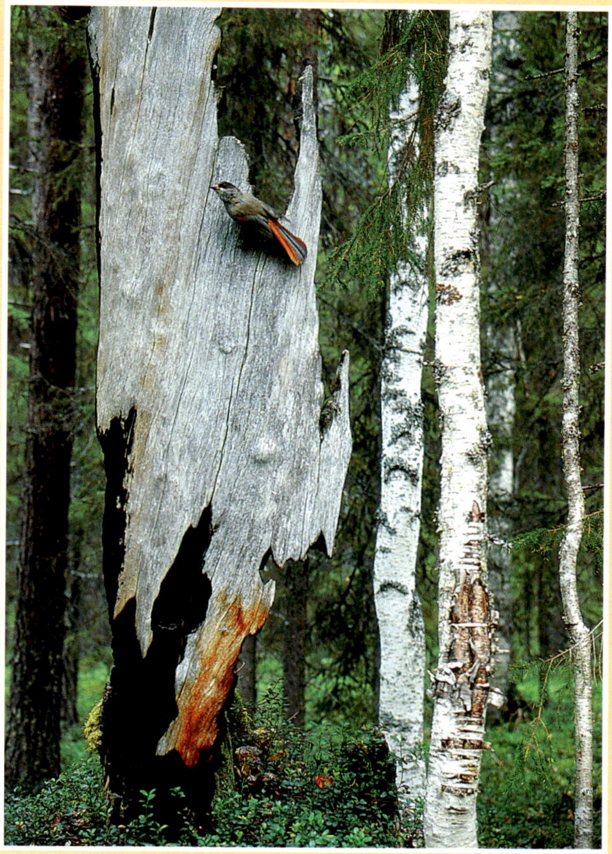

The chronicle of the woods: a forest fire that raged centuries ago transformed an almost entirely burnt pine into an enduring monument. The generations of Siberian jay come and go in teeming swarms, but, silver-grey, pitch-impregnated and preserved in carbon, the tree defies time and the forces of nature. Prior to mechanized intensive forestry, regeneration occured largely by means of fires.

Autumn leaves are in particular favor among bacteria and micro-fungi. A bacterium consumes ten times its own weight in biomass in a day; in the same time humans eat the equivalent of one-fiftieth of their weight. Comparisons between bacteria and human beings are, of course, impossible, almost absurd for no other reason that only one of them is an organism indispensable to all life. One small clod of dirt contains as many bacteria as there are people on earth. The fungi responsible for breaking down biomass are in the same category of abundance: in a spadeful of soil there are so many hyphae that, joined together, they would reach many times around the globe.

The micro-organisms that break down litter lead their inconspicuous existence year-round, beneath the snow as well. The ground, varicolored when it retires in autumn, wakens grey and lifeless in spring. The agents of decomposition have converted part of the leafmass into a form that benefits trees and other plants. The tiny members of this immeasurable demolition crew are rewarded anew at the end of the growing season with a fresh supply of herbage.

Peeping from among the leaves are caps, the visible representatives of the fungus community. The dome of the boletus mushroom, the trumpet of the chanterelle, the russulas and the wax caps with their Chinese-like...surface mushrooms are the tip of the iceberg. The caps growing from mushroom stems are the fruit bodies of fungi living out invisible lives. And many of them are among the greatest of delicacies; this is known not only by human beings, but also by crows, squirrels and deer. However, the larvae of fungus gnats are often the first on the scene. In counterpoise to this are the inedible and downright deadly poisonous toadstools. The only mushrooms fit to eat are those the picker recognizes as such.

Fungi are neither plants nor animals. They contain none of the chlorophyll necessary for photosynthesis. Some of them survive by feeding off dead vegetation, some are parasites on living plants, and some live in symbiosis with them - for example, when a tree receives minerals from the earth from a fungus and in turn provides the fungus with photosynthetic products.

A restless flock of titmice accompany a mushroom hunter. The great tits and blue tits fuss boisterously; a willow tit, crested tit and coal tit are busily employed in some branches. Among them moves a treecreeper, using its curved beak to extract meals of insects from cracks in bark. A softly twittering covey of goldcrests is along as the titmice's' travelling companions. The shy whistling of a willow warbler sounds from some brush. Out of sight, a hazelhen takes flight, the whir of its wings betraying a bird that is otherwise a master of concealment.

But an even more unusual whirring sounds from the air, drawing nearer. It isn't possible to pinpoint the sound, but before long its source is revealed. Having become entangled in one's hair, a deerfly crawls out onto one's neck. This tough louse-fly lives on the skin of

A subfreezing night assails the soft fruit of the northern bilberry.

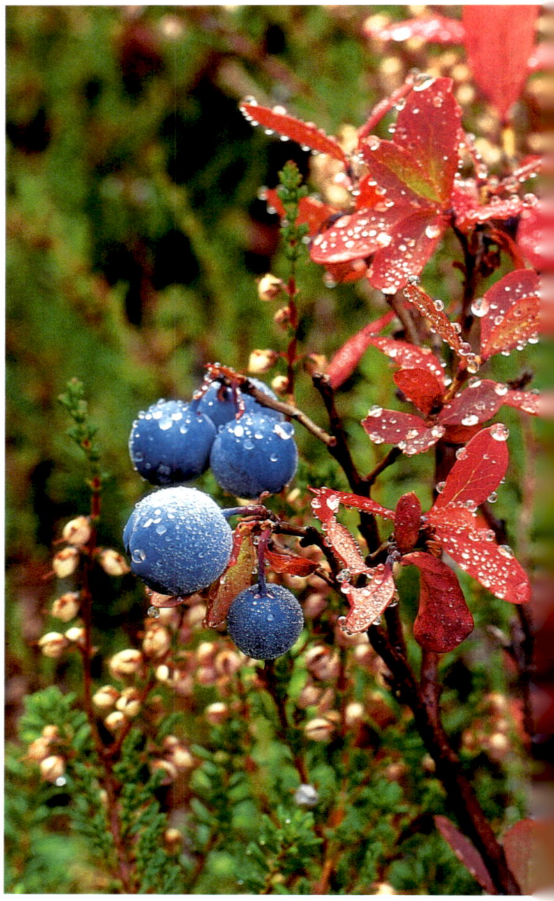

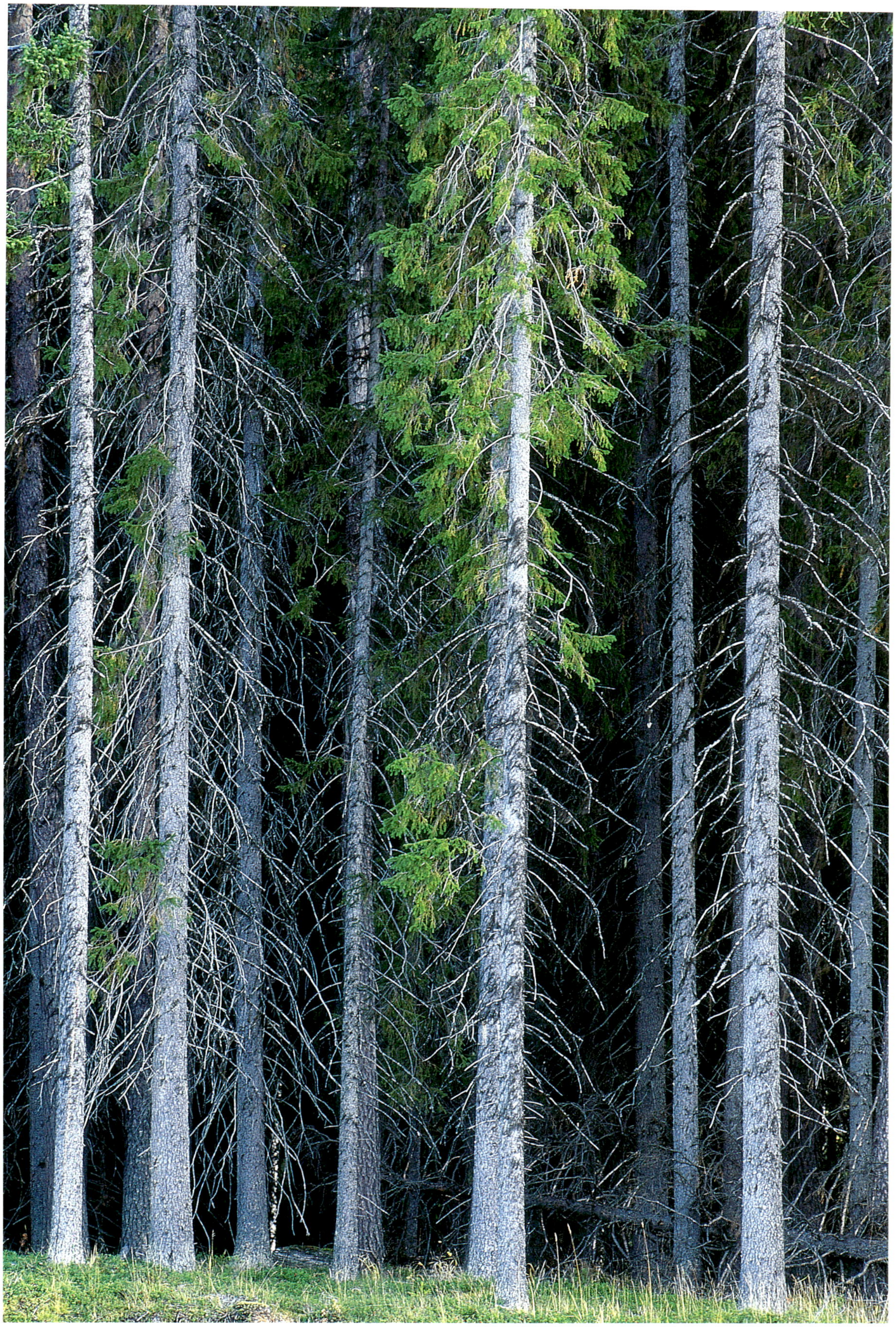

Spruces in a dense stand are wiry, straight and have few limbs.

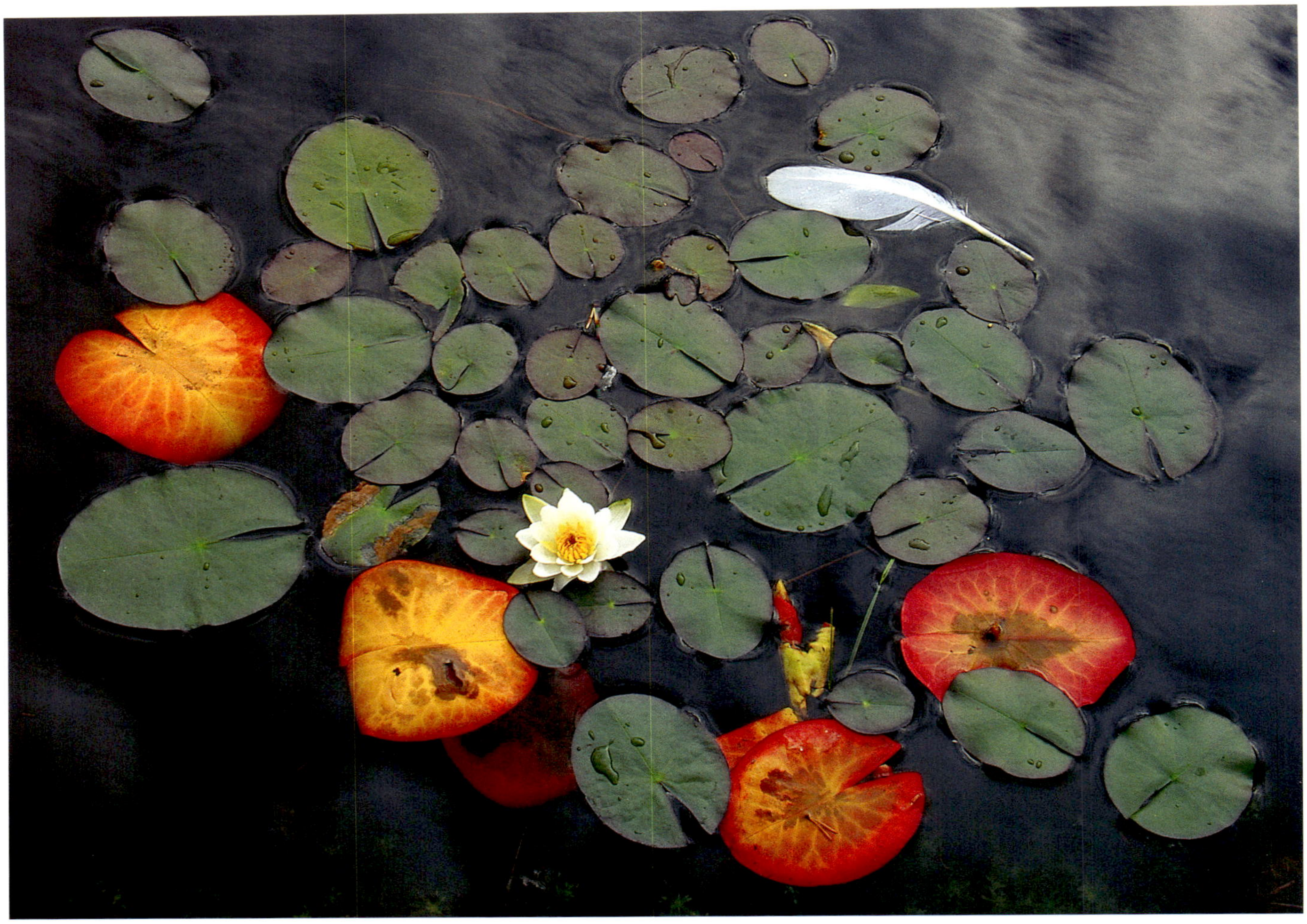

deer but, while flying about in the autumn, may seek its requisite meal of blood from any warm-blooded animal. Wintering in deer fur, the deerfly larva falls to the ground and develops over the summer into a flying insect which, soon after finding a new host, sheds it wings and, as they say, makes itself at home.

Brown beds of leaves reveal that swans have consumed the water lilies of the wild marsh pond.

Morning dawns ever later, day begins to be the duration of night. Wagtails twitter at dawn on the rocky shore. They snatch night-numbed insects and skitter about restlessly. There is the sound of quarrelling in the birds' sharp voices; there is no vernal ardor in their bickering. Nor do they dare each other as was their wont in the spring. Dozens of wagtails dart about the vicinity and they all seem to be more or less of one mind.

A small group of birds sets out across the water. The birds seem to fuel each others mood with agitated exclamations. Their long tails bobbing, a wagtail and its young launch themselves southward. One flock after another follows the first. Eventually the shore becomes deserted but for a few birds which pay no heed to others of their kind.

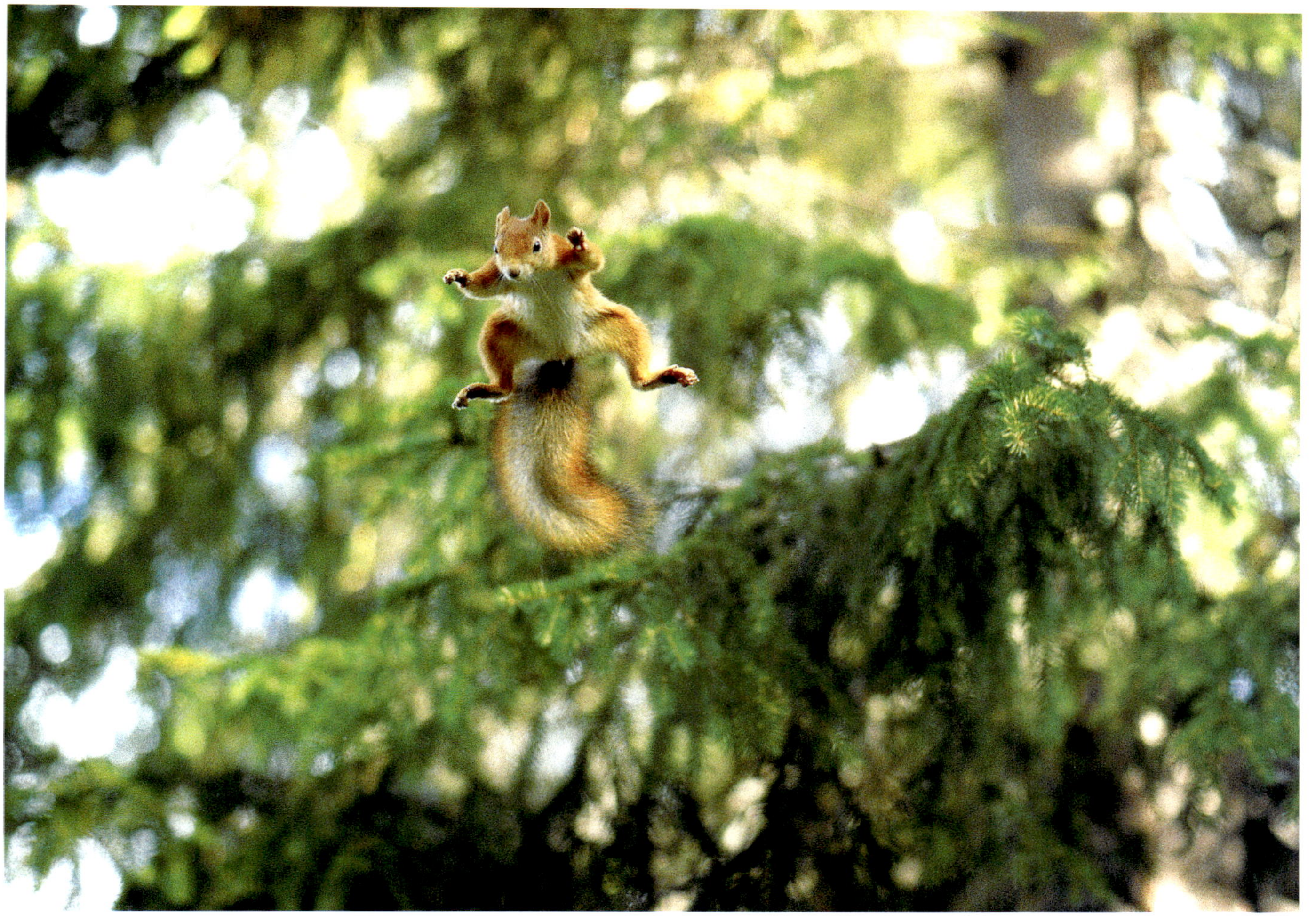

Full points to the squirrel for this leap. Daily practice hones the skills of this champion jumper.

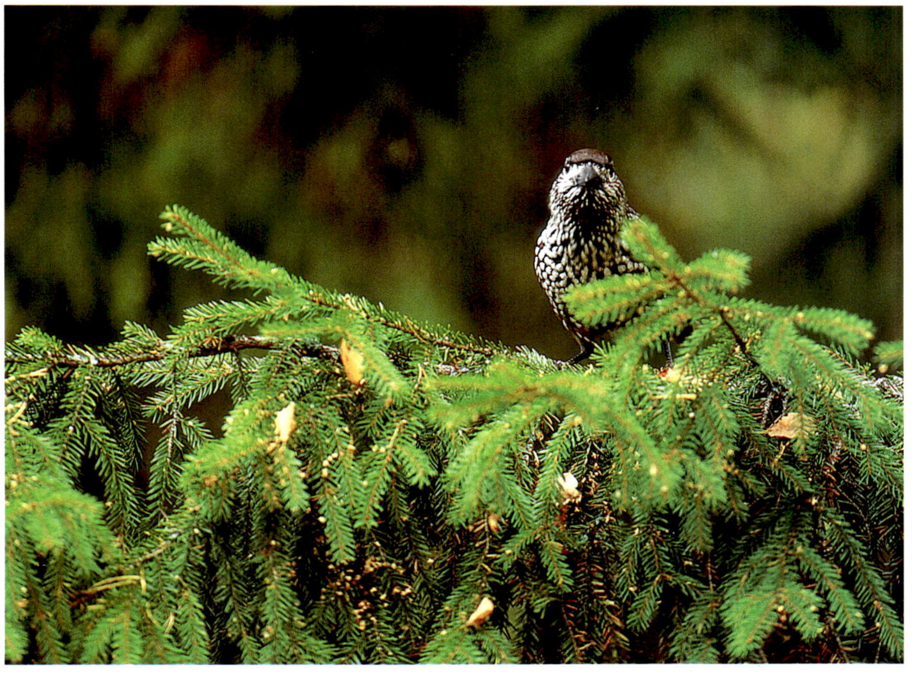

The nutcracker is quite a concealer of goods. The stores it lays up in the fall also feed the young born to it in the spring.

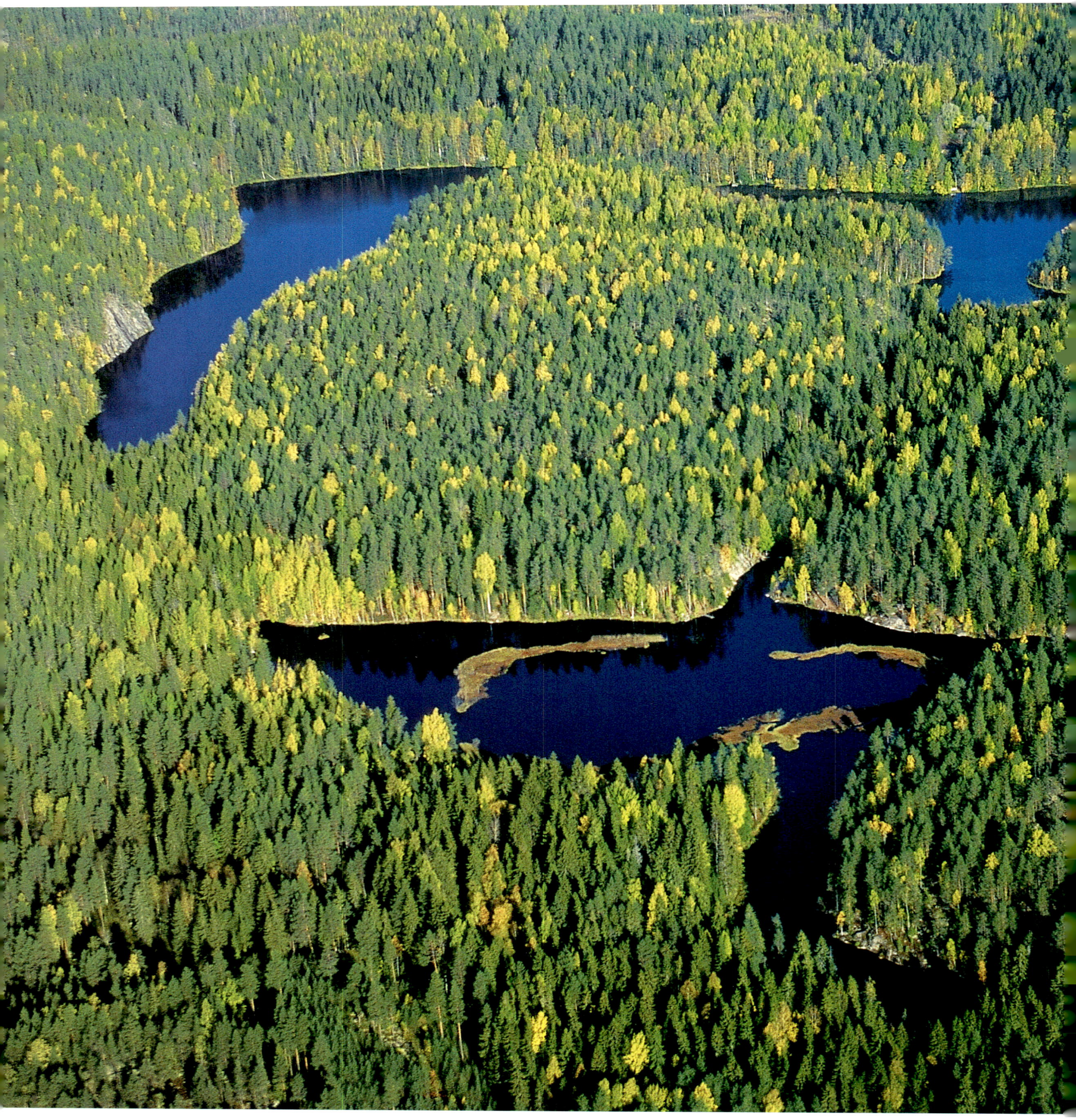

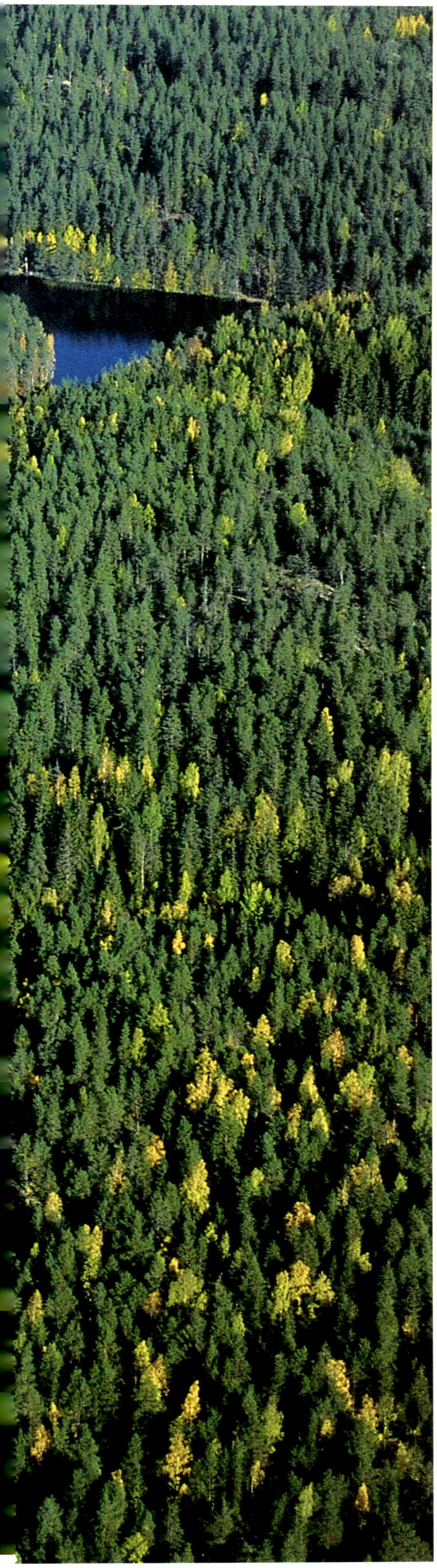

But it isn't long before the recently embarked seafarers return. One lot after another comes back, now in silent groups, to the familiar rocks, their chatter subdued. By midday nearly all have returned.

This behavior is typical of the wagtail: the migratory impulse triggered by bright autumn weather clashes with loyalty to its native haunts. Crossing large bodies of water – they must cross the sea when migrating – is such a hard chore for these poor fliers that they must muster their forces and courage. Those leaving in the morning often return by noon. They may give it another try in the afternoon, and thus migration proceeds very slowly at first: two steps forward and one step backward.

After two or three weeks' practice the wagtails finally get in a mood for true migration. Clear weather and the slightly favorable wind they prefer propels them forth, without even the sea crossing giving them cold feet. On the best sites it is possible to count thousands of wagtails sprinting southward on a good migration day. The country empties very quickly of these rumba dancers, though the odd individual does hang around until winter is about to arrive. There are even cases on the southern Finnish seaboard of a wagtail braving out a mild winter until January or February.

A chill autumn shower drenches a level landscape that is grey and lifeless. Water turned brown by loose soil floods a river from ploughed fields. The entire brimming channel is murky with clay. Large drainage ditches hurl into the current a cocoa-like sludge containing field sediment and left-over fertilizers. Willows and clumps of sedge along the banks glow with the mellow hues of autumn.

The river flowing through the plain has been stepped with dams to form a chain of reservoirs. Where the current has not been harnessed to produce kilowatts or untreated water for population centers, the river channel has been rebuilt with weirs that prevent its complete drying up when water is in short supply. In addition to power generation, the objective of river engineers has been flood prevention, but autumn downpours and spring meltwaters often push the water over the limit. The draining of watershed marshes and water-logged woodlands and the efficient drainage of fields have managed, if anything, to increase the susceptibility to flooding.

A bird's-eye-view of wilderness mirrors. Finland is a land of forests.

On the coast, at the lowest dam, the flood boils, for all the world like natural rapids. Below the dam a large fish skulks, occasionally lifting its head above the surface and gauging the height of the dam with its gaze. The noble fish's dorsal fin slices the flowing water, though it has chosen to lie in wait in an eddy, where staying in place consumes little energy. In suitable backflow a meter-long salmon can tread water for long periods without straining its fins. In the roiling water the fish's handsome flank is occasionally revealed completely: elegant dark spots fleck its burnished silver covering of scales.

Having visited the Baltic basin to feed, the fish travelled over the summer to the mouth of the river and inconspicuously came upstream to the pool of a former falls. The fish has bonded with the water into which it was introduced as a smolt. Its spawning run is futile, however, for the channel is unsuited to it. The obstructions of dams form insurmountable barriers, and the tampering with rapids upsteam has left them unfit as spawning grounds – even those not blocked by concrete.

The fish does not know that its efforts are in vain. Nature has created in it a readiness for reproduction, and driven by instinct it strives, as a salmon should, to reach fresh water to spawn. Its body cavity holds several kilograms of coarse-grained, oily roe which belongs on the gravel bed of a flowing stream. Fertilized there, it would develop into fry. In a few years' time a flood would carry the smolt, now just under a span in length, to the sea, from which after one, two or three years of roving they would again run upstream to spawn.

The salmon eyes the roiling dam for days on end; it lifts its head, assessing the force of the falls and the height of the dam's crest. Other salmon and a few wildly leaping brown trout show up, all of them likewise homeless transplants, sexually mature bearers of roe and milt. Each has behind it a long journey: the salmon have trekked hundreds, if not thousands of kilometers from feeding grounds, the trout have been cruising local waters in pursuit of Baltic herring and European smelt.

The capercaillie's morning flight generally ends on a branch.

October

The autumn assembly of cranes adjourns.

Wildfowl shift to woody sustenance.

Animals change their white winter coats.

Frosty weather insects swarm.

Ants retire beneath their hill.

A convocation of thrushes in the night sky.

The busiest season for birds of passage.

Reindeer and forest reindeer in rut.

Permanent snowcover comes to Lapland.

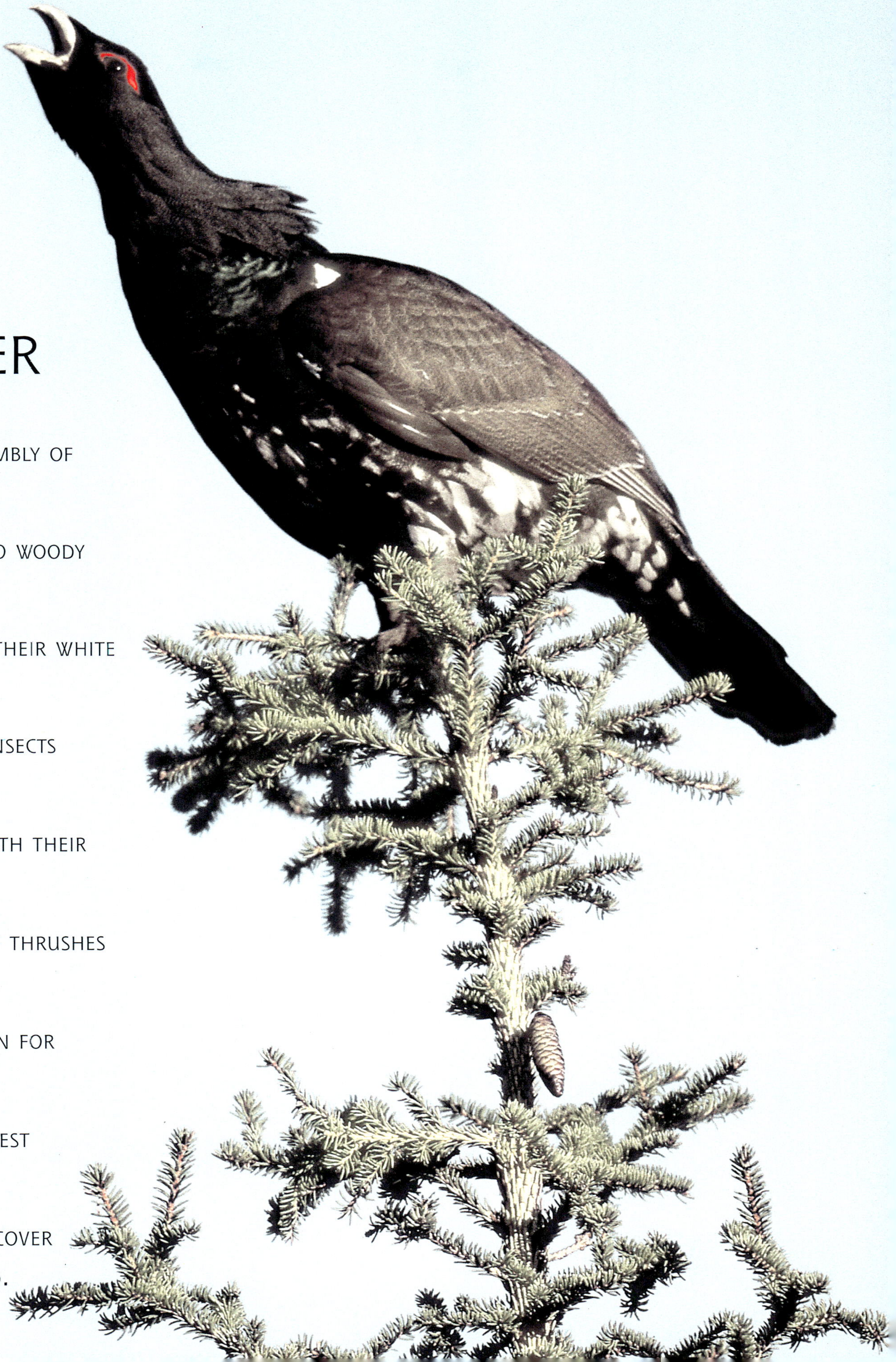

Awaiting Winter

The limpid morning dawns sedately. A few grey fleecy clouds drift across the sky but without dimming the sun. Cranes cry out: the adults croak huskily but the young, fully grown over the past summer, twitter like songbirds. The large birds have maintained their meeting in this place for weeks, their numbers increasing as autumn's grip grows firmer. The wind has already stripped the trees of their yellow, and thousands of cranes trumpet ruefully in autumn convocation.

Cranes from a broad area have gathered on the plain: from Ostrobothnia, from Lapland and probably from beyond the eastern and western borders. The first flocks appear as summer draws to a close; and many farmers regard them with disdain, for these dagger-beaked beanpoles are inclined to browse on their crops. However, the true masses arrive during the harvest, when grain and other leftovers from the combines are all that is on offer.

The cranes toil in the fields from morn till night, shifting now and then from one furrow to another to avoid the tractors pulling ploughs that glint as they turn the soil. Ploughed earth does not attract the cranes, for turning it hides its delicacies. Small flocks take wing in the middle of devotions, climbing to the heights and disappearing southward, aided by a favorable wind. But the main body of birds stubbornly holds its ground for some time yet.

As evening flushes the sky, the flocks of cranes make short flights to the archipelago and coastal shallows. The cloudless autumn night banishes warmth from the entire plain; the mercury drops below zero. Thus, the cranes eagerly seek to spend the nights along the sea. The huge body of water stores heat and relinquishes this energy slowly. The sea warms the cranes. The islands are also a good refuge against predators and other troublemakers. Through the morning mist, the cranes set out for their feeding grounds, the fields shimmering silver with hoarfrost. Between meals, they bicker and even break into dance.

And eventually the day of departure rolls around. One morning the big birds are more restless than usual. A few running steps, a few beats of outstretched wings, and one bird after another is up and away. Flock after flock congregates over the plain to gain altitude. The cries of the birds on high fade gradually and are masked by the hubbub of those babbling further down or on the ground. A brisk southwestern wind provides good sailing for the cranes. Forming wedges, the flocks vanish into the distance.

The bear's final meal before winter sleep and a long fast. Nothing remains of the reindeer calf but one cleave and some hair.

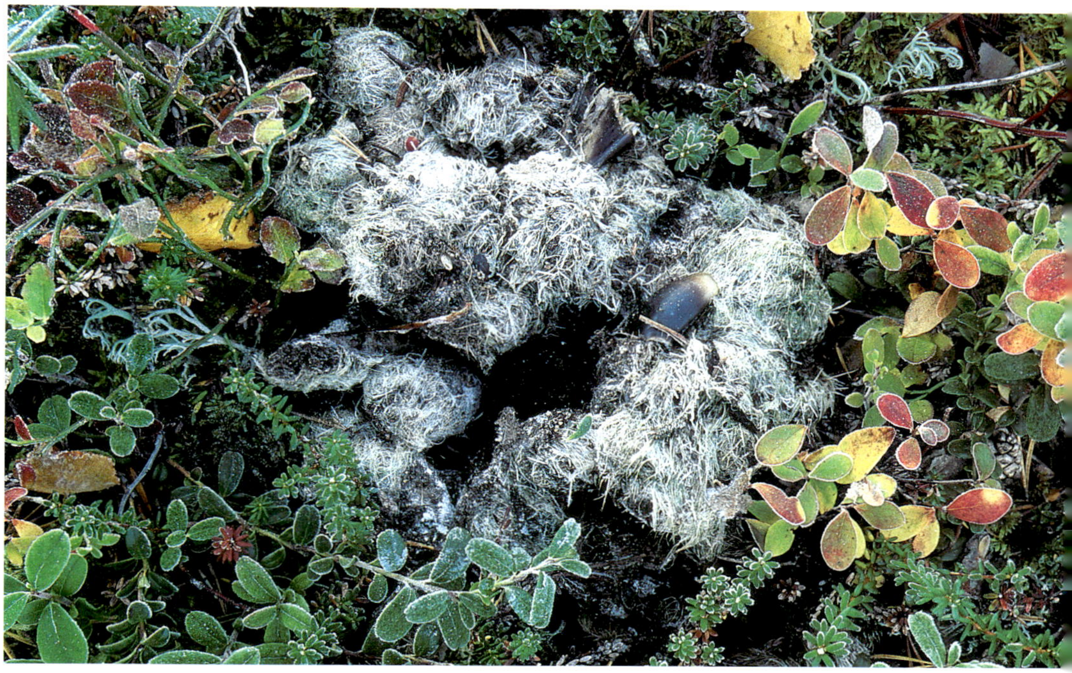

The first snowfall illuminates the shortening day.

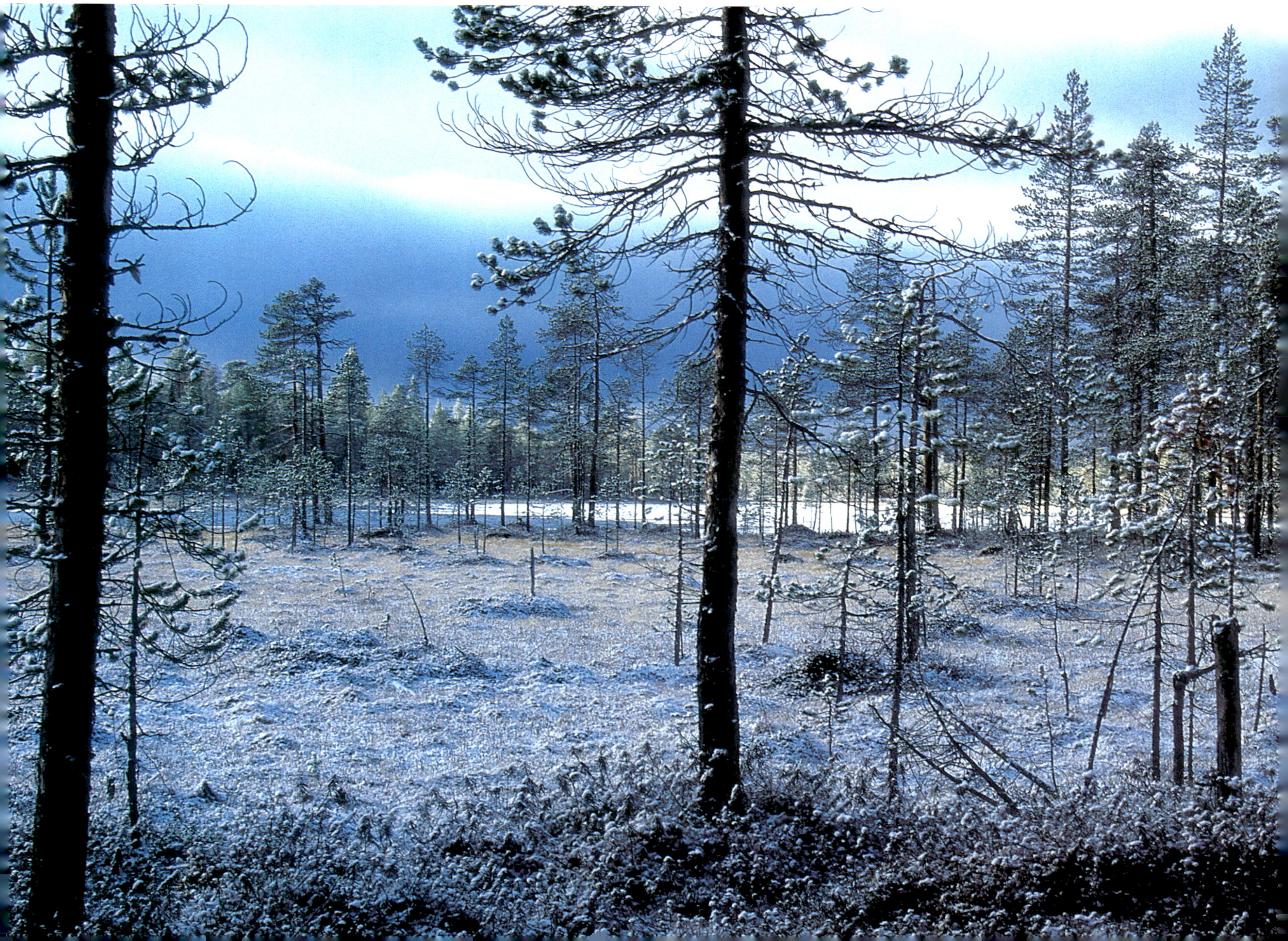

The fields make up an singular patchwork quilt to cover the entire region. Here and there a serpentine river glints, to the west the dark blue sea and a city shining white on its shore. Stripped bare, the hardwood forests are clearly distinguishable from the deep green stands of conifers. Marshes glow yellow; wet hollows reflect the light of the sky as a silver sheen or skulk almost black in shadows. Ditches slice straight through bogs slated for forestation.

The cranes head swiftly and resolutely south or south-southeast. The high-flying flocks gradually descend. Gliding on a tailwind conserves energy. Before long the formation approaches the ground, at which point, aided by a favorable current, the birds again soar aloft. The flock breaks up into a confused swarm but eventually organizes anew into a skein, the bird that assumed point position soon relinquishing lead to the next in line. The leader drops back to serve as tail, and thus the heavy burden of cleaving the air shifts from one individual in the flock to the another. The journey is accompanied by easy chatter and the twittering of the young, which in days of yore was thought to come from songbirds; it was believed that swallows travelled on the cranes' backs.

October 9, memorial day
for writer Aleksis Kivi,
a flag day, the national birds.
In the forest a bear prepares
for sleep.

With the freezing cold,
an elegant greyness cloaks
the shores.

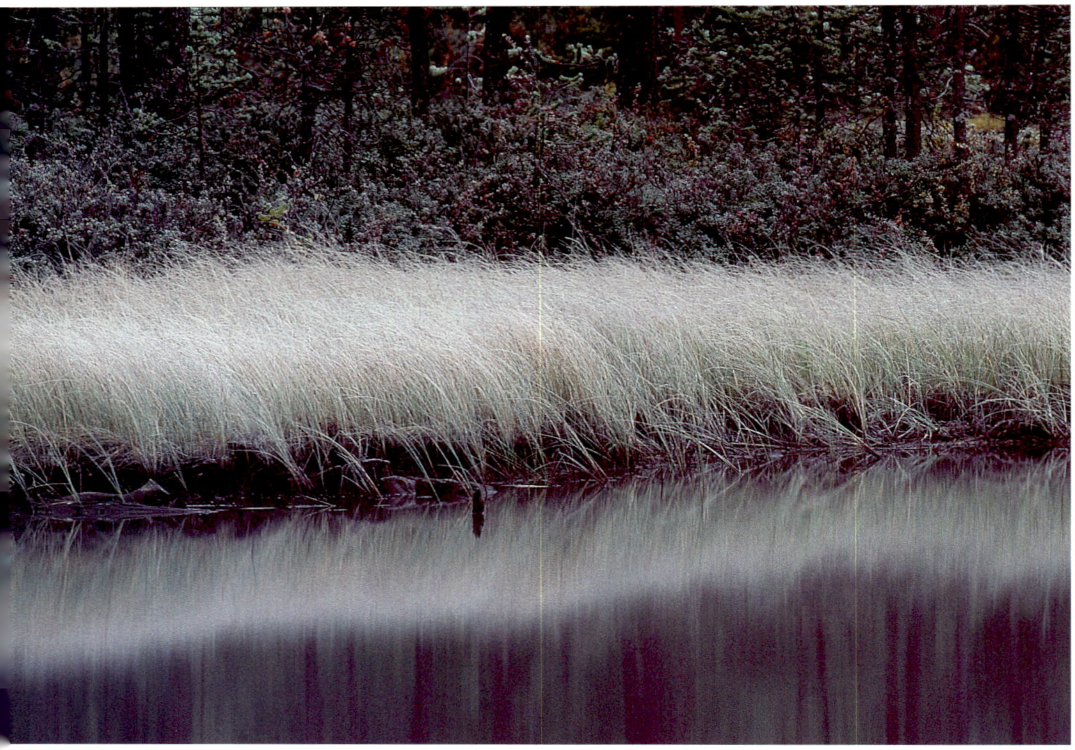

By midday the cranes are far inland and during the afternoon they reach the south shore of the Baltic, whence they continue on over Estonia. From a single position it is possible to count fifteen hundred and even two thousand cranes within the few hours before evening. Once across the Baltic, the noble birds rendezvous with cranes from elsewhere into a even larger autumn assembly. And the journey continues again when the time is ripe – within a week or two.

In Estonia the flock splits up. Half cuts across Belarus to Hungary and on across the Balkan peninsula and the heel of Italy to Tunisia. The other half flies through Poland and Germany to France and from there to Spain and, spurred on by a hard winter, across at Gibraltar all the way to Morocco. Some individuals even follow unknown routes to the Sudan, to the source of the Nile.

Leafless branches reach their dark limbs into the greyness. It is showering. Silvery droplets glisten on the tips of branches. The constant trickling swells them, and in the end gravity triumphs: faster than the eye can see, a droplet plunges to the ground, to break up into inconspicuous moisture on boughs and sedges. The glimmer of pearled water adorns the stark landscape. The faint thundering of water and the random patter of raindrops accompany the silence.

A covey of dark birds bustles in a birch grove bordering a field. Black grouse pluck provisions from branches bent under the big birds' weight. The supple boughs bow as the birds peck buds to eat. They occupy themselves silently a good while until, as if by common consent, they fly off to other business a few hundred meters away. Having seen to it, the grouse again take to wing and disappear into the forest.

The ground beneath the birches is a dreary brown. The leaves, a blazing yellow only a moment ago, are now faded and most have even darkened into a slimy mass. The brilliance of the willows and ashes has also waned, and the aspen too no longer glows. But the naked boughs are hardly lifeless switches; they already show signs of a fresh burgeoning to follow the impending winter.

The buds that have surreptitiously developed on the boughs over summer hold everything the tree needs in the spring when its vital processes start up again. The buds contain the rudiments of both leaves and shoots, and in many species, of blossoms as well. Conditions over the previous summer influence the quantity and quality of buds. Abundant flowering and seed production consume energy, with the result that a tree rarely yields two good crops in consecutive years; and this is also reflected in the production of buds.

The chrysomyxa rust fungus that afflicts young spruce needles every few years is a fungal disease whose pearly fruiting bodies, freezing with the first frost, colorfully reflect sunlight.

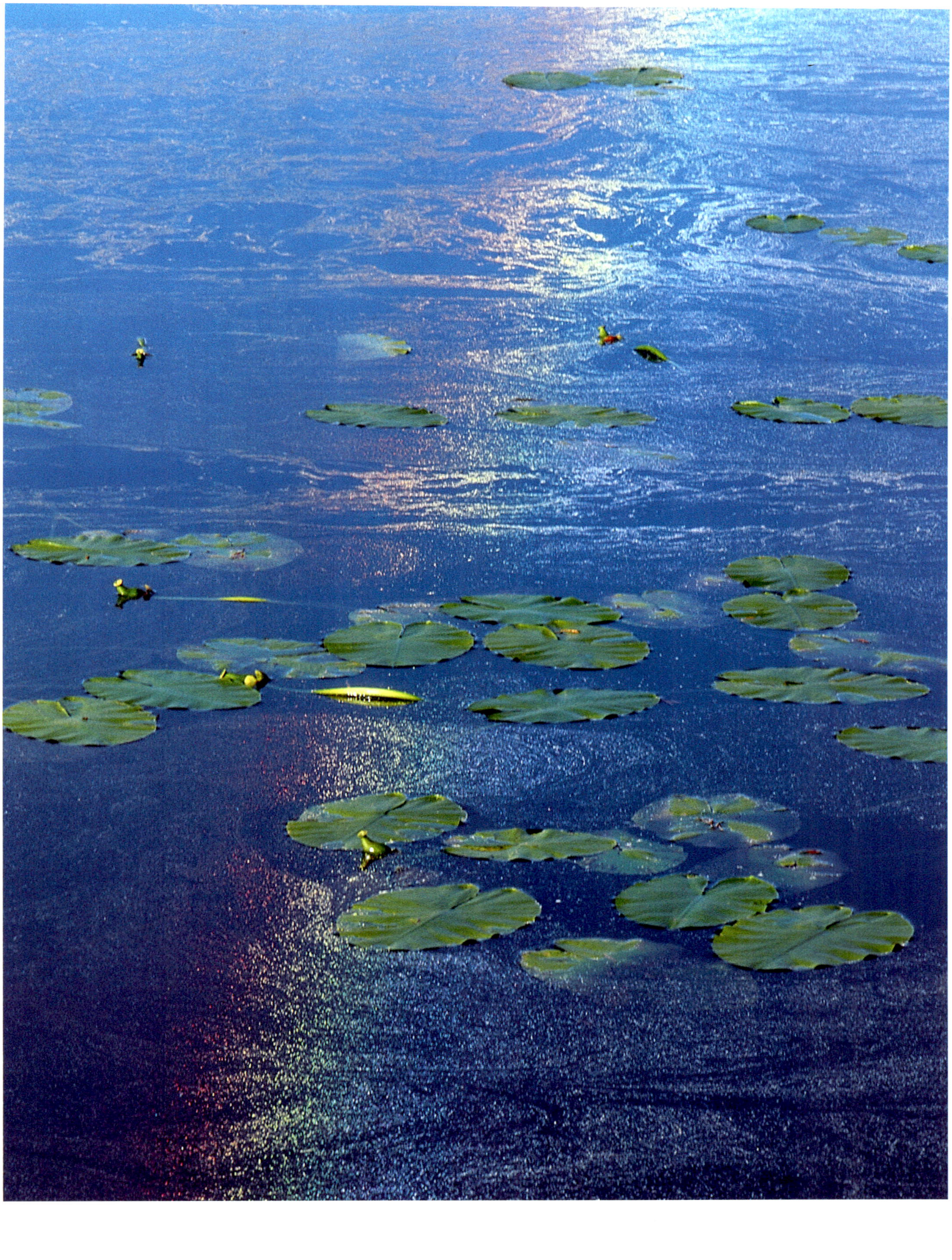

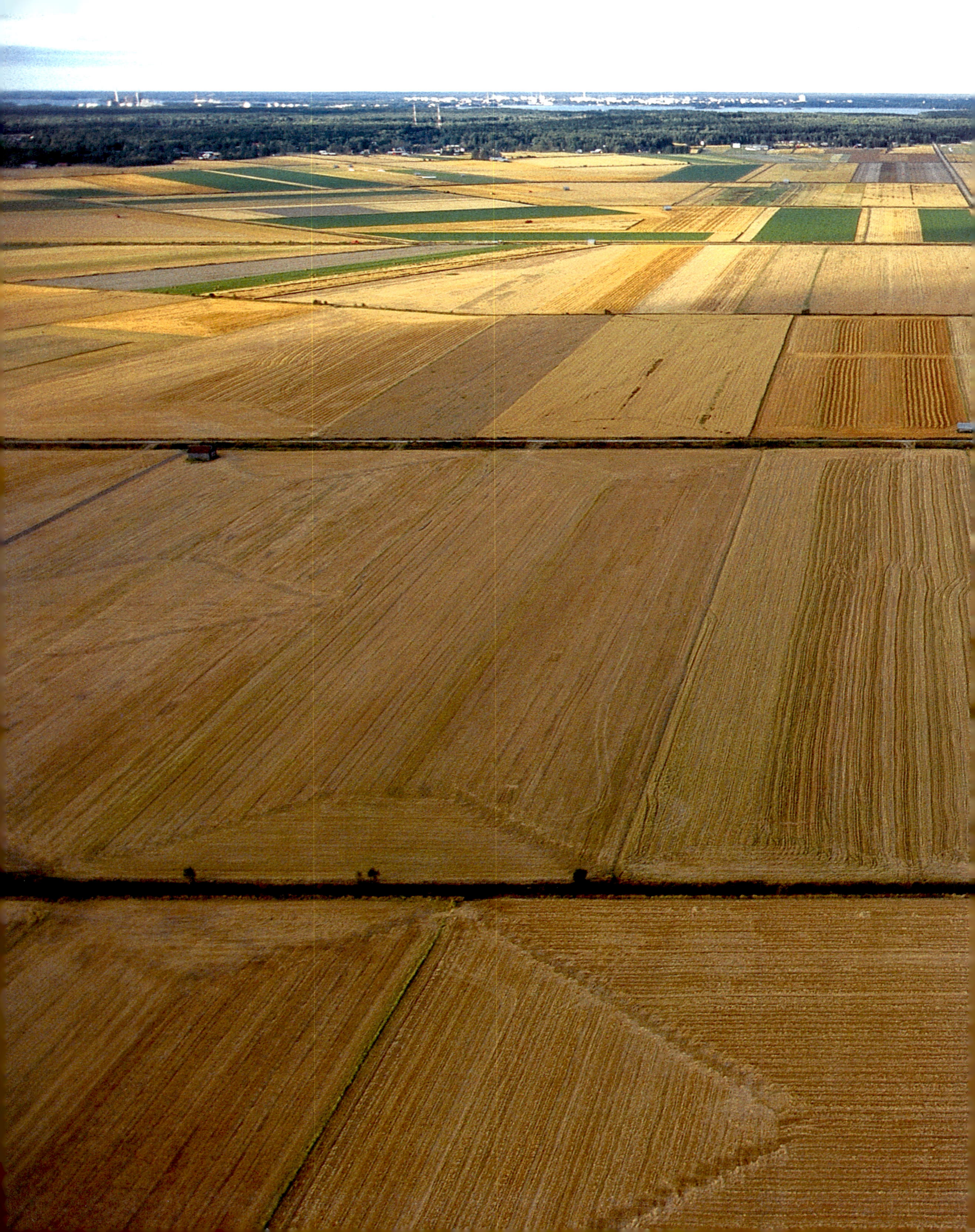

Not all fields lie fallow. Those spreading out near Vaasa make up an intensely cultivated plain.

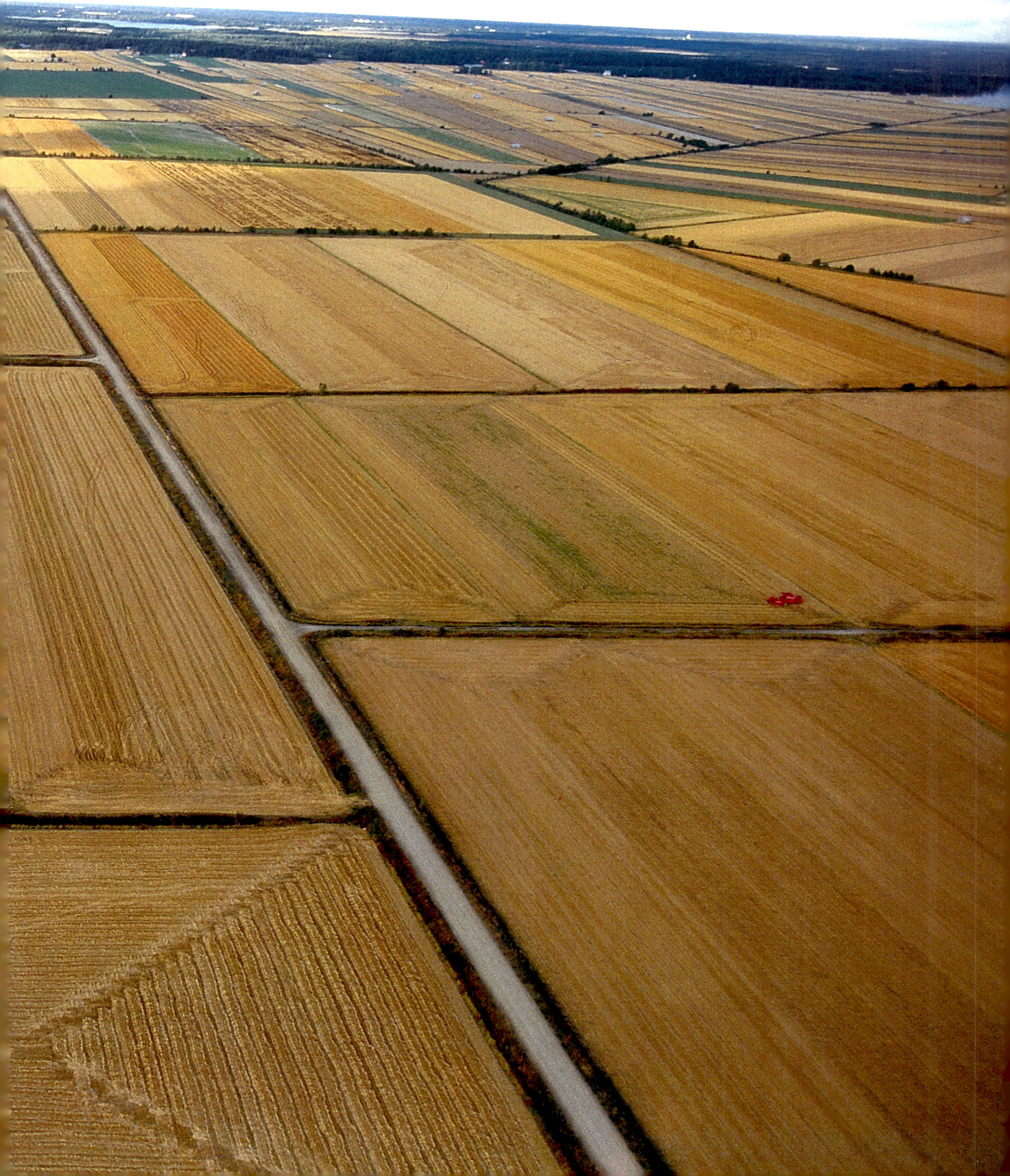

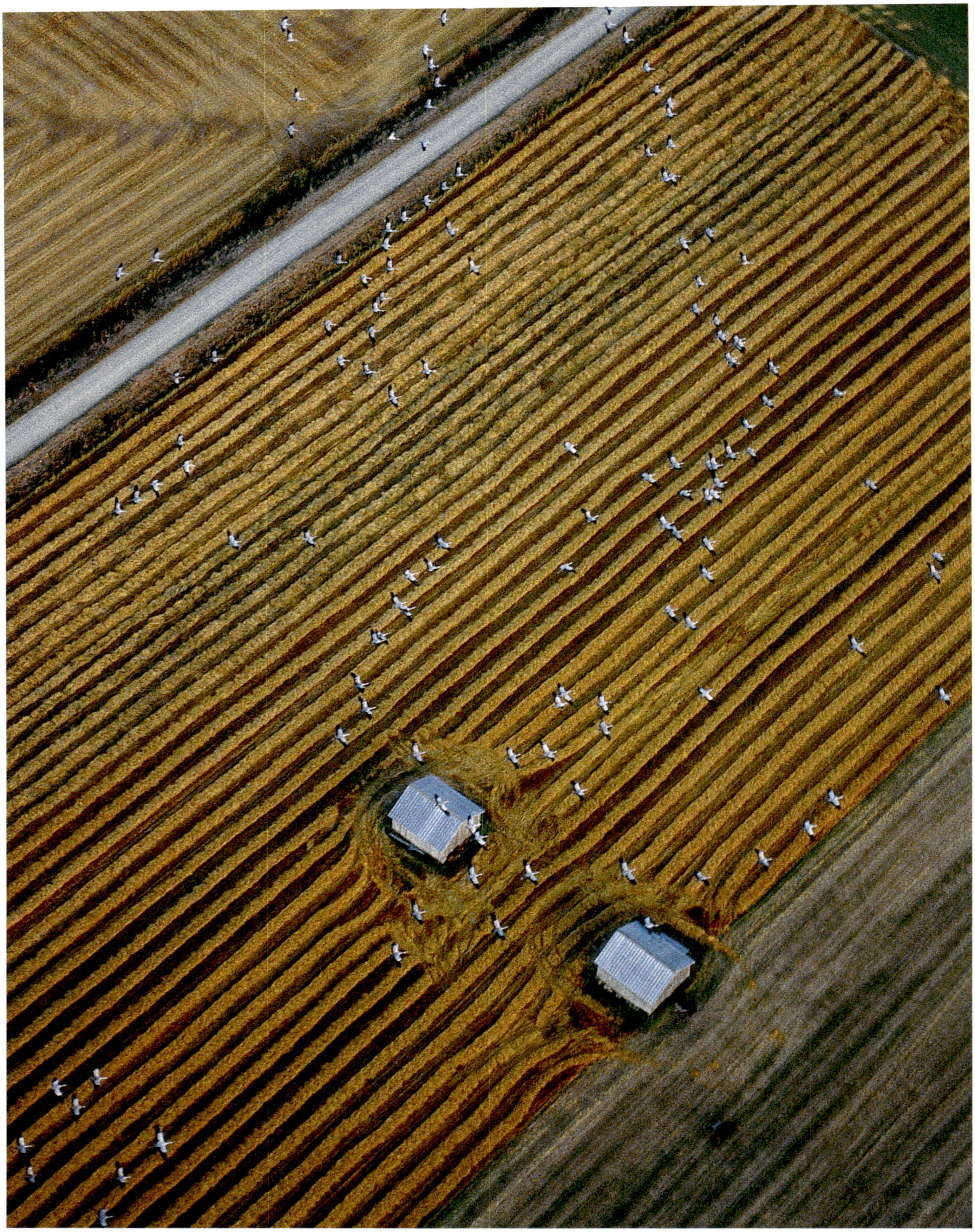

A gathering of cranes betwixt havester and plough.

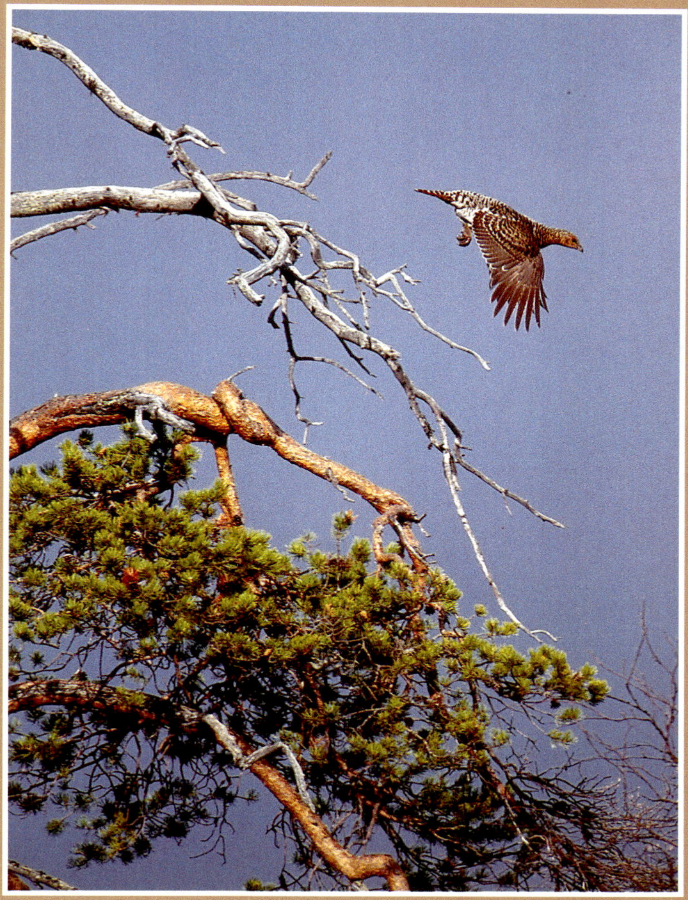

As autumn mellows, the capercaillie transforms the landscape.
Having dined on berries in mixed forest, the birds shift to pine woods
and brave out the winter on pine-needle nutrients. The habitat and sustinence
of the capercaillie changes radically with the season of the year. For example,
having sought out a felled area to nest after the lek, a hen directs its brood
to backwoods swarming with mosquitos and then
to berry-producing land.

Hard, thick and, in some species, even hairy scales protect the buds from the cold and the dryness of winter. Well protected against desiccation, the buds contain sticky resins which function as an anti-freeze. The sugar-rich fluids of the cells are condensed and low in water content; their freezing point is well below zero degrees Celsius. These protective substances also act to repel animals that use trees as food. A covey of black grouse will dine in one tree for but a moment or else get stomach pains from the one-sided diet.

First snowfall covers the northern regions; large flakes fall, painting the landscape white. With steady brushstrokes the sky changes thickets to grey and then to white. The windward sides of pines are also grey for a moment but they too are soon covered in delectable looking icing. Glacial erratic boulders look like glazed pastries, rocks are soon transformed into unrecognizable mounds. The forest receives a snowy mantle.

For the mountain hare roving the area, with its brown and white coloration finally turning completely to white, the first snow means a marked upgrading of life insurance coverage. In a bare landscape of even greys and browns, a white winter coat is like an exclamation mark, inviting predators. A hare is not carefree, though, even in the

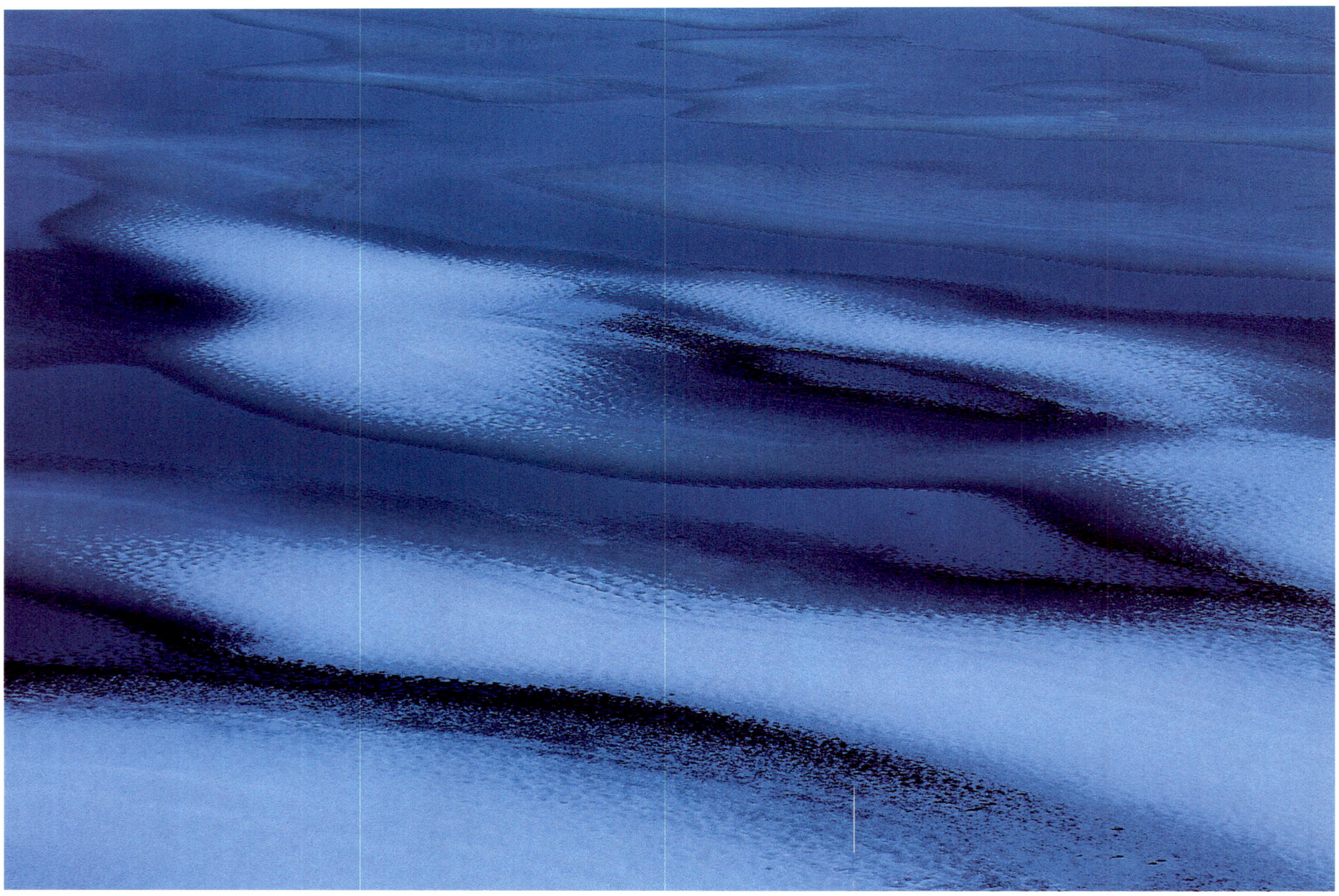

The ice of one night transforms the landscape.

season of snow; the degree of difficulty for predators merely changes.

The white winter fur is not simply camouflage. The underfur is thicker than in summer and the guard hair longer; the winter coat holds more air and is thus better insulation than summer fur. That the hairs are hollow enhances their insulating capacity. In summer there are a good two hundred hairs per square centimeter in a hare's coat, whereas in winter the average is over five hundred.

The other mammals beside the mountain hare that dress in winter camouflage include the arctic fox of the fjelds and the stoat and the least weasel, both found throughout the country. The length of the arctic fox's fur doubles and even the pads of its feet, which are bare in summer, become covered in fur. The squirrel's winter coat is thick and grey in color, an excellent protective hue for a creature that climbs about on frosty tree trunks. For protection from the cold, the squirrel curls up in a tail grown thick and dense.

The brown hare, a 20th-century arrival that has spread throughout Finland, attempts to survive winter in its brown coat. More and more grey has begun to appear in the winter fur of these hares; natural selection favors the survival of those individuals with good protective coloration. This creature of fields with scant snow cover may not even need to acquire completely white camouflage. A frosty grey may be a better option during the virtually snowless "greenhouse" winters that have come to prevail as the climate changes.

Birds also dress for winter. The ptarmigan of the fjelds and the willow grouse of snow-clad spruce marshes turn pure white. The worn summer plumage must be changed anyway, so the birds, stationary for the winter, restore their feathers and also adjust their colors for protection. Featherless in summer, the feet of the ptarmigan and grouse acquire a centimeter to a centimeter-and-a-half covering of feathers which serves both as insulation and as a kind of snowshoe. Lengthening claws also improve carrying capacity.

The plumage of birds does not thicken as much as the fur of mammals does. The feather mass of a bullfinch or a tit may nonetheless become one and a half times greater, and birds may enhance the insulating properties of their thicker plumage by fluffing it. If necessary, they will dig a cubbyhole beneath the snow to protect themselves from the cold and increase their energy production by putting to use the reserves of brown fat under their skin. As an extreme measure, some bird species lower their body temperature in an effort to survive spells of subfreezing weather.

Length of daylight regulates the changing of winter coats. For many birds the change of attire, which consumes energy and raw materials, commences as early as in summer; migratory birds molt before departure. The change to white winter plumage generally coincides with the coming of snow; because of the fall berry crop, wild fowl are at their strongest. Temperature and hormonal activity are of little significance in triggering color change.

The Big Dipper lies in the northern heavens; the serrated silhouette of the forest can only just be distinguished from the sky. A yard light hampers celestial observations, but tweetering sounds echoing in the darkness indicate that life has not come to a standstill. A cloudless blue sky presages a night freeze; and thrushes, after restless hubbub in the twilight, have set out in the dead of the night on their migratory journey. The cheeping of redwings is the most common sound; there is also the constant ticking of song thrushes, accompanied by the chuckles of fieldfares and the jeers of blackbirds.

A green grasshopper trills intermittently in the bushes; the serenader of balmy nights is winding down. The trilling that dominated early autumn nights has dwindled to the jaded swan songs of a few individuals fighting the inevitable approach of death. But the mission has been accomplished: the future of the green grasshopper species rests as eggs in the ground. The adults will not live into a second year.

But there is a real commotion in the wan light of the lamp. Gnats hum, a grey veil in the halo of light; among them flutter large butterflies, and harvestmen tread the walls in hopes of landing prey. Most insects and spiders are in winter dormancy, but several species are not activated until winter is on its way.

The last gnats to fly in the autumn seek out fissures in bark as winter comes on and hunker down in their hideouts in dense mats. The hardiest species can even survive temperatures of minus forty degrees; when spring arrives they are among the first to dance in the change of seasons. Over the winter vast numbers end up as food for woodpeckers, tits and treecreepers, but enough also survive to carry on the gnat line.

The butterflies and moths roused by the frost are mainly geometrid moths, along with the occasional Noctuidae and a couple of prominents. The winter moth fluttering in the lamplight is a member of the moth population that is active in late autumn. The winged males search out the wingless females creeping about on tree trunks and transmitting chemical scent signals to potential mates. The female climbs up to lay its fertilized eggs in the leaf buds of trees.

The butterflies are traditionally considered creatures of high summer hot spells, but late autumn has its advantages: the later the autumnal butterfly lays its eggs, the better their energy reserves will last through the winter. And it is also advantageous that the risk of diseases and parasites is smaller during the reign of frost than in the sultry swelter of late summer. The eggs contain little water and have a protective sheath, so they are well able to weather normal winter conditions.

A northland field lies silent beneath winter whiteness.

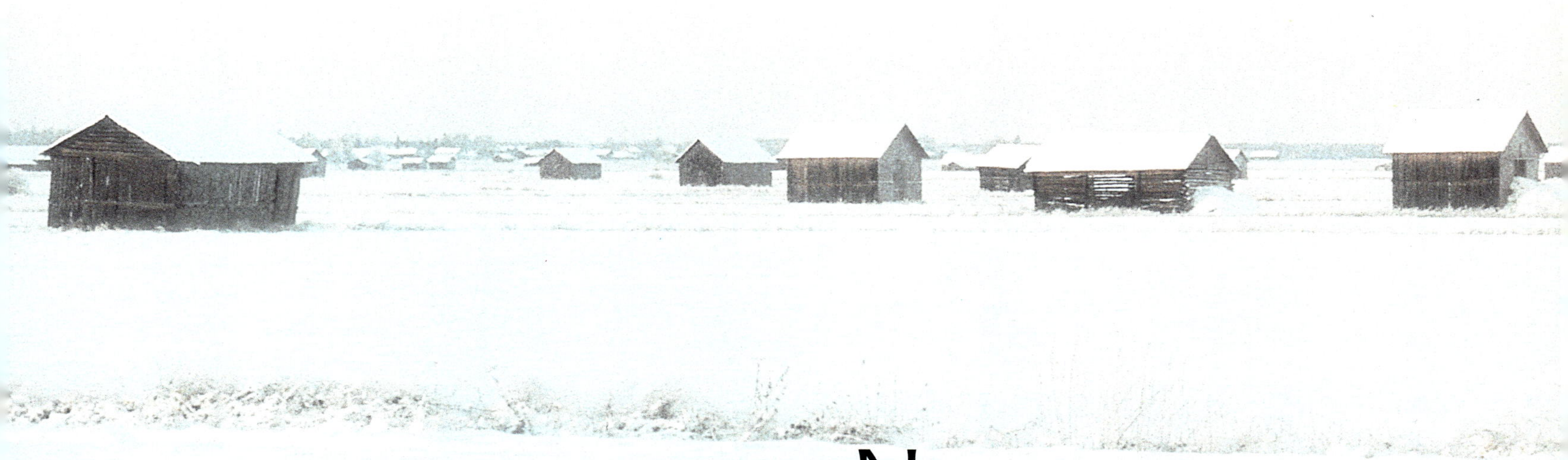

November

Mice head indoors.

Birds bolt seeds from weed stalks.

Northern lakes freeze over.

Swans make for the coasts.

The cold bites deep into the earth.

Flocks of waxwings pluck rowanberries.

Rain, sleet and snow throughout the land.

Animals store up for winter.

The season of darkness begins in the north.

THE BARREN SEASON

Grey morning. Water droplets glint on leafless birch boughs like minuscule magnifying glasses. Drizzle falls. There are scattered showers. A glance out the window indicates that autumn's first attempt at winter has failed. The night's rain has washed the snow away. Only a few piles heaped beside the path in the yard remain and even these have shrunk to dirty grey patches.

A squirrel has settled in to sup on the bird feeder. Its fur damp, it nibbles sunflower seeds. There is no sign of titmice. The mild, rainy late autumn day is quiet. The flock of bullfinches perched in the crown of a spruce doesn't seem particularly interested in the seeds either, though the squirrel gobbles them with gusto.

A yellow-necked field mouse scampers by beneath the feeder; long-tailed and big-eared, its legs are bright white, as if it sported gym socks. The wee tim'rous beastie frantically stuffs fallen seeds into its mouth, swelling its cheeks. Soon the grey-coated rodent runs for cover, a leafy compost heap airy with twigs, to lay up provisions for winter.

A gingerly quivering snout appears first as the mouse sets out on another hoarding expedition. Soon after, a pair of large eyes assess the surroundings and then its ears thrust forth, taking aural soundings. In a few smart lopes the mouse is at its feeding site again, cramming its craw with seeds.

A wet day is a perfect time for a mouse to run errands. The neighbor's comfort-loving cat doesn't deign to go on its daily prowl, but a pigmy owl may be lurking about, which is why the vigilant rodent scrutinizes its surroundings before darting from its hole.

Though the yellow-necked field mouse caches considerable hoards of seed for winter, the first proper cold spell drives it indoors. It gains access to human habitation with astonishing ease: if the stone foundation offers no suitable hole, the uninvited guest will climb clear to the roof and squeeze through an appropriate opening in the structure. When needed, it will enlarge the hole by gnawing at it.

And so it is that one day things begin to disappear from the kitchen pantry. A hole appears in a sack of potatoes and little toothmarks on the tubers. Someone is pinching the gingersnaps! It knocks spice containers from a shelf, nibbles bread, fouls the sugarbowl. It strews tiny droppings all over the house. It squeals with others of its kind in a nook behind the kitchen cupboard. Soon the house is home to a family of mice, a whole clan which is particularly mischievous in the nighttime.

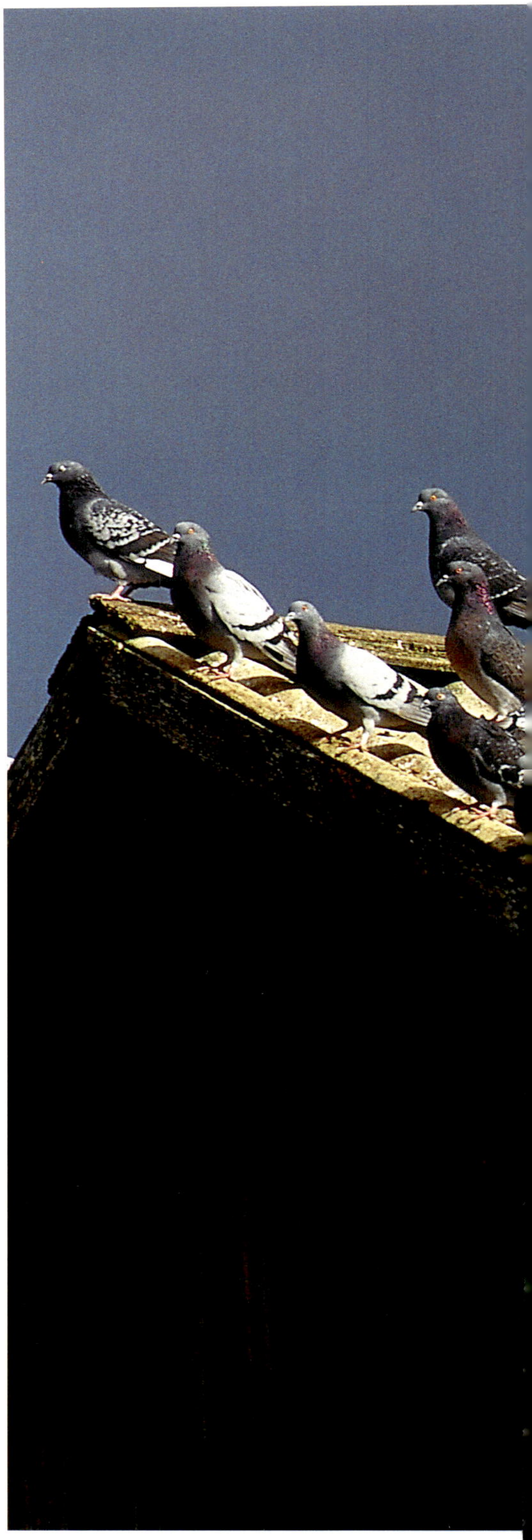

A goshawk's meal on the roof.
Toward spring the pigeon flock is depleted
for the good of its betters.

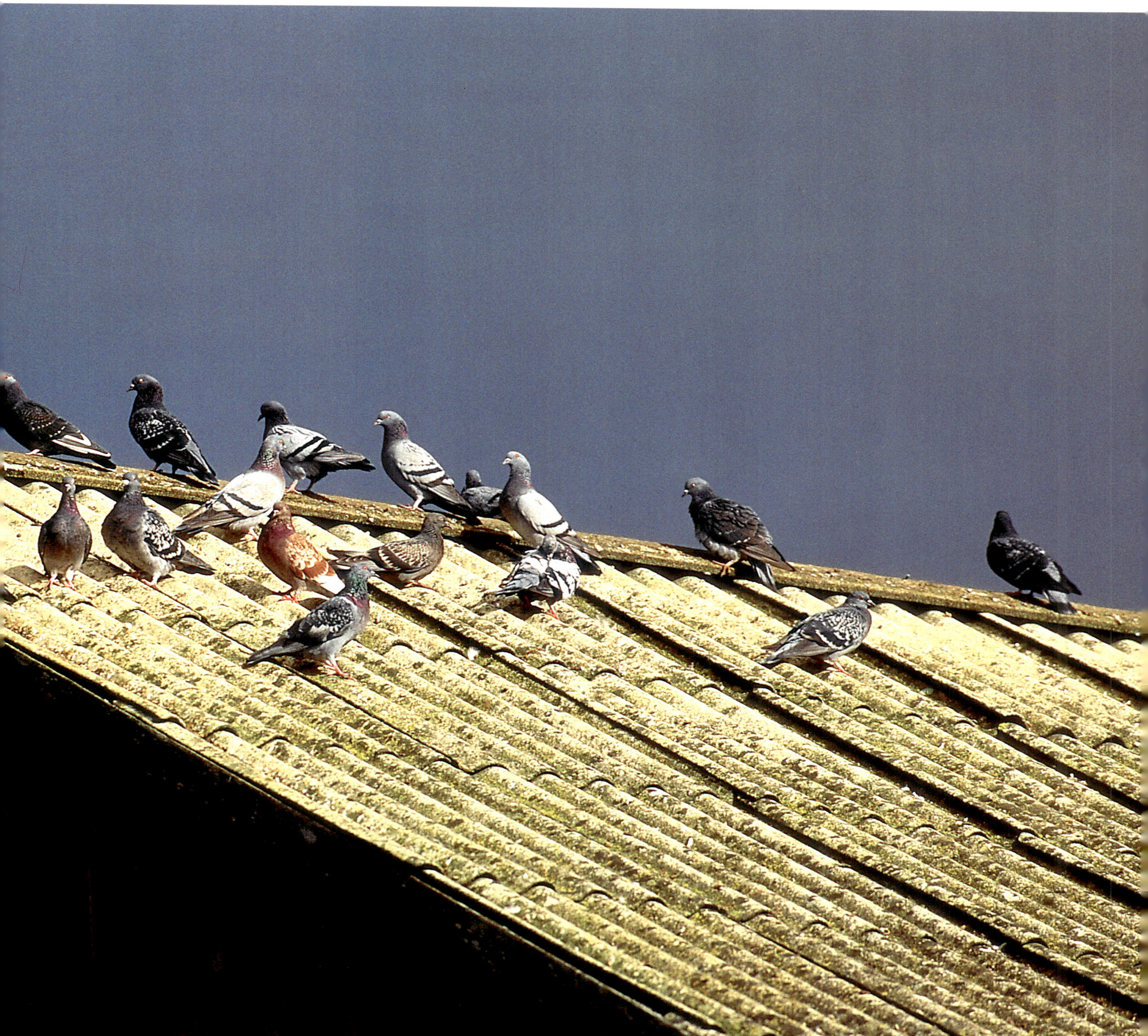

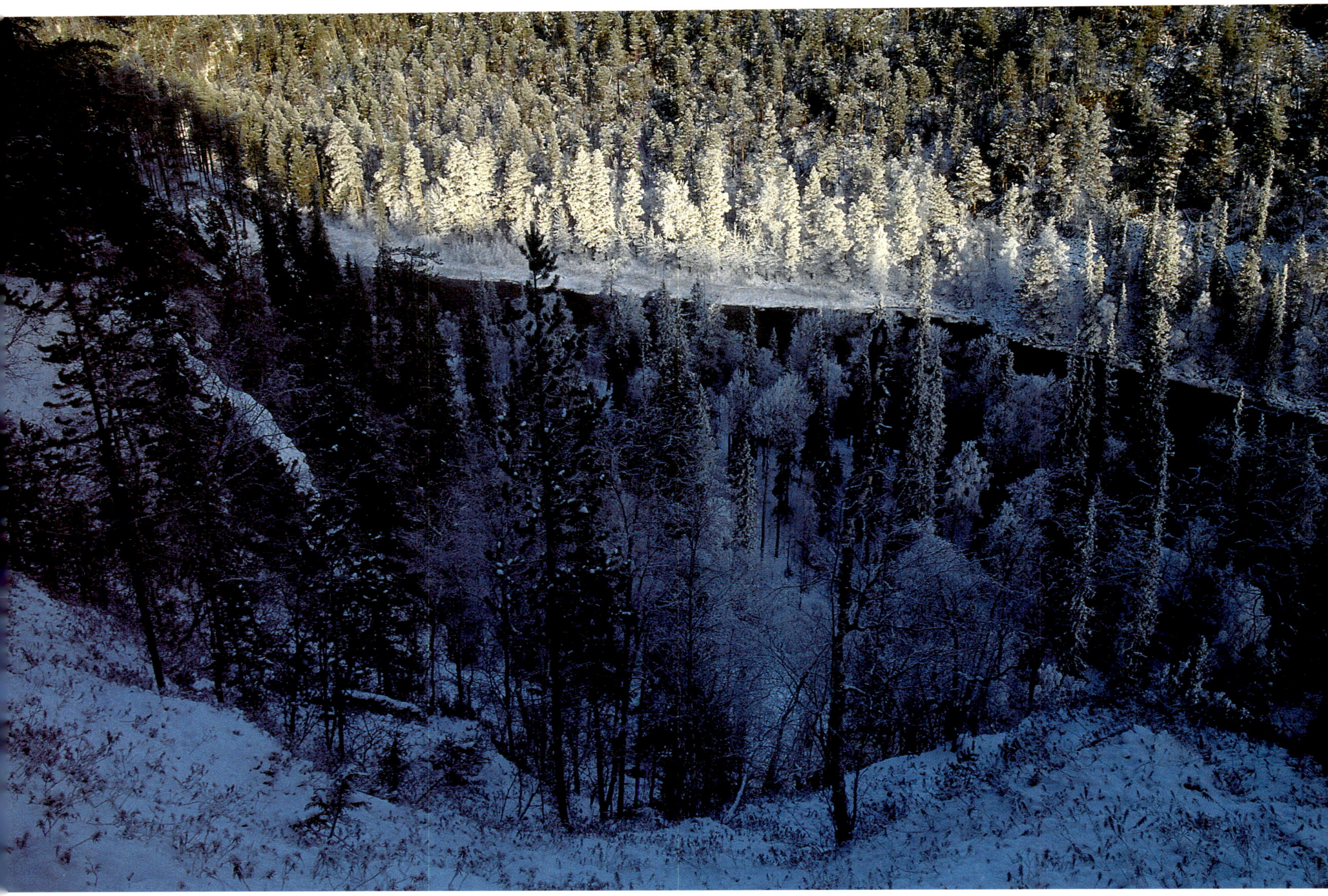

The white of winter again characterizes the landscape. From the southwest and west one low-pressure front follows another; the earth is awash with endless rain. The sky offers cold rain, sleet and slushy snow in seemingly never-ending supply, accompanied by energetic, sometimes even gale-force winds. Sudden changes in the weather typify this transitional period: a gloomy shower is instantly transformed, through the mediation of a bright sunset, into a clear, frosty night which freezes puddles and rimes shores until a fresh squall comes barging along.

Darkened plants poke up through the mantle of snow. The crop in a fallow field is always left for nature to reap. Weeds, parsleys, and grasses stand stiffly in the storm. Their dead stems survive well the uneven load of snow and severe buffeting by the wind. In summer the plants' blossoms sought to reach the heights to catch the attention of pollinators: there were thistles, tansy, cow parsley... among them the odd, svelte bellflower, a clump of nettles, burdock.

Winter tightens its grip; soon even flowing water will yield.

Having lost their kaleidoscopic splendor, they now lift there fruit high over the snow, but they have not yet fulfilled their function. The yield of the growing season must be sown before the entire being may fall to earth to rest. And snow is a good place to cast seed: the wind conveys the seeds far from the parent plant, the crust acting as a runway. Ripe seed is highly tolerant of the rigors of winter: cold and dryness.

At the very outside, the seeds are borne to new growing sites by spring meltwater. Thus, the plants ensure diversity in their gene pool and gain a foothold wherever conditions permit. The plant kingdom advances with less speed and more stealth than do animals, which can colonize a new region in one clean sweep or in easily traced, purposeful migration.

When snow blankets the ground, the rear guard of migratory birds throngs marginal land rank with withered plants. The glut of seed produced by weeds provides an ample food supply for the cone-beaked denizens of the air. Softly chattering linnets, timidly whistling bullfinches, brightly chiming and strikingly clad goldfinches, greenfinches expressing themselves sonorously, and redpolls chirping dolefully and softly all stop by for a snack. Sometimes a group of chaffinches and bramblings joins in. For the grey partridge the seed offerings from wasteland are a crucial component of its preparations for winter.

Winter tightens the screws. The short day has passed with astonishing swiftness. The aurora borealis dancing in the northern sky flares, its crown reaching toward the zenith of the sky. The solar wind sweeps the outermost layers of the atmosphere at phenomenal speeds, the magnetic storm conveying its singular salutations from afar. But the resplendence of the fiery fox traversing the firmament does not warm the earth.

Heat escapes into space through a cloudless sky. The freezing cold pops in telephone poles; the day's moisture is extruded from wet plant stems and rotting limbs. The ground frost runs deeper, and the wet surface soil freezes into needles as thick as a finger, forming a curious bed of spikes on the decomposing litter. Unless the protective snow cover builds as winter tightens its grip, the deepening frost will damage the frail roots of trees and, before long, the main roots of such vital importance to survival.

The average daily temperature has remained below freezing for some time now, in the winter range, but the earth's heat reserves, aided by rain, have melted nearly all the snow that has fallen thus far. It would now begin to stay put, but a high-pressure front pushing in from the east brings a snowless cold that freezes the ground and chills the waters. Small ponds already crackle with frazzle ice and on still, frosty nights the surfaces of even the broadest reaches are spread with a veil that is driven ashore, tinkling, by the morning breeze.

Moisture condenses into frost in subfreezing cold. Ice crystals formed on stalks of grass indicate the wind direction; there are no crystals on the downwind side.

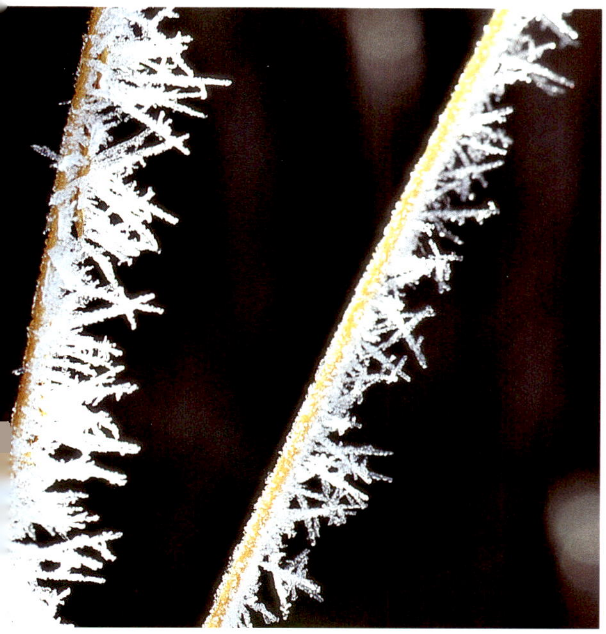

The seasonal changes wrought by winter in water are even slower and, in the end, also less significant than on land and in the air. The sea and lake basins are large heat reservoirs that are slow to cool down. Under the influence of cold weather, the surface water cools and eventually the entire body of water is equally cold. At the same time, the water mixes, and oxygen-rich surface water sinks into the oxygen-starved depths.

As water is at its heaviest at four degrees Celsius, surface water eventually cools to a lower temperature than bottom layers, and at zero Celsius it begins to condense into ice which quickly spreads over entire expanses in a sort of spider's web. Gradually the thickening ice and the snow falling on it also come to act as insulation which prevents some heat loss from under the ice. In fact, conditions beneath the ice are fairly stable and secure for any animal adapted to them.

During a winter of little snow and of bitter cold in particular, shallow waters may freeze to the bottom, an ordeal for even the

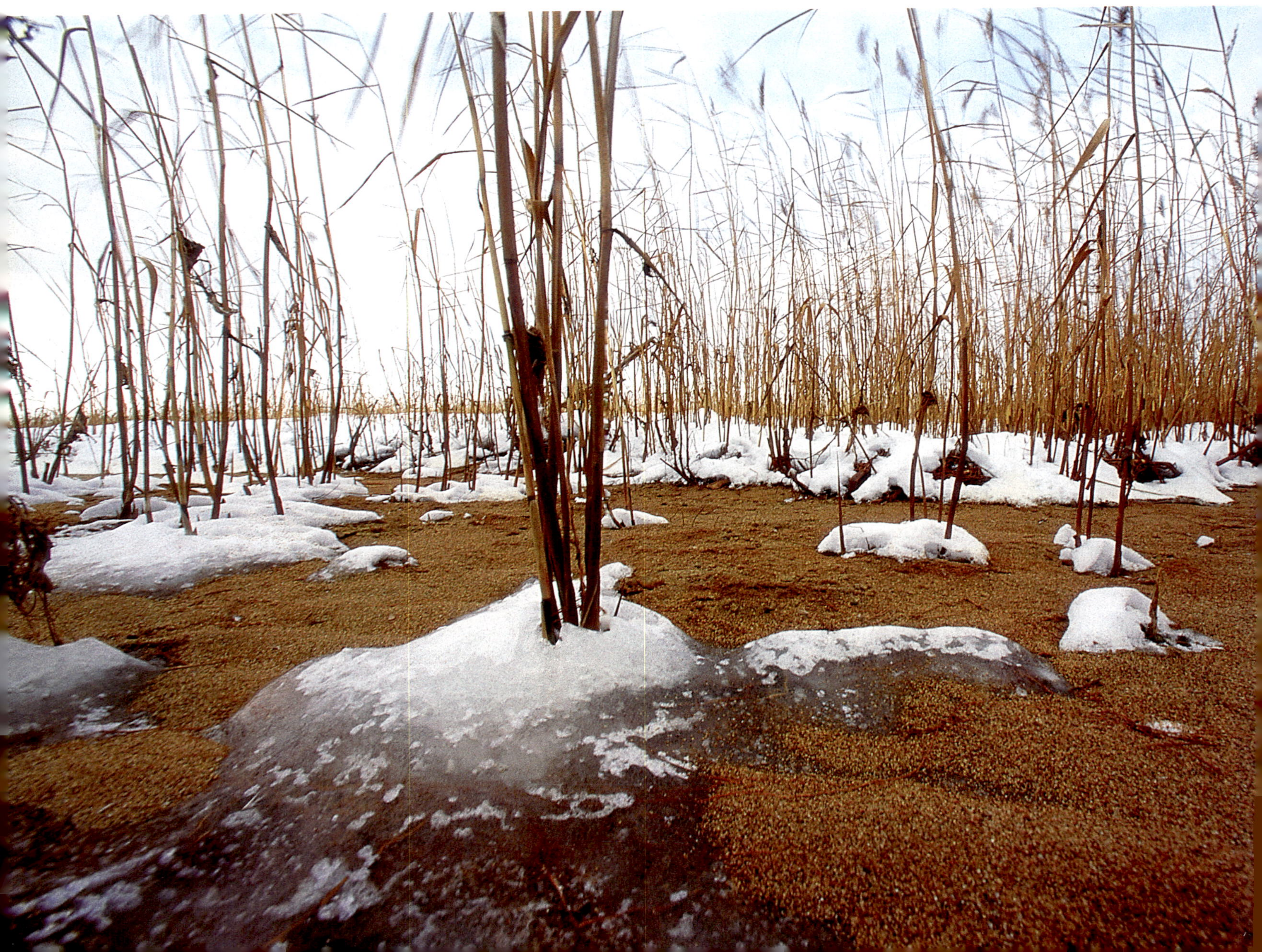

Winter steals over the lowland coasts of the northern Gulf of Bothnia.

hardiest of beast. Due to the complete circulation of water in autumn, oxygen reserves in the mass of water beneath the ice layer are generally good.

In naturally eutrophic lakes, or those eutrophic through pollutant stress, biological breakdown continues briskly beneath the ice and, in the worst case, oxygen reserves are depleted before the spring thaw frees the water to circulate again. In the most severe cases, winter oxygen depletion is manifested in extensive fish mortality. Usually, however, lack of oxygen affects only the depths and damage is largely local.

In small bodies of water survivors are few, but the crucian carp serves as an excellent example of an animal species that is tolerant of extreme cold and a nearly total lack of oxygen. In winter it produces alcohol in its organs as antifreeze agent and may burrow into the nearly oxygen-free muddy bed, where it braves it out until spring fills its home pond anew with meltwater.

Rifts split the strengthening ice sheath out on lake expanses.

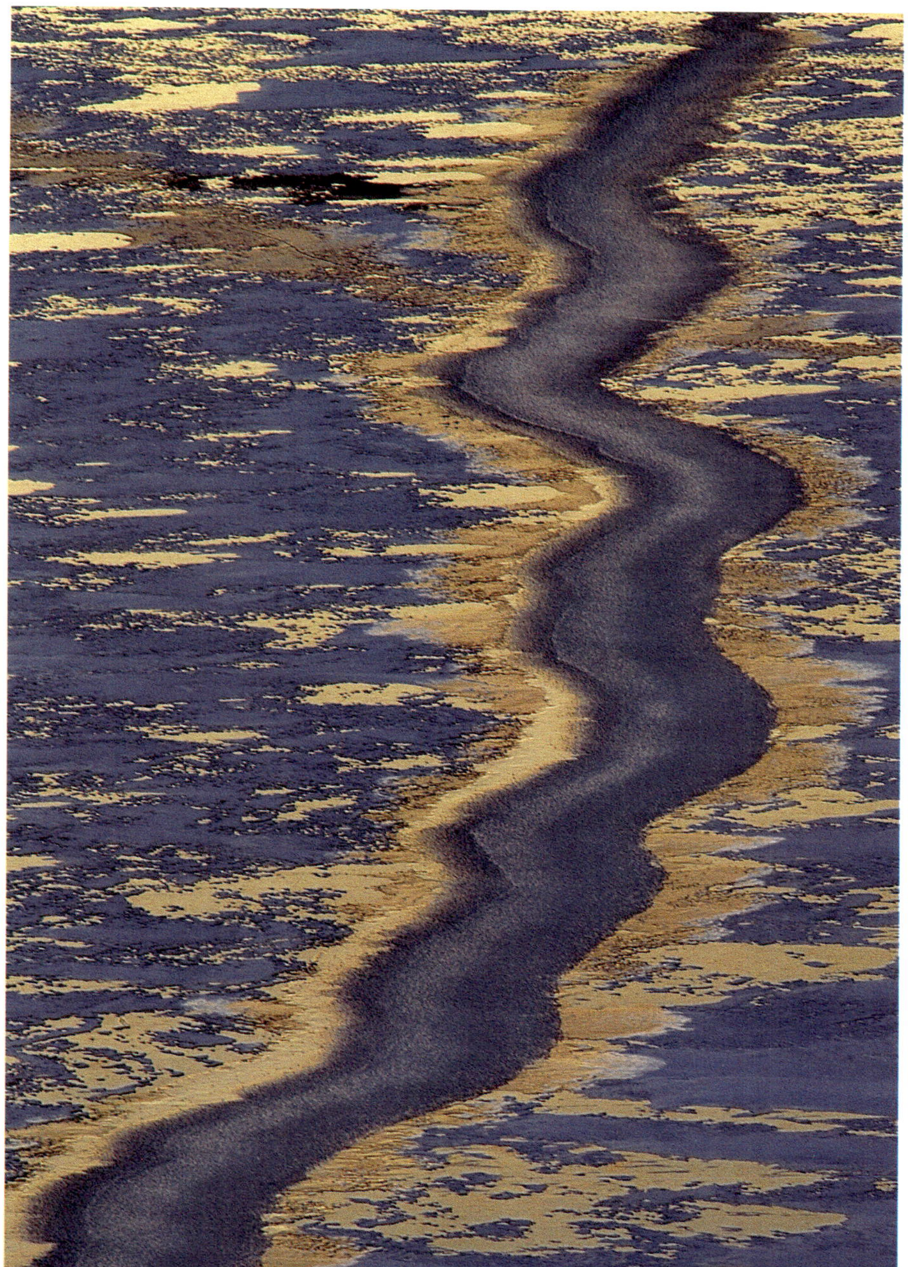

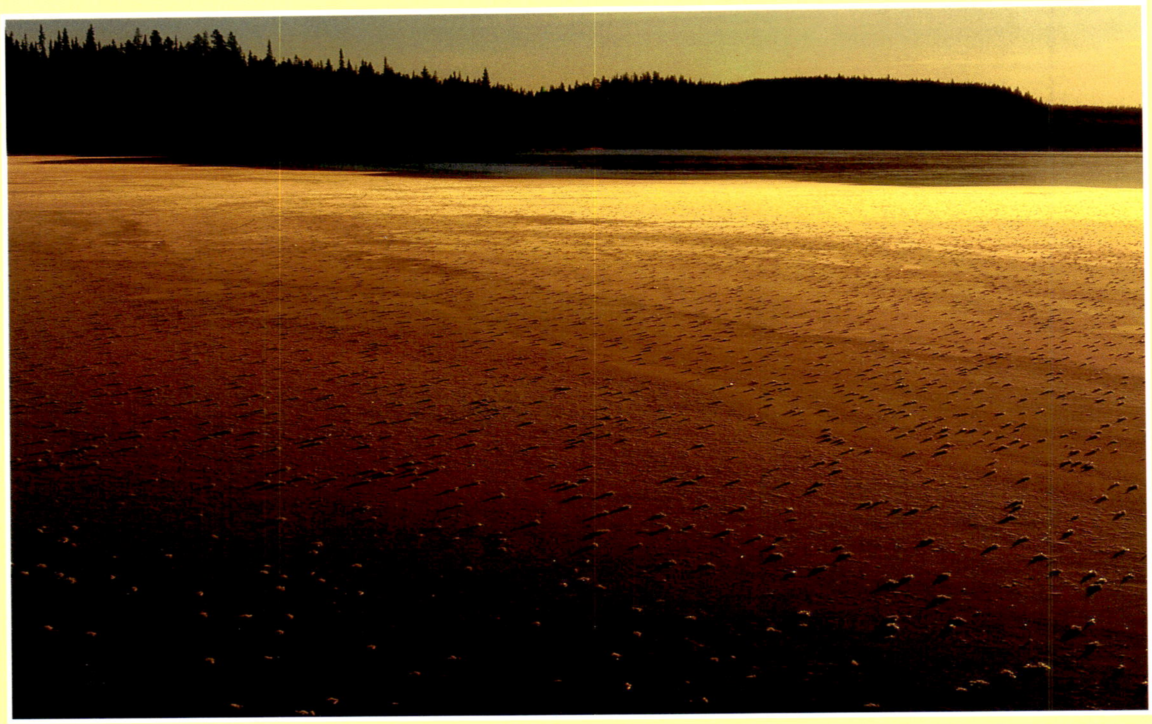

Frost blossoms on overnight ice. Under normal conditions water has only one solid form, ice. An ice crystal forms around a dust particle in the water when the temperature falls below freezing. Expanding crystals adhere to one another, giving rise to a film which eventually hardens into a solid sheet. Growing in thickness from beneath, the crystals of ice form splinter-like structures which only spring exposes.

A wistful silver tinkling chimes from the forest. A flight of greyish birds sweeps the tops of the trees, scours the area, and with surprising ease finds rowans that still hold a few shrivelled berries. The flock of waxwings systematically cleans a tree and flies off at once to seek the next one. An failed berry crop means hard times for a bird with such a highly specialized diet.

The flock strays onto the terrace of a private home and strips the bunch of rowan berries picked as decoration. And on the journey continues, over field and stream, accompanied by cheery chatter. If rowan berries are lacking, these crested birds will also pluck juniper berries; but it's the red rowan berries they pounce on most eagerly. Hawthorn berries will do; those of various ornamental shrubs and of elders gone wild also find favor. And there is even a flock that pecks at the plastic ornaments on a Christmas wreath nailed to the door of the community hall.

Known for its crest, the waxwing is an elegant bird whose grey plumage has a rusty cast. A thin streak runs from beak to neck, crossing the eyes like a black mask. A black bib also graces the waxwing's being. There are white stripes and a bright yellow pattern on its wings. A red rear underside and a yellow tip to the black tail complete the artistic impression.

The beard moss of the south and the horsehair lichen of the north meet in northeast Finland.

A groaning board for winter birds. Fungus gnats winter beneath the bark of a dead-standing pine.

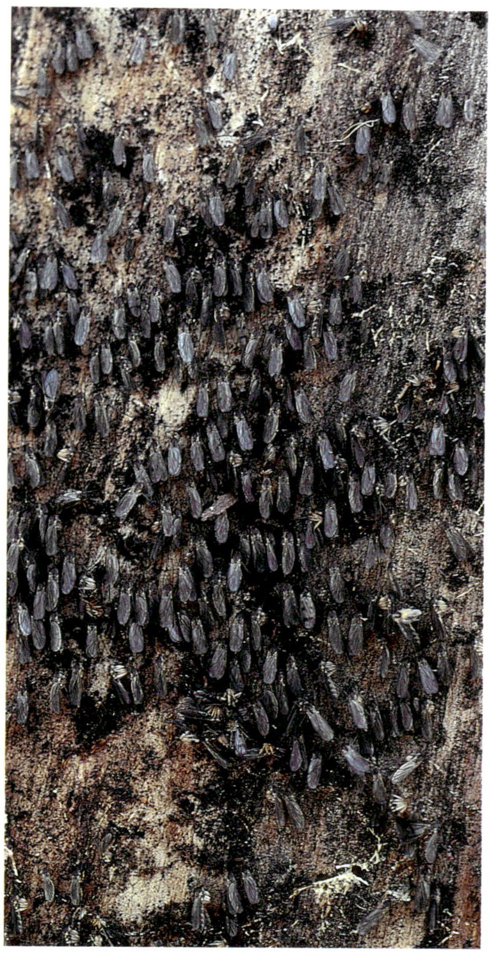

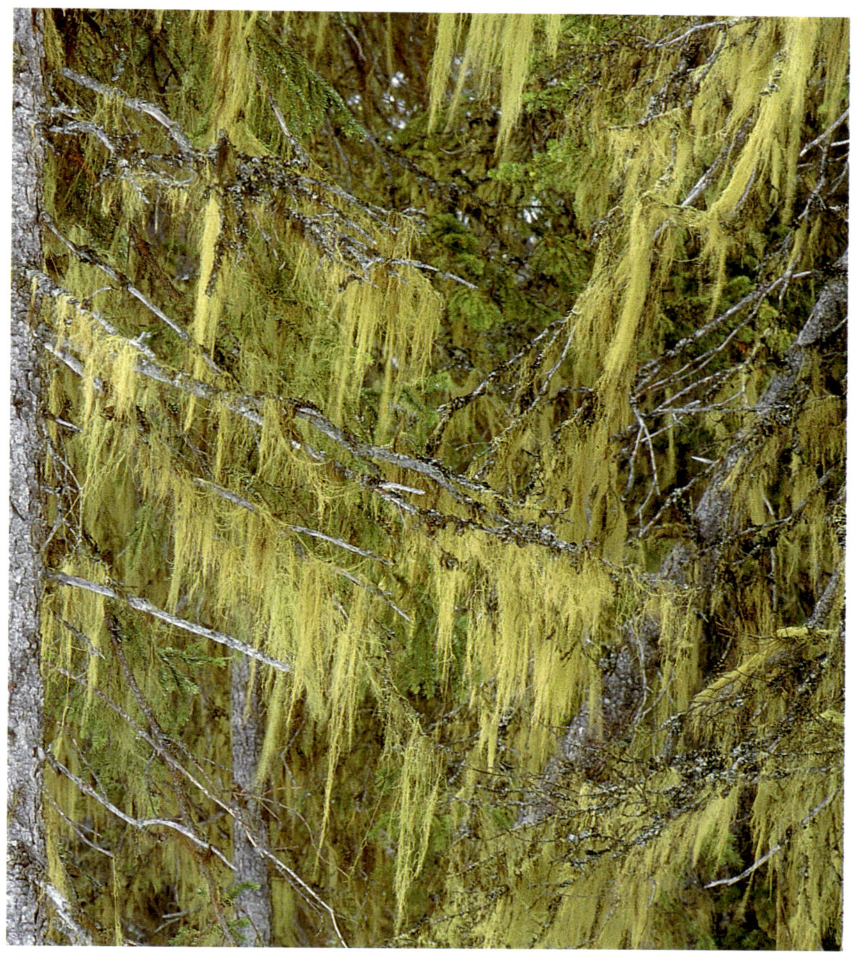

The summer blossoming of the rowan and the quantity of raw fruit hanging on the trees in late summer are indications of the number of the chiming birds fall and winter will bring. A plentiful crop ensures that the waxwing theatrics will continued well into the new year, while a poor crop or a failure means the waxwing review, accompanied by plaintive chatter, will be a quick one.

Waxwing admirers in Finland may sometimes have to content themselves with small groups rather than gatherings by the thousands. This is when the crested songsters are bringing joy to central Europeans. To them, these comely birds of the northern forests are a more exotic sight than they are to Finns, who may enjoy the waxwings' charming features every year. Their migratory journey may take them as far as the Mediterranean, but generally it ends in the northern reaches of the continent. As they are a hardy northern species, waxwings can endure harsh conditions and, being robust travellers, cover fairly long distances rapidly.

The waxwing is the only fruit-eating bird in Finland. It does not extract the seeds from the rowanberries as the bullfinch or the pine grosbeak does, but swallows them whole. Only the flesh of the fruit, its pulp, is of use to the waxwing, and only its easily digested sugars at that. The seeds pass quickly through the bird's short alimentary canal, in perhaps only half an hour. During a brisk flight, the bird may carry a rowan seed far from its parent tree: kilometers, even dozens of kilometers away.

The frost-bitten, fermented berries may contain alcohol. It has been suggested that waxwings are alcoholics. The birds clamoring in a berry-laden tree may act fearless, sometimes downright familiar – jovial raconteurs who may, upon leaving their tavern, go bumping into cars and windows. There truly is something of the inebriate's lackadaisical mien in a flock of waxwings' careering through the air.

But if a waxwing is big on knocking back intoxicating berries, its usually large liver is good at dealing with fermented products that affect the central nervous system. If its alcohol content soars momentarily to a dizzying extent, it also drops quickly. Nothing is known about the waxwing's potential for alcohol dependency. It is unquestionably only an occasional user, for fermented berries are only available temporarily in the autumn.

By mid-winter old moose too have shed their antlers.

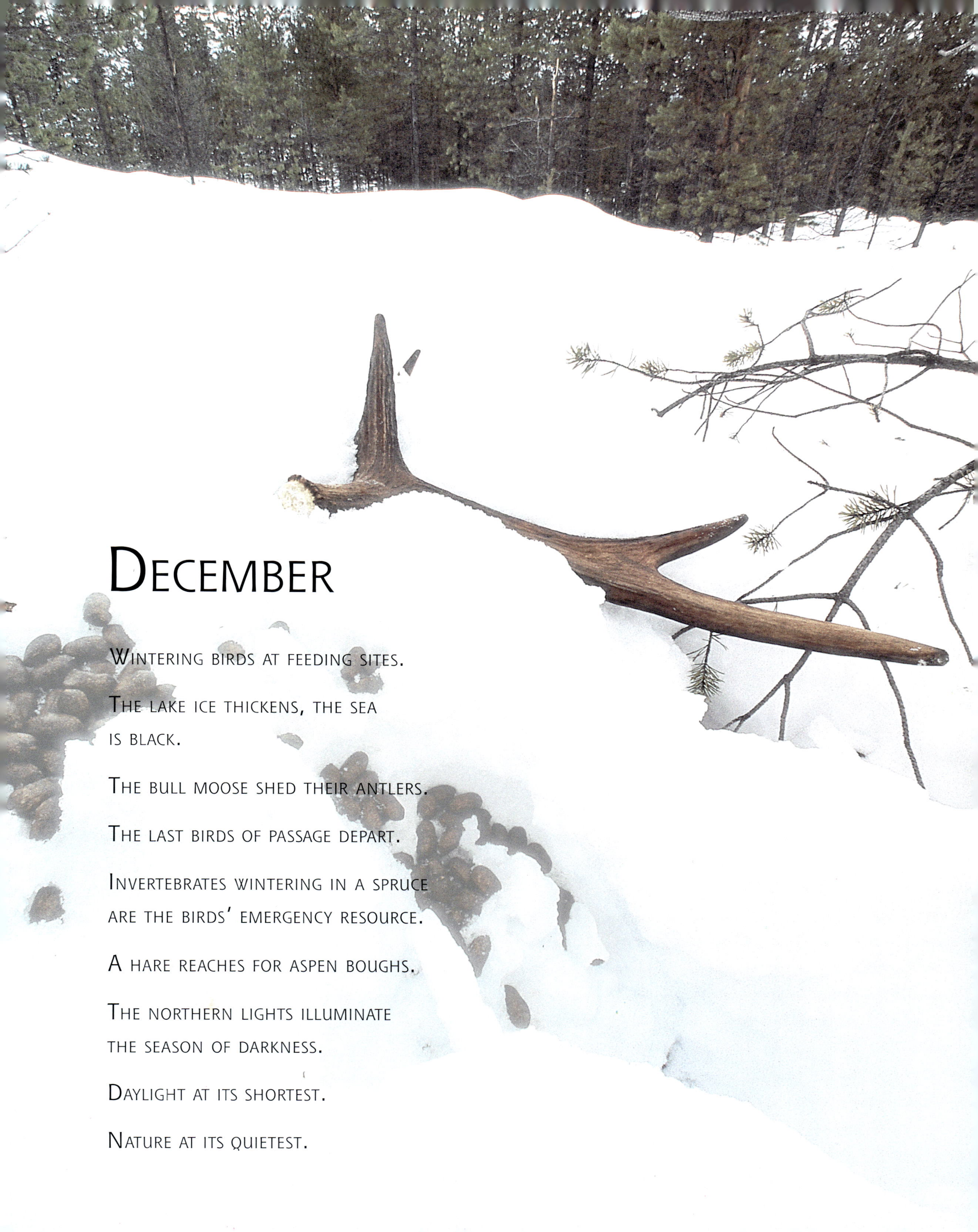

December

Wintering birds at feeding sites.

The lake ice thickens, the sea
is black.

The bull moose shed their antlers.

The last birds of passage depart.

Invertebrates wintering in a spruce
are the birds' emergency resource.

A hare reaches for aspen boughs.

The northern lights illuminate
the season of darkness.

Daylight at its shortest.

Nature at its quietest.

Daylight at Its Shortest

When the time comes to wake up, it is still dark; yellow light pours out of the window, illuminating the bird feeder set up beneath the birch in the yard. The sky is overcast, emphasizing the effect of the darkness. A breakfast fire crackles in the stove; the morning paper, smelling of printer's ink, rustles as it is opened: garish Christmas advertisements, minor and major news, what are supposed to be entertaining columns. The coffee has a more authentic smell.

There are fresh hare tracks beneath the window; new snow has given the animals a clean slate on which to write their messages. The hare was glimpsed a few times in the fall, but in the snow it is possible to follow its activities daily. It has gnawed the aspens bordering the forest, beginning with the most slender of them. By bracing itself on trunks, it has also sought to reach lower boughs higher than the shoots – to no avail. Each night it appears to make a pilgrimage to the house, to the apple saplings protected by wire netting.

The thermometer shows a few degrees of frost, so the snow will stay feathery. The pendant boughs of birches sway in a light wind which scatters the snow from the trees. The coating of snow, shattering into crystals, is wafted by the breeze to the ground, where it gathers in drifts at the foot of trees, beside rocks and in depressions. The snow softens the shapes of the landscape and conceals the objects in the yard. Even the bucket overturned on the well cover has been given a white collar.

One's thoughts stray to the excesses of summer: the flood of light, the teeming richness of life. This offsets those. Nature looks dead; the light of the short day takes its time coming and then beats a retreat far too soon. Rife with verdancy in summer, the vista now shows as minimalized shapes clad in black and white. But this inert silence has its appeal; without winter, summer too would lack something.

The day dawns so slowly as to be imperceptible. There comes a moment when the gaze simply carries farther than the light cast from the window. While twilight still prevails, the morning's first bullfinch arrives to feed. But the elegant grey female must make room at once for the male, which alights and pushes the earlier arrival out of its way. After a few frantic flaps of its wings, the female also finds a foothold on the feeder and begins to gobble sunflower seeds.

In the dim light the feeder is already in complete turmoil. More bullfinches appear in nearby trees, along with greenfinches. A group of yellowhammers settles to the ground below the feeder to collect what others have flung down. Titmice stop by to fetch seed, one at a time, and flit off to quarry them among the branches. A great tit acts with firm resolve, paying the bullfinches no heed. A diligent blue tit eagerly pauses at some suet held to a tree with fishtrap mesh; and a great spotted woodpecker which has set up shop in a split goat willow also pecks at it with gusto.

The solar wind sweeps the outermost atmosphere. The northern lights flare in the arctic sky.

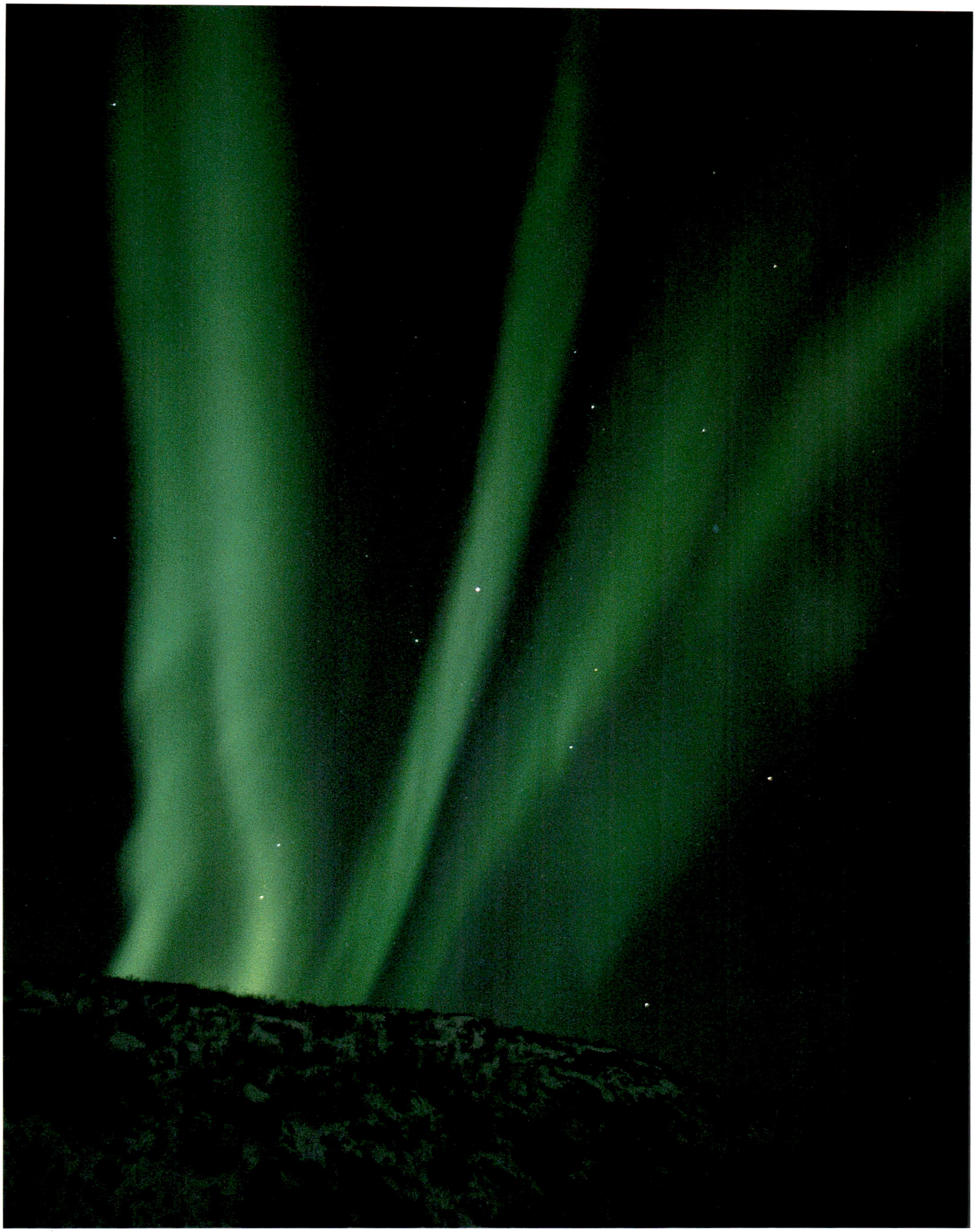

Magpies chortle in treetops around the yard, as if from a safe distance. They are cautious and don't dare come to feed when there is movement indoors, a human at the window. There is no sign of any hooded crows, but both of these crow varieties drop by the instant humans look the other way. Tracks in the snow give them away. Also the jay that emerges from the woods for a snack is rarely seen; but rounded marks of wing strokes in the snow betray the uninvited caller.

Suddenly the birds scatter. From somewhere the sharp warning of a tit shrills, and the bullfinches, greenfinches and yellowhammers shoot off in all directions. The titmice freeze in odd positions among the branches; heads cocked, they survey the sky. The great spotted woodpecker closes up shop for a while. A predator stalks the skies; outlined against the sky, the grey silhouette of a sparrowhawk darts from the clouds, but this time its scouting flight is to no purpose. Gradually the birds return to their seed feast, squabbling among themselves, flinging shells to the ground, and occasionally fluttering off in retreat for the pure pleasure of flying.

People who wish to view nature's theatrics in their yards help the birds through the coldest season by feeding them. Established with the first frost, the avian restaurant remains open until spring, when its patrons are able to manage again on what nature offers. Feeding brings birds together in people's gardens in large concentration, which is why it must be kept up throughout the winter without interruption. Cutting the providing of food short means insuperable difficulties for birds accustomed to a groaning board.

Widespread feeding has affected the populations of some bird species: the blue tit, the greenfinch and, quite clearly, the blackbird as well have profited from human hospitality. The occasional chaffinches and bramblings that remain in Finland – often ailing or injured individuals - may with the aid of feeding survive until spring. During some "greenhouse winters," robins and blackcaps have lingered at feeders on the south coast well into the winter.

A squirrel peers from a hole hollowed out by a black woodpecker, its whiskers quivering, its eyes squinting. Dazzled by the glittering frosty morning, the creature has halted in place to savor the winter light falling on its face. The sun, blazing low in the sky, offers comforting warmth. A bitter cold night has passed; the grey on the dead-standing trunk and the thick frost fringing the hole are its mementos. Moisture from the squirrel's respiration has condensed in a glinting ring on the opening to its winter nest.

Having sunbathed for a while, the squirrel exits, beautiful, busy-tailed, grey-furred and tufted-eared. It stretches its limbs, head down, grasps the rough trunk with its hind feet and reaches for the ground with its forepaws. And then a few lissome leaps toward the heights. At the first fork the squirrel stops to rub its muzzle – a morning dry-wash – and another mad dash up the trunk to the next limb, where it springs to an adjoining tree. On it goes, effortlessly, from tree to tree for a few hundred meters until it is confronted by a stand of sapling, into which the squirrel descends.

The creature vanishes into a dense spruce grove, a trembling treetop now and then betraying its whereabouts. The squirrel will busy itself with the stashes it has in the grove: boletus mushrooms wedged in the forks of limbs. It has good taste. Protected by the thick branches, the delicacies are well preserved; an American species shifts the mushrooms its dries in the fall to the security of a hollow, but for Finnish squirrels, open storage sheltered from the worst rains suffices.

Over the autumn the squirrel creates random food stores here and there, secreting cones and nuts in the ground, hoisting seeds and bits of apple onto branches. As it empties its caches over the winter, it overlooks some of them. Thus, a hidden tidbit in time develop into a lovely hazel bush, unless another squirrel or, say, a yellow-necked field mouse stumbles on a seed that escaped its hoarder.

Hoarding is vital to the squirrel, particularly when there don't happen to be any human providers of food in its territory. On a bird feeder, a squirrel retains its right to the best offerings. It may sit down for a bite to eat at dawn and go on snacking for hours. Following a brief midday break, it will return for supper before climbing to its nesting hole for the night.

The capercaillie's winter menu is meager: nothing but pine needles. But quantity makes up for quality.

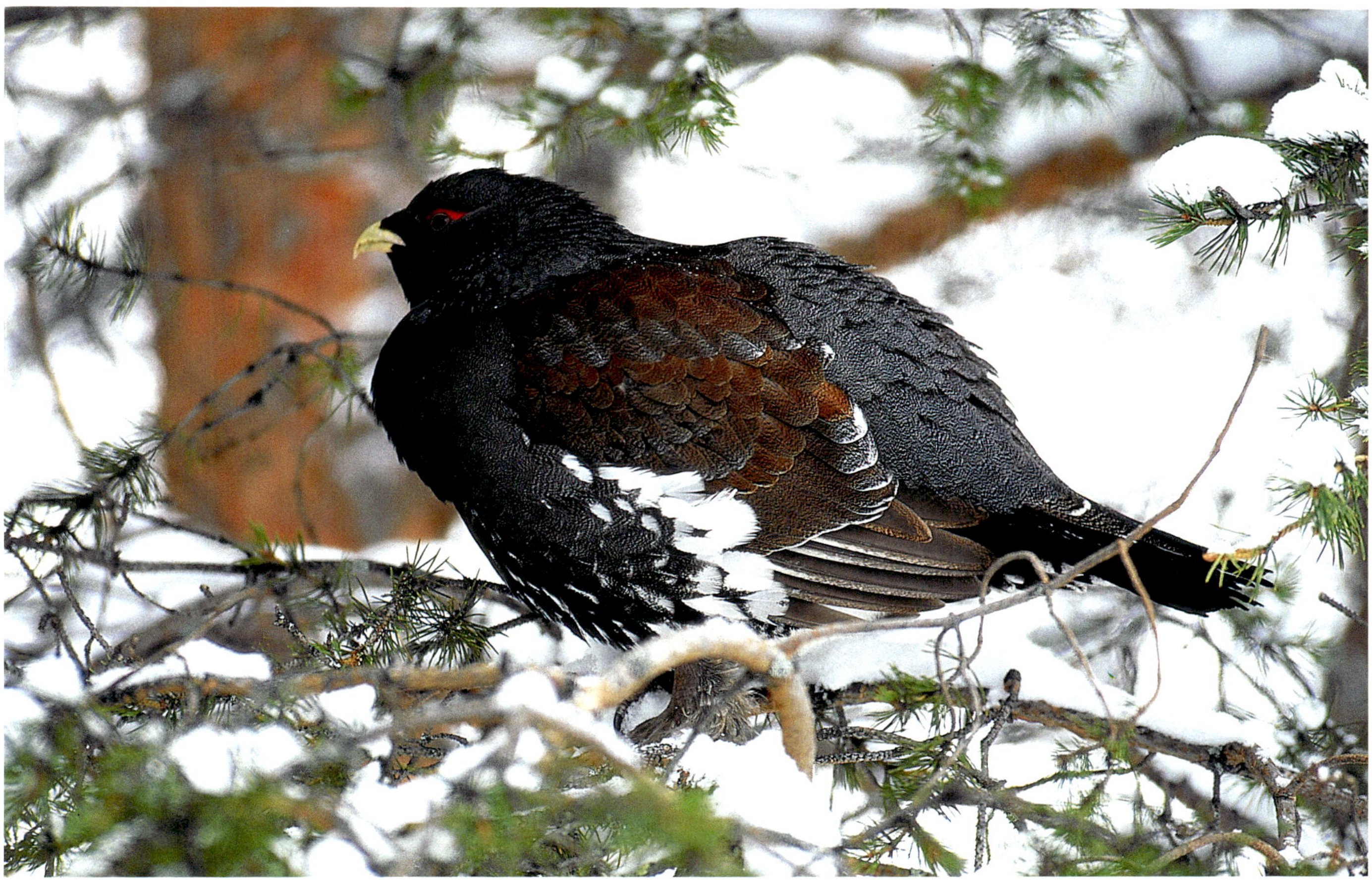

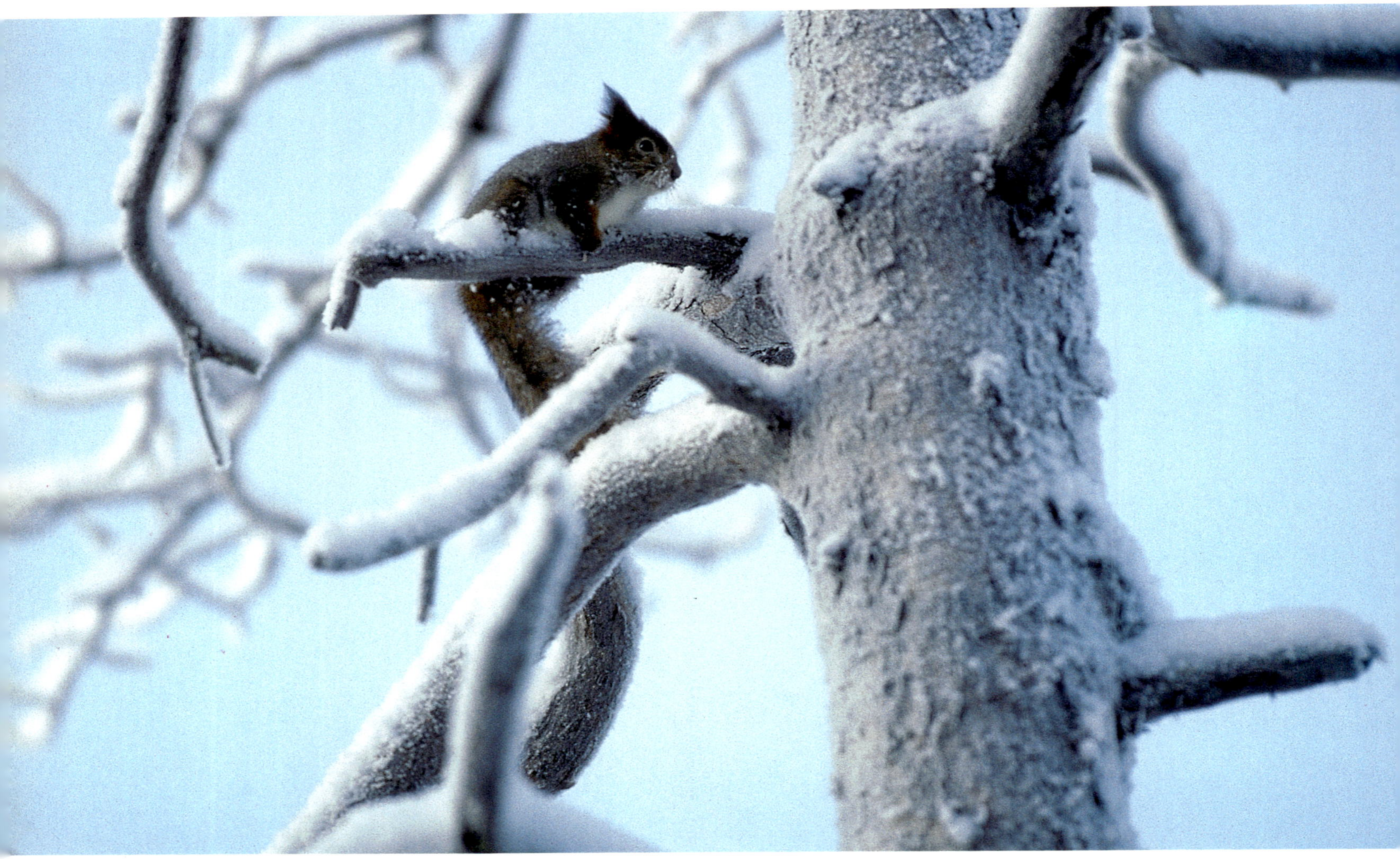

A squirrel's winter day is just as busy. Threatened, it freezes in place.

The winsome flying squirrel also feels at home near people, but does not care for the provisions on feeders, preferring instead to rely on winter food it gathers itself. To sustain it over the winter, the small, silver-grey creature gathers the catkins of hardwoods into hollows, old thrush nests and sheltered nooks among spruce branches. It conserves energy by not moving much; if well fed, it can lounge for days in its beard moss-insulated hole without so much as putting its snout out into the cold.

The northern water vole is a veritable master of stockpiling, refusing to scatter at random the food is gathers in late summer and throughout the fall. It builds a separate larder in its subterranean network of tunnels, storing all manner of morsels in safe keeping there. Dandelion roots are what a vole eats, but it will also avidly pinch root crops from fields. Fifteen kilograms of potatoes were discovered in the stores of one assiduous northern water vole. That would tide an even bigger animal over the winter.

The bank vole, on the other hand, stores lingonberries, seasoned with a few fungi, in hollow stumps for the winter and rolls beard moss

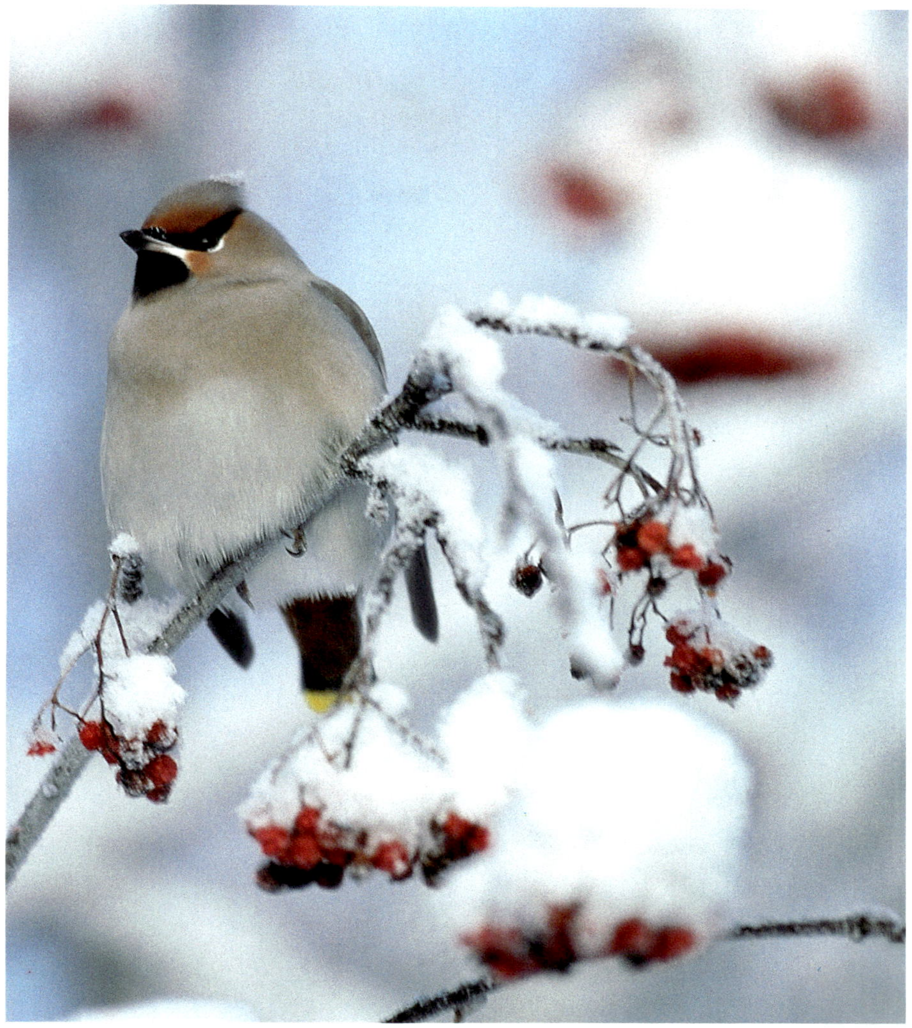

A waxwing's winter is one big party as long as the berries hold out.

into little balls, like heads of lettuce. It does have to come up every so often onto the snow to chew bark from branches, putting its life at stake. Should a hawk owl come upon the prey it seeks, it doesn't miss.

Nor does the pigmy owl, one of the bird world's stockpilers. As the temperature drops below freezing, the owl begins to stow prey in woodpecker holes and birdhouses. Dozens of voles, shrews and birds may accumulate in one hollow. These this dwarf among owls devours to sustain itself if it fails to obtain fresh quarry, and in this it often succeeds around a bird feeder.

There are many stockpilers among the birds. All corvids stash surplus provisions. During the fall some titmice hide insects and spiders on branches and tree trunks, where they may be found in winter. Some birds remember their caches; the common nutcracker, for example, is considered very astute at recalling its hoards. In contrast, an individual titmouse will forget its own stash, but, since all its companions employ the same tactics to store food, they all benefit from behavior typical of the species.

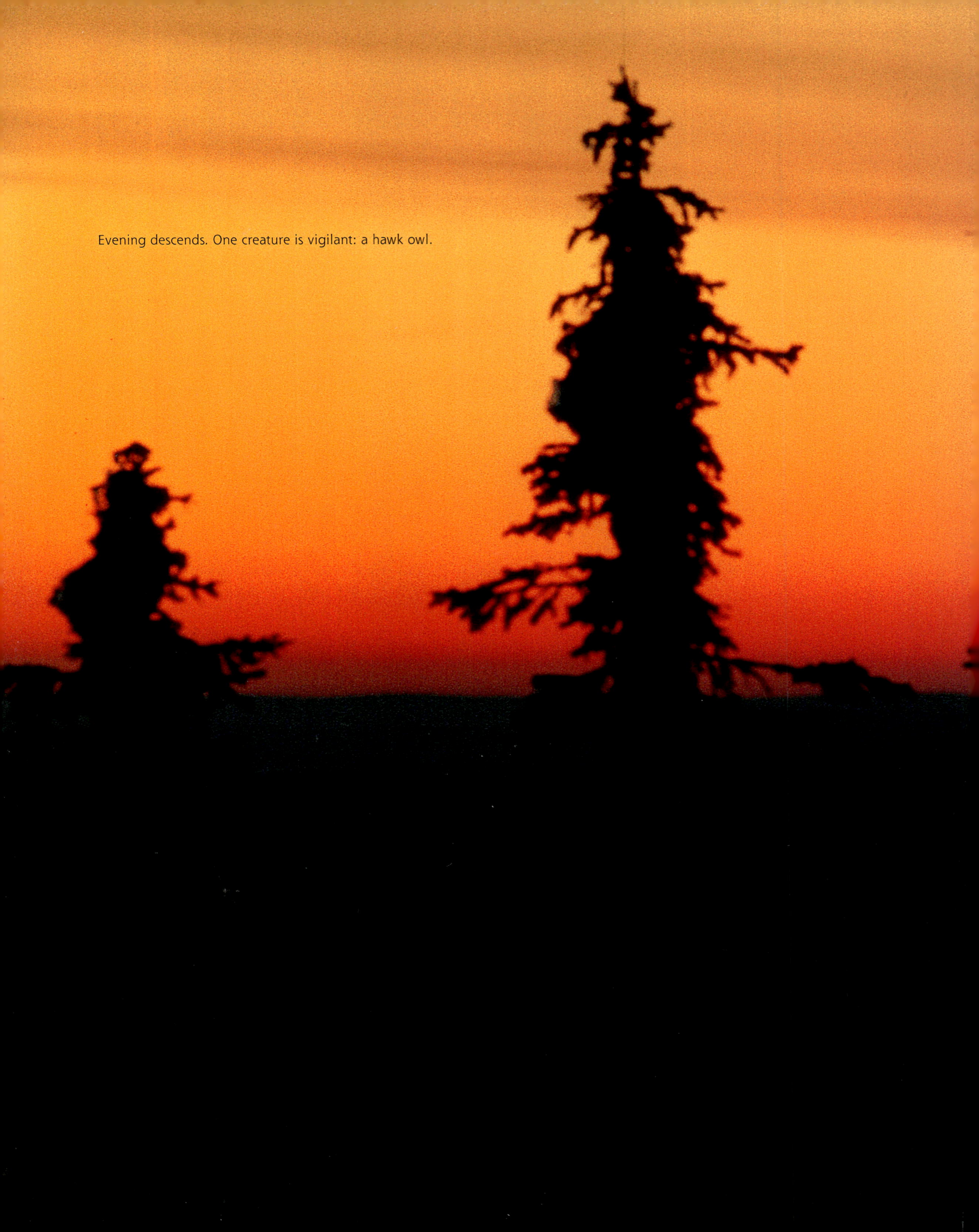

Evening descends. One creature is vigilant: a hawk owl.

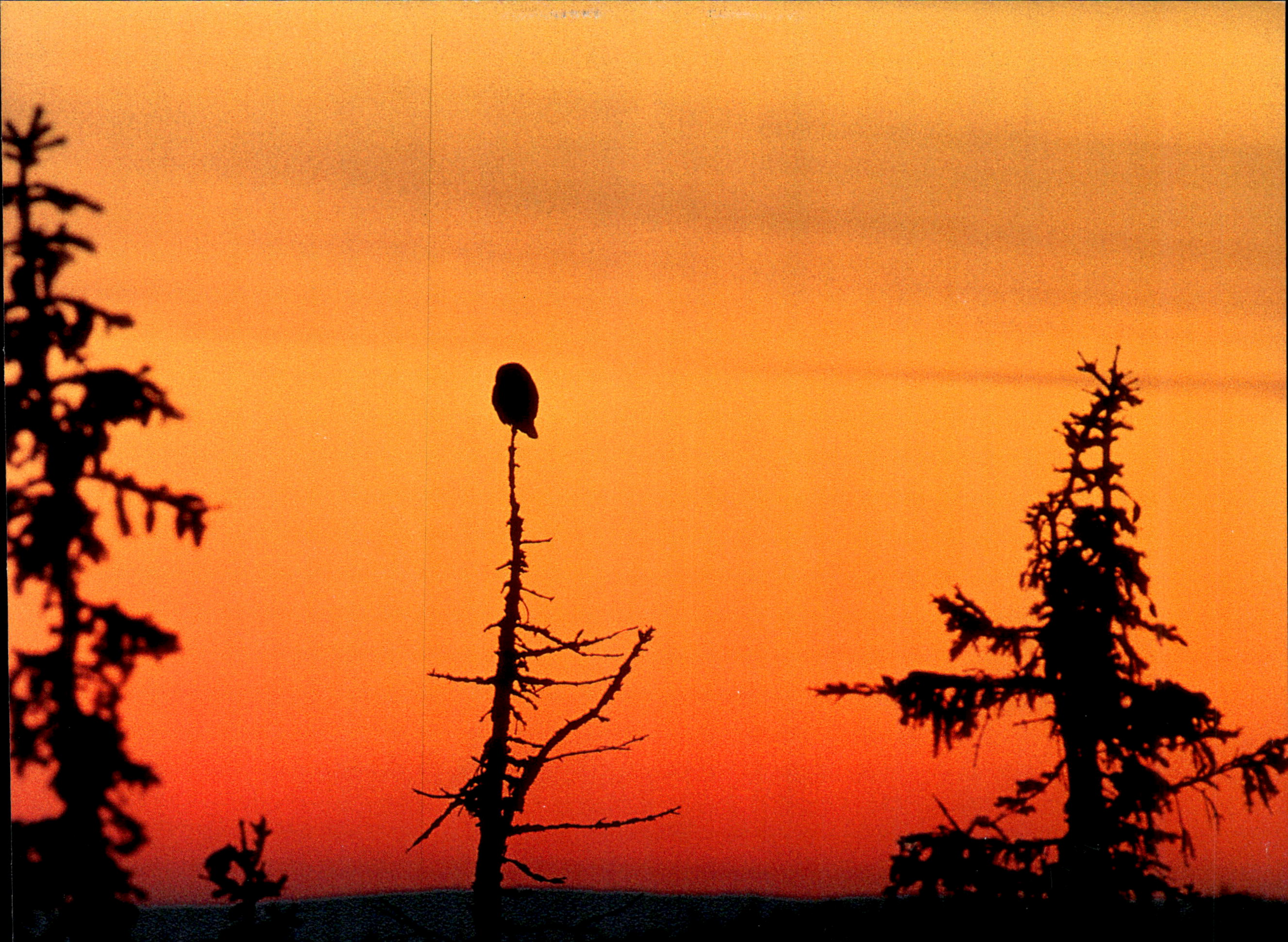

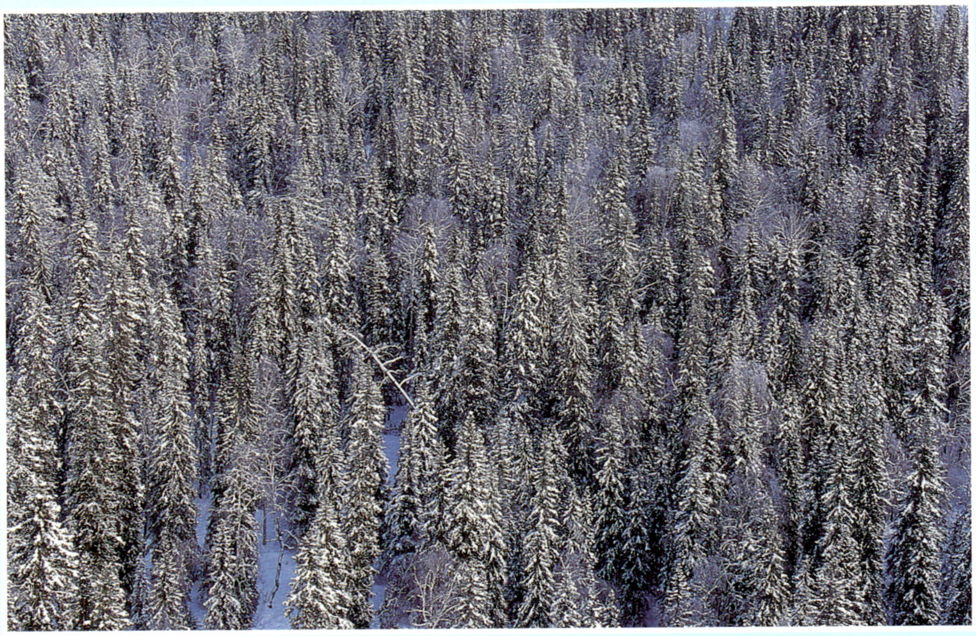

A wintry spruce teems with life. In clefts in the bark, in the crotches of limbs and in cones there winter insects whose names boggle the mind: jumping plant lice, psocides, froghoppers, flea beetles, lathariddidae beetles, leaf rollers, true bugs and of course spiders. The bigger the tree, the more life there is. Not even a Christmas tree is deserted. Piling in with it comes a host of uninvited guests – like elves.

Animals generally store more food than they require for winter. Much good food goes to waste, though it's not a total loss. Seeds get sown in new surroundings, scavengers obtain nourishment from animals, as it were, killed in vain. Microbes also need food, and this the surplus stores provide them with. Nature wastes nothing in this case either.

The sea roars ashore in white-capped waves. Low pressure brings stormy greetings in from the Atlantic. The wind roars and chill raindrops draw horizontal streaks in the grey air. The short day is grey and dispirited. The earth is black. For the umpteenth time an try at winter has foundered in a rainy southwestern wind. With the greenhouse effect getting stronger all the time, one has to get used to such winters. The sea will freeze late, if at all.

Large white birds swim the waves, mute swans, and with them greyish-brown signets. To mute swans, a belated winter is all the better. The arrival of real winter is hard on the half-tame population, gone wild from domesticated stock. The slowly developing young don't always manage to become fully fledged while the ice is out, and then death takes its toll. But hard winters have become rare in the archipelago, and the mute swan is doing well. To this long-lived bird, the casualties of one or two hard winters mean nothing, if they are followed by several mild ones.

Gulls float in the sky, most of them sturdy herring gulls; but there are a few thumping great black-blacked gulls and graceful common gulls. These patrollers of local beaches will keep themselves fed as long as the water remains open. There are waterfowl carcasses and fish aplenty to peck at. The birds hector their share from fishfarms and the fish-cleaning sites of the few year-round island inhabitants. Herring trawlers trail escorts of gulls, adults greyed for the winter and brown juveniles.

The goosanders are now dressed in their best, the males in their handsome mating attire. A few goldeneyes make their ricocheting sound in the greyness; some mallards wander by. And not all of the whooper swans that left the inland regions in good time have fled further that the open inner bays of the coastal region and the margins of open water in the outer islands. Among them are white adults and the grey juveniles of the past summer. The calls of whooper swans, the national bird of Finland, sound through the gales from time to time, their black-tipped bills, flashing golden yellow as they give out to a comely bugling.

But visitors from afar are also swimming on the open sea. Steller's eiders from the Arctic Ocean have taken to wintering in the outer archipelago. In groups of a few birds, sometimes in flocks of hundreds, they paddle about the open sea. Overhead wheels a glaucous gull, massive resident of arctic shores, an individual clad in juvenile beige. And along the shore skitters a third arctic bird: the purple sandpiper also winters over in Finland, weather permitting.

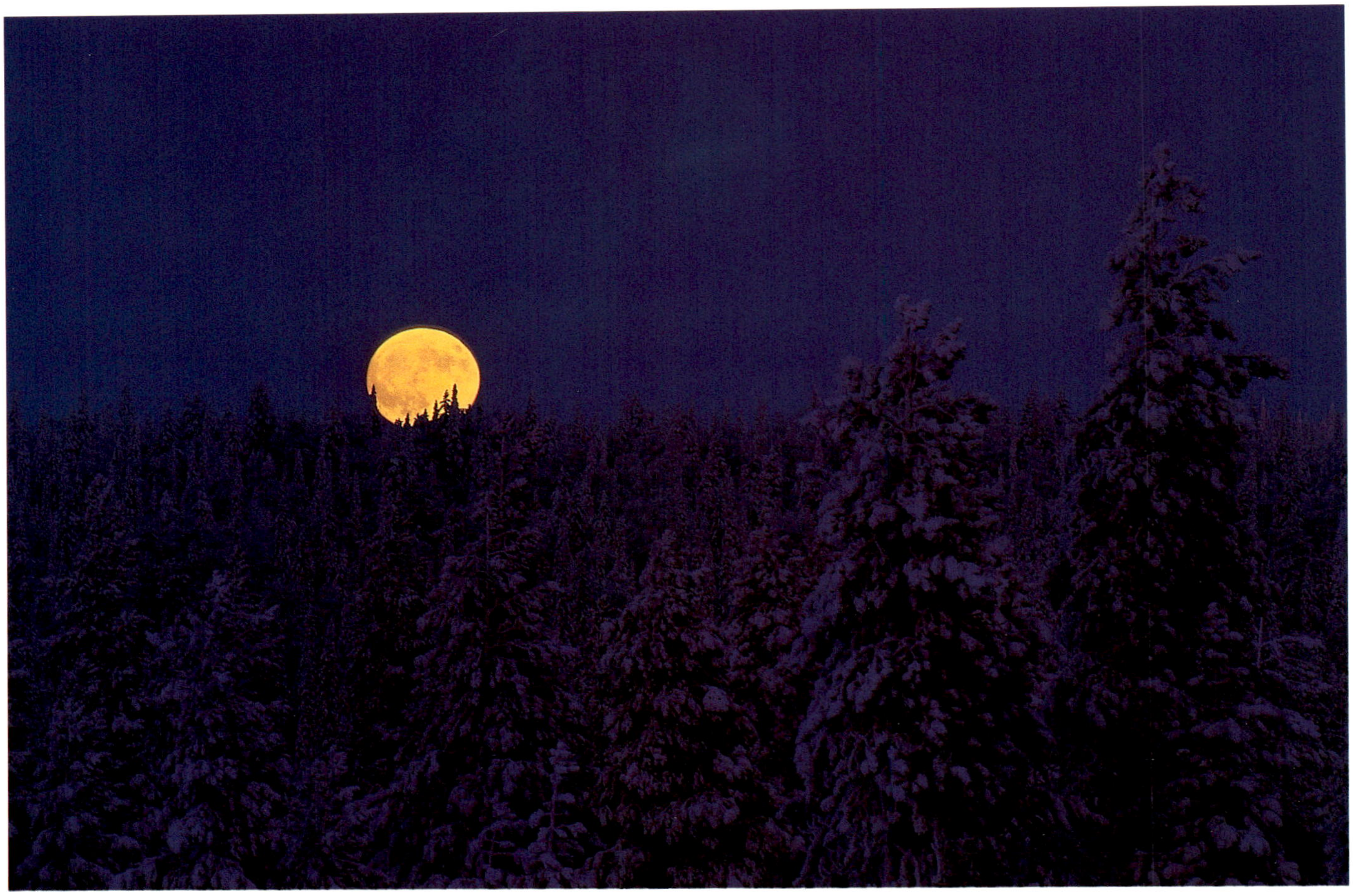

Some northern passerine birds winter on the southern coast. The twite, which inhabits Fennoscandinavian mountain ranges, spends its winters on wasteland. The snow bunting is also partial to such environs. As modest songbirds, they lead an inconspicuous existence in areas dominated by the dried stems of weeds.

The birds that winter among the outer islands set out the instant the sea freezes. Likewise, twites and snow buntings shake the snows of Finland from their plumage when winter tightens the screws. The visitors do not necessarily go far: the aquatic birds to the rim of the ice, small passerines to the Baltic countries. And they are also among the first to travel north when spring begins to show signs of making headway.

Total silence, with only the cold snapping in the tree trunks.

According to the clock, it's midday; dawn turns directly to dusk. A yellow wedge is thrown into the even grey sky for a moment as the headlight of a snowmobile climbing a fjeld sweeps the area. Details of the blue-grey landscape are engulfed by twilit mounds. The wailing of the machine is the only sound, and even that is smothered. The putter of the engine is muffled by its deep track; snow is also excellent sound insulation.

The low, blazing winter sun glints like stars among boughs.

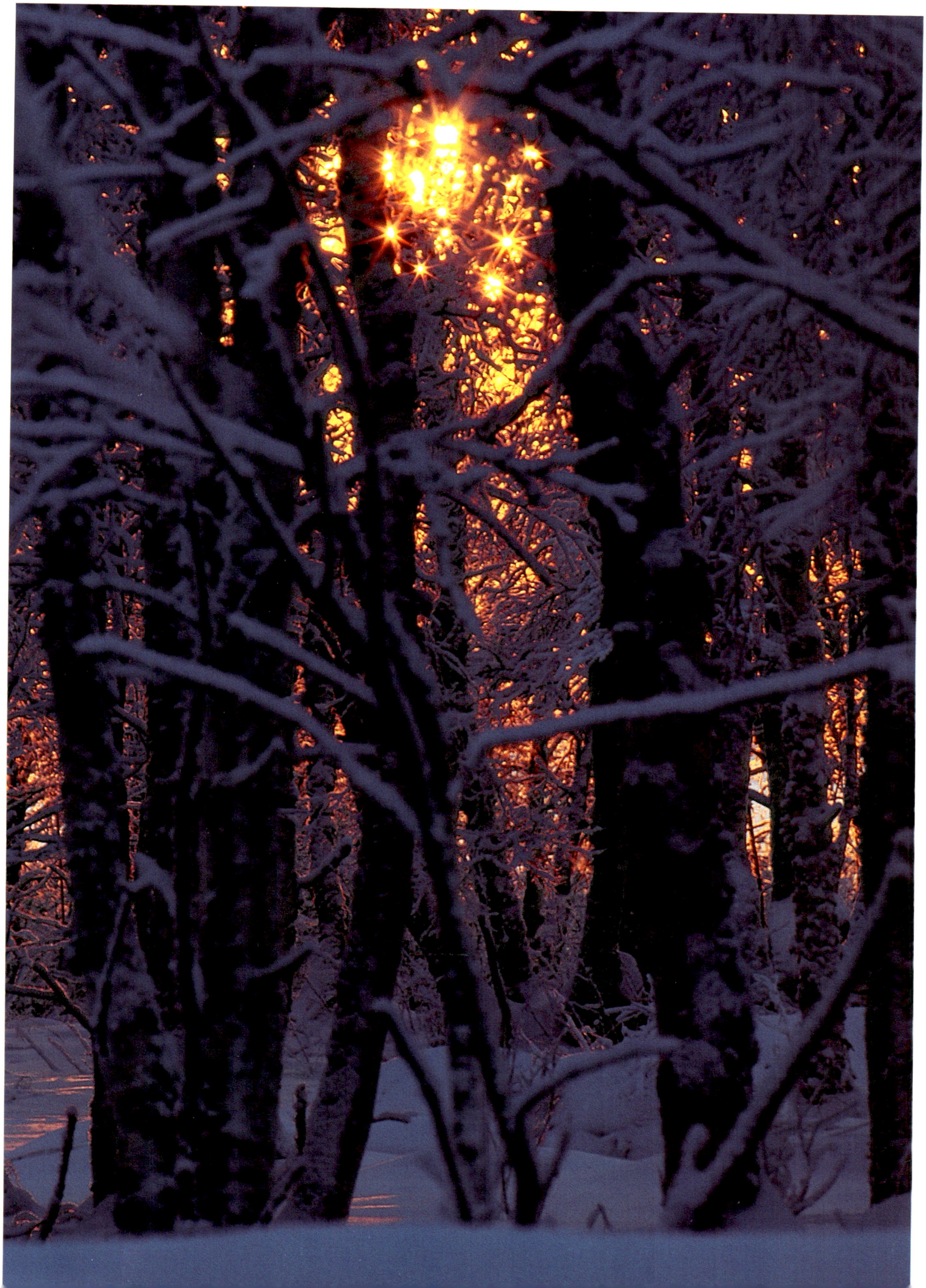

Somewhere beyond the fjeld there is the clatter from the hooves of reindeer released after sorting and marking. The half-tame domesticated animals delve for lichen and browse beard moss from trees. The size of the reindeer population is controlled by butchering in accordance with the carrying capacity of the north's meager pasturage – or at least that's how it should be done. There are many indications, however, that the intensity sought by reindeer husbandry is depleting the pasturage. Nature becomes exhausted and the reindeer suffer as well. To offset this, perhaps, there is somewhat more in the way of transactions.

Ravens flap about the vicinity. The black scavengers always show up wherever there is life. The reindeer marking means knives flash and blood spews; this the ravens know from experience and they return faithfully to inspect the possible pickings. They fly effortlessly for tens

The sun does not come up; living conditions are at their harshest. In northernmost Finland the season of darkness last from November to January.

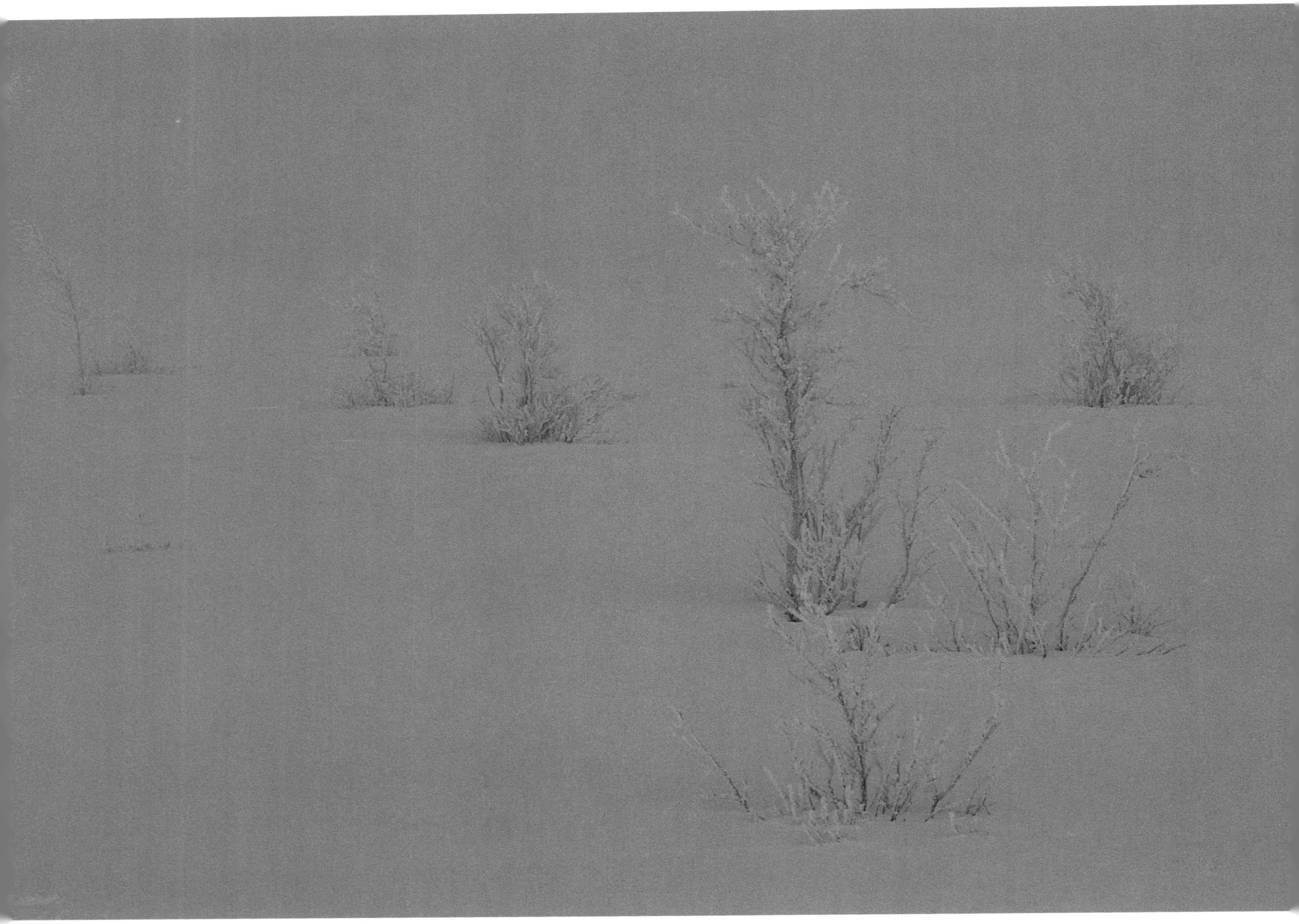

of kilometers and on their daily patrol flights discover with amazing ease both the carcass of a reindeer that fell over a cliff and remains left by humans after a butchering.

It must be added that most ravens have learned to exploit the fruits of our overflowing dumps. They scrounge in a black cloud through humankind's discarded delicacies. The ski resort vying with the northern lights to paint the sky has taught the birds to expect goodies the likes of which these wanderers of the fjelds would never have dreamed of before. The skiing music playing on the brightly lit slopes doesn't bother the ravens.

But the true master of survival lives on the fells: for all practical purposes, the ptarmigan, camouflaged in its white snow suit, spends its entire life above the tree line. On only descends from the treeless fells in exceptional circumstances, when afflicted by extreme cold and when snow covers its feeding grounds. Plump due to its thick plumage and trusting implicitly in its white camouflage, the ptarmigan scratches a living from fell slopes swept clean of snow by the wind. The wind may pile drifts on its feeding sites, but it opens fresh patches elsewhere; and these this tenacious bird tours in small bevies.

The willow grouse – it too a stout, white-clad wildfowl – lives further down the fell, in the birch zone and lowland moors. Its winter forage consists of birch buds that, when frozen, are heavy food; and the bird must use vast quantities of energy to ingest them. During a couple of morning hours it consumes its daily provender, and then, snug in cubbyhole in the snow, defrosts and digests the meal in its crop.

It is when the day of darkness turns to night and the night sweeps the clouds away that the northern lights flare in the star-studded sky. The cosmic solar winds licks the uppermost layers of the atmosphere over the polar regions, producing a blaze that fills the sky in a belt that can span thousands of kilometers. The constantly transformed fans of flame flash greenish yellow, white, sometimes even blood-red.

At midday a warm red glow creeps over the horizon, but the sun has now business in the Lapland sky. The northern sky takes on shades of blue and turquoise then, and these velvety hues lure the gaze. The prominences of the fells lie white, in the valleys the mysterious shapes of the frost-clad trees stand motionless. The moon rolls slowly into place, a pallid disk.

Only Change Is Permanent

It is pouring down rain, the day is short and the sea is black. According to the calendar, it is winter but the information conveyed by the sense indicates something quite different. October seems to have drawn out. The ground has already frozen a few times, snow flurries have swept the coast, but real winter stubbornly holds back. One low pressure front after another brings heavy rains to bathe the fields. Water stands on clay ground and the river floods, brown from the earth washed into it.

At the same time, a few hundred kilometers away, the earth is engulfed in snow. Dense snowfall streaks the greyness. The trees are clad in snow, the fields and open stretches of lakes are deserted expanses of snow; only the mouth of a flowing river gapes black in the whiteness. The calendar is correct: it is winter, right on time, fit and proper. Inland from the coastal plain the showers turn to flurries the instant the land begins to climb to the altitude contours inland.

The bitter cold pops in the blue-grey emptiness of the undulating tundra landscape. The snow- and frost-mantled trees loom as ghostly forms, sentinels of the darkness. Though the sun remains below the horizon, crisp shadows are cast on the snow as a bright moon illuminates the surroundings. The darkness of this season is relative: even the signature of a fox is easily legible on the luminous snow covering these northern ridges.

In southern Finland May changes spring to summer, its verdancy quickly mantling the play of early flowers' color. In the best-suited places lesser celandine, in the manner of wood anemones, forms extensive carpets.

In northermost Finland the nightless night begins in late May. Spring advances in leaps and bounds. Meltwater streams from the fjelds to the valleys, where the breaking up of the ice often makes for brief and violent drama.

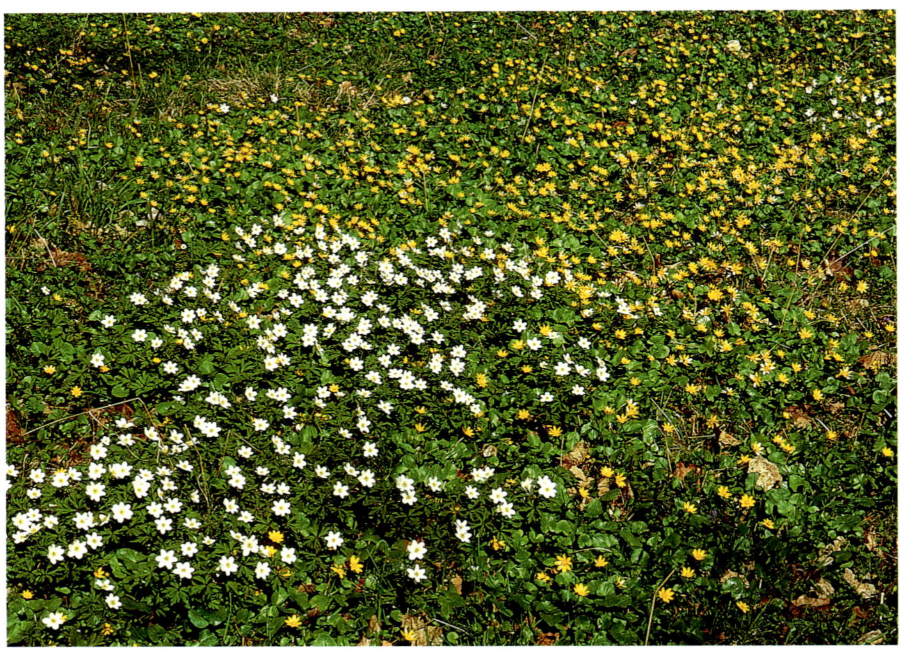

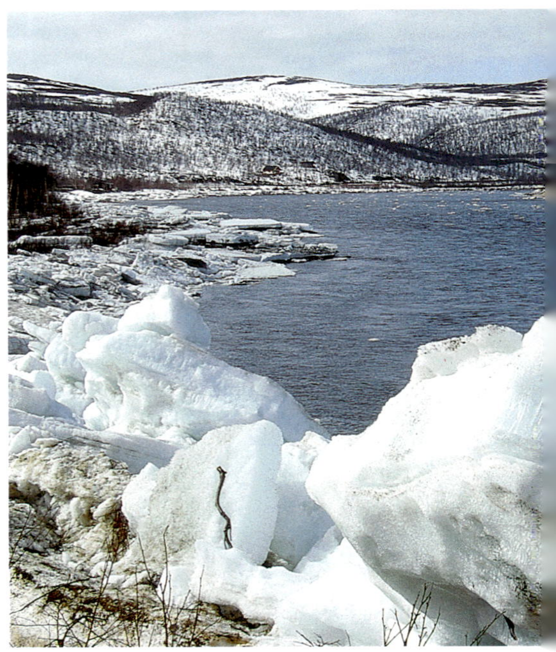

It is a long way from the southernmost Hanko peninsula to the northern reaches of Finland, over a thousand kilometers. This leaves its mark on the seasons. The amount of light, temperatures, rainfall and climate type all vary, along with vegetation, fauna, everything that life comprises. There are also differences between the east and west, though not as marked, but perceivable nonetheless.

On Midsummer Day along the southern coast the sun stays up from nineteen hours. On the Arctic Circle the orb is visible around the clock, but in northernmost Utsjoki the summer day comes to measure more than two months long. Similarly, at the winter solstice just prior to Christmas, the day is six hours long in the south, while in Utsjoki the period of darkness, illuminated only by snow, the aurora borealis and moonlight, lasts seven weeks.

That the season of darkness is shorter than sunlit night results from the shape of the earth's orbit around the sun: in winter we swing closer to the sun than in summer. The slant in the earth's axis, in turn, means that despite this "proximity" the winter sun warms less than in summer: as our native planet rockets through space it careens away from the sun, as it were.

Finland's interior seasonal variations spring from the same phenomena that mark the country's climate as a whole. In the southwest, the maritime climate predominates; toward the north and east there are more and more continental features. The effects of the Atlantic, the Gulf Stream and the Baltic wane as the geographical distance to them increases. Although Finland belongs to the western maritime climatic zone, at times the eastern influence dominates for long periods.

No two years are alike. Nor is the timing of the hare's molt always perfect. Its white winter fur changes gradually to brown summer garb, starting at its head.

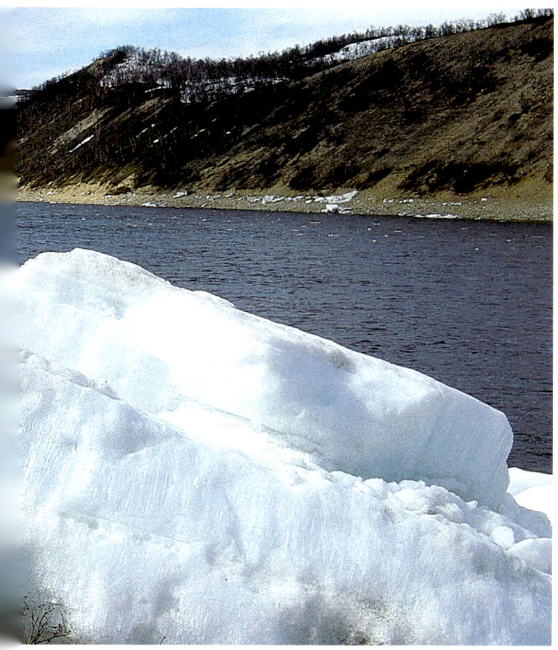

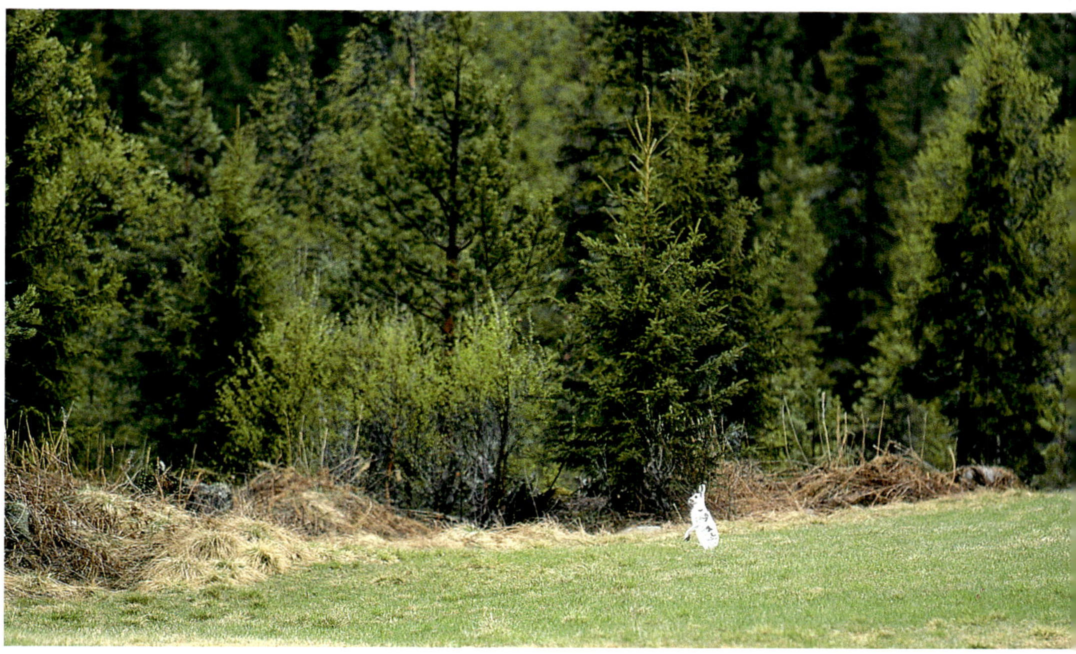

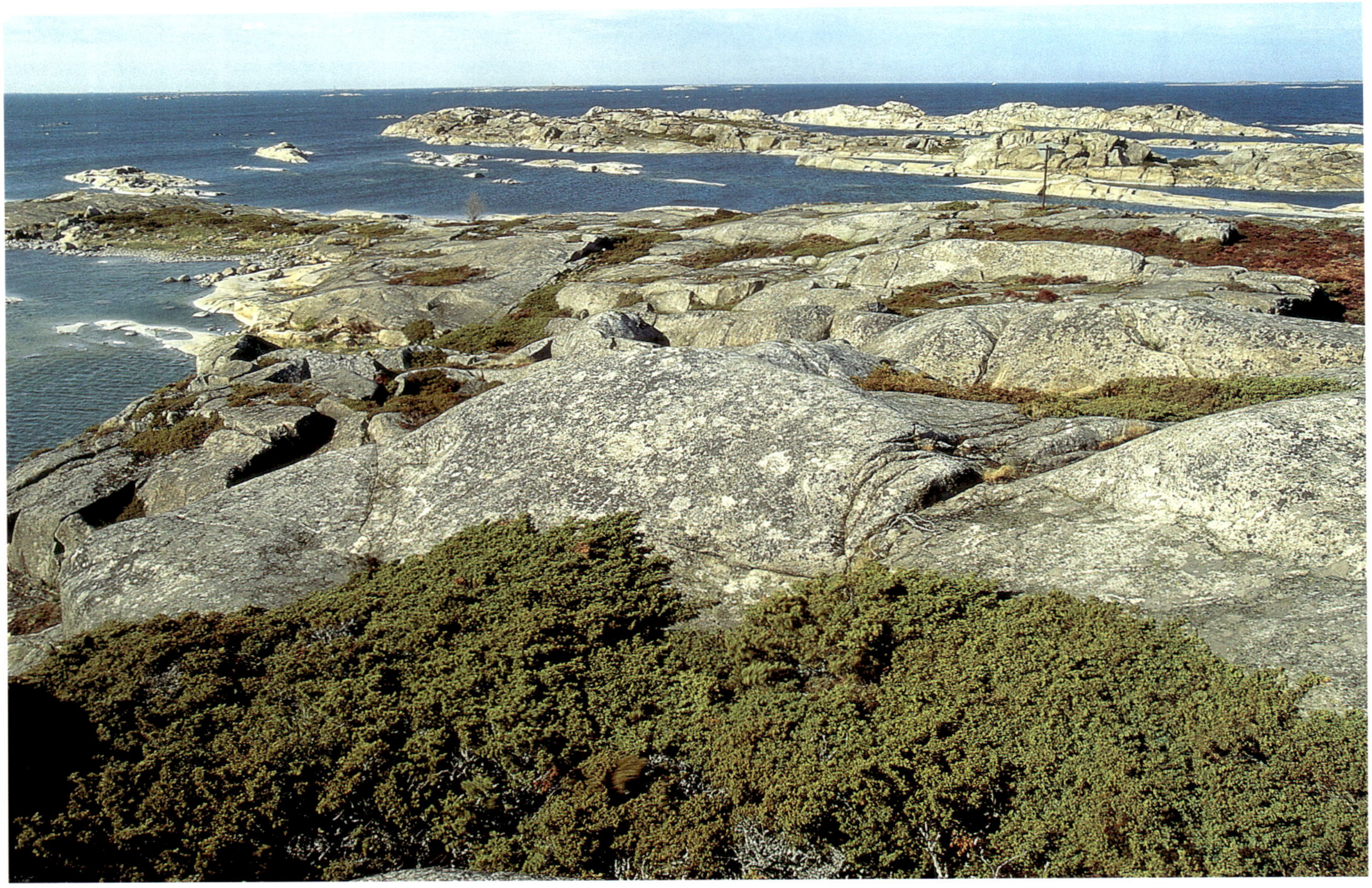

The outer skerries of the archipelago are Finland's extreme south. The sea laving thei- shores leaves a strong stamp on al life there.

In the vicinity of the sea, spring and autumn are long because large bodies of water store both the warmth of summer and the cold of winter much more efficiently than does the earth. Spring arrives suddenly and intensely on the mainland; autumn too sweeps over the mainland with great speed. During the summer season of sunlit nights the temperature range between north and south is smaller than in winter, during which arctic conditions firmly grip the north.

Winter is something of a key season in Finland. Adapting to it is an absolute prerequisite to survival for all life forms. Winter comes – the temperature drops permanently below freezing – at different times in different parts of the country. The season of subfreezing temperatures begins in October in Lapland, but not until December in the densely populated south. Variations in the quality of the winter, the degree of frost and quantity of snow are even greater.

On the other hand, summer arrives when temperatures rise to above ten degrees Celsius. In inland areas of the south this happens during the final third of May, in the outer archipelago and southern Lapland, the first third of June, but in Utsjoki it often doesn't arrive until after Midsummer, if not as late as early July. Summer's triumphant advance through Finland takes a good month.

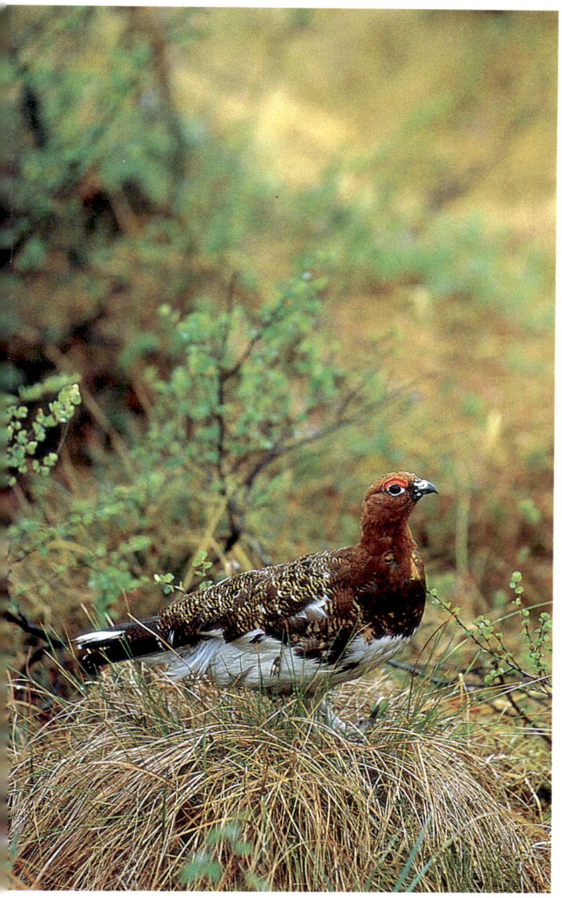

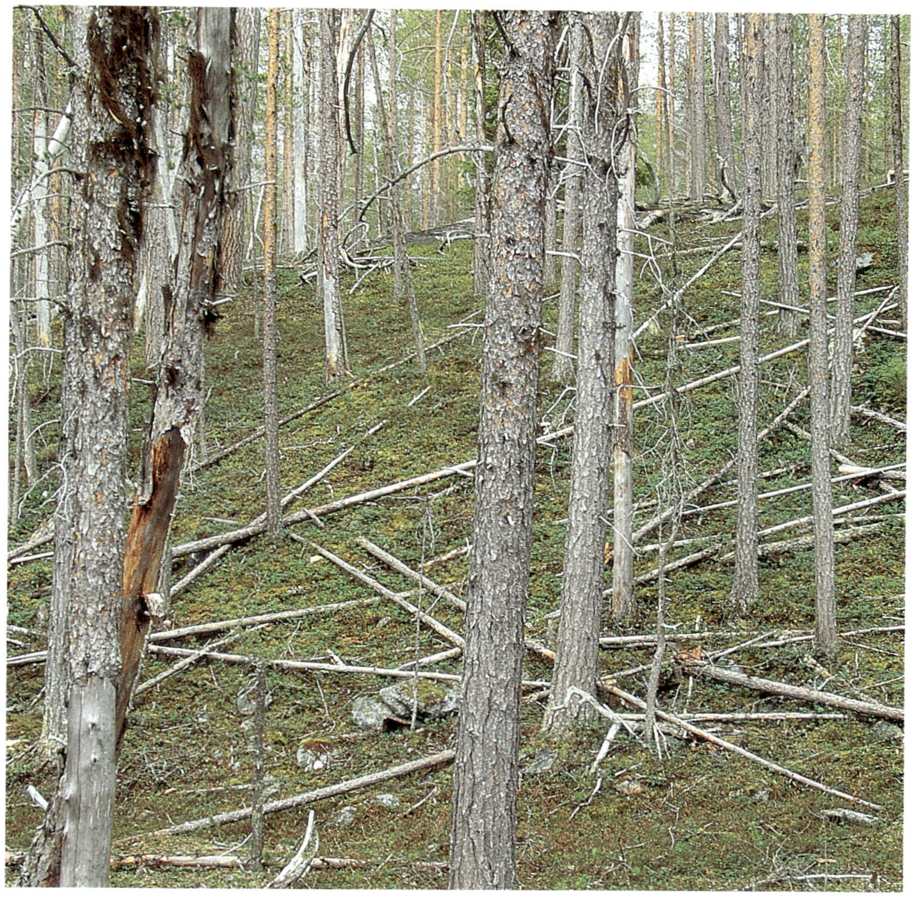

The willow grouse is ingeniously camouflaged in all seasons.

Fire once spread through the old forest. New growth has occured at its own pace. Growing conditions have shaped the character of a forest untouched by the ax. In its timeless manner, nature sees to its own.

Spring is defined as the period in which the temperature rises above freezing but not over ten degrees Celsius. Among the islands it begins at the close of March and in Lapland, the beginning of May. Fall, in turn, is the period when the temperature drops to below ten degrees but does not stray into winter – that is, below freezing. In northernmost Lapland autumn begins in mid-July, on the southern coast toward the end of September.

The seasonal phenomena of nature vary in accordance with temperatures, but the time lags are not as great: living things in the north are hardier than individuals of the same species in the south. So, for example, a birch in southwestern Finland will burst into leaf in mid-May, but not until a month later in Utsjoki. In September and October the pace is the same, but the order, quite naturally, is in reverse. The season of autumn colors marches across the country in a month and a half.

The appearance of the earliest migratory birds varies with the region. Our national bird, the swan, appears in some of its northern nesting areas as well as its nesting sites in the south in March and April. The skylark comes home to the south a month to a month and a half earlier than it does to the north, but the cuckoo begins calling in almost the same week in the provinces. Only a passage migrant in the south, the bluethroat can be observed at more or less the same time throughout the country.

Averages do not tell the truth about seasonal change. Between different parts of the country there are great differences that are merely emphasized by yearly variations. The year is always the same length, the sun rises and sets in keeping with a schedule set by planetary forces. They form the framework for events, what is called the main thrust, which the innumerable interactions of the commonplace shape as they see fit. The years truly do not make up a brotherhood.

The diversity is accentuated in the seasonal transitions. Winter takes backward steps, the first snows fall and thaw many times before whiteness finally takes over the landscape. In the north the pace is quicker, but along the southwest coast winter may feel like one long October, while among the fells it can stretch out to eight months in length.

Spring always suffers setbacks when vast fronts vie for supremacy in Finland's air space. In the end, however, winter relents, bit by bit in the south, more like a shot in the north. Not even summer, characterized by delirious growth and reproduction, advances in keeping with a detailed script. In the north wintry relapses and early summer frosts lie in ambush, a constant threat to nature. In the south the contest is between continental heat and maritime moisture.

Autumn's features depend a lot on the past. The severity of the winter gone by, spring weather conditions, and humidity and warmth of the growing season affect the capacity of plants to adapt to the change of seasons. During dry summer archipelagic birches store precious constituents away as early as midsummer and yield prematurely to the fall color change, due to thirst. Conditions during the breeding season are also reflected in the faunal autumn. For example, avian autumnal migration is set back if nesting was retarded due to bad weather.

In nature the only permanent thing is change. Finland is still living in the period of recuperation following the Ice Age that withdraw ten thousand years ago. Nature continually tests is limits. As a rule these experiments are, from the human perspective, unsuccessful, but every so often these experiments also produce positive results: a plant finds a new habitat, a bird a niche in which to winter over in place of the arduous migratory passage.

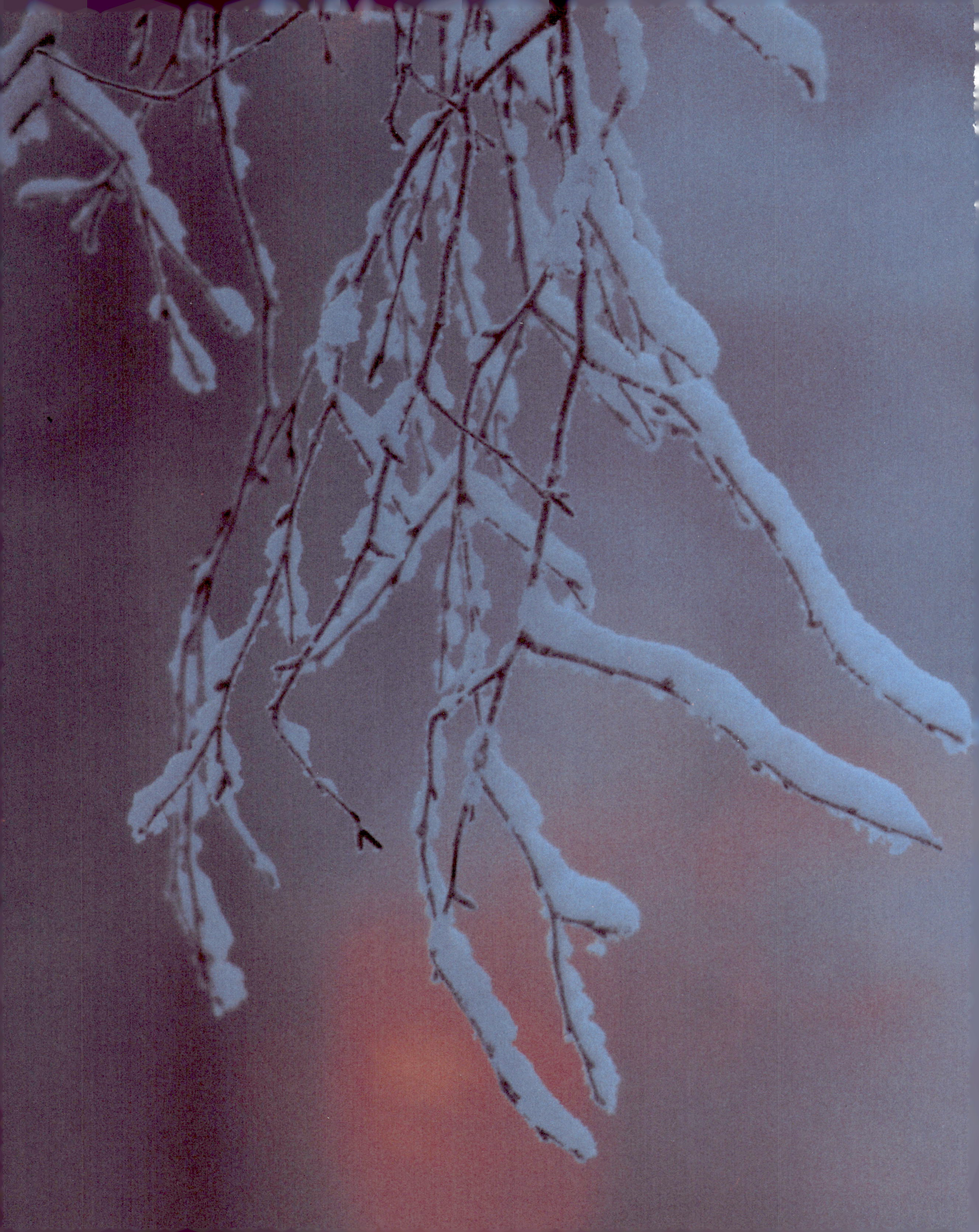